1

MORALITY: HOW TO LIVE IT TODAY

MORALITY: HOW TO LIVE IT TODAY

*Contemporary Moral Issues
in the Catholic Church, with an
Introduction to Traditional Doctrine and Principles*

by
Rev. Leonard F. Badia, Ph.D.
and
Ronald A. Sarno, M. Div.

ALBA · HOUSE   NEW · YORK
SOCIETY OF ST. PAUL, 2187 VICTORY BLVD., STATEN ISLAND, NEW YORK 10314

Library of Congress Cataloging in Publication Data

Badia, Leonard F.
    Morality, how to live it today.

    Includes bibliographies.
        1. Christian ethics—Catholic authors.
    I. Sarno, Ronald A., joint author. II. Title.
    BX1758.2.B24   241'.04'2   79-20498
    ISBN: 0-8189-0391-0   *1979*

Nihil Obstat:
Martin S. Rushford
Diocesan Censor

Imprimatur:
†Francis J. Mugavero D.D.
Bishop of Brooklyn
January 25, 1979

The Nihil Obstat and Imprimatur are
a declaration that a book or pamphlet is considered
to be free from doctrinal or moral error. It is not implied
that those who have granted the Nihil Obstat and
Imprimatur agree with the contents,
opinions or statements expressed.

Designed, printed and bound in the United States of
America by the Fathers and Brothers of the
Society of St. Paul, 2187 Victory Boulevard,
Staten Island, New York, 10314, as part of their
communications apostolate.

---

4 5 6 7 8 9 (Current Printing: first digit).

DEDICATION

Dedicated to Pope John Paul II
whose first encyclical the *Redeemer of Man*
teaches the dignity of man
and summons all to live a moral life
in today's world.

PREFACE

Religious Education has been involved in many changes during the last decade. Whether you were aware of it or not, your religious education classrooms were the targets of hot debates among Catholics. The Baltimore Catechism, with its question-and-answer format, had taught most of your teachers and parents. But the Catechism did not meet modern requirements, especially after the theological revolution sparked by Vatican II. You live in a Church with many viewpoints about theology, morality, and religious education. Your parents and teachers, for the most part, lived in a Church with set agreement about these issues.

Some religious educators, especially the conservatives, want a return to the older-Catechism. They believe it would provide you with all of the content which you missed in the last ten years. The liberals, however, are unsure. Most of them wish to convey content to you, but they are uncertain that a century-old Catechism will prepare you for the Church of the 21st Century.

Below are two passages on religious education. Both are written by Catholics who could be termed "liberal." Both emphasize the need for content today. However, the two different views show the difficulty in planning out a suitable textbook for you, the student.

When I began teaching in 1963 there were still some nervous parents who questioned my not using a catechism. I assured them the new approaches were far better because they combined the best in theology and pedagogy. It all seemed to be true initially because the children did well and the parents became avid learners along with

them. Then, as the pedulum continued to swing to the left, a
gnawing suspicion began to form. As each year passed and series
upon series of student religious books appeared and then underwent
revision it became apparent that a vacuum was being created. The
children all knew that God and Jesus loved them, that they were
continually being enlightened by the Holy Spirit, that all the
Church is Jesus' gift to us. After eight years of religious education
that was still all they knew. I don't deny that these concepts are
fundamental, but they are certainly not all that someone should
know about one's faith. Another factor became increasingly
evident—the religious milieu which has provided the realization
and support for the content was becoming weaker and less visible.
The children were becoming more and more religiously rootless as
the pendulum hit the far left swing in the arc. (Diana Grieco,
"Hickory-Dickory-Dock" The Alternative, Feb., 1977 Vol. III, No.
3, pp. 2-3).

Ms. Grieco uses the image of a swinging pendulum. The
conservatives are on the right side and the liberals on the left. The
pendulum began on the right, and after Vatican II moved steadily
leftward. At first Ms. Grieco welcomed this change. Now she
doubts about her original position. What made her change her
mind?

Most liberal Catholic educators see a genuine value in what
was done new in religious education. They do not want to lose all
the benefits of the new system. At the same time, they are painfully
aware that the liberal position needs some important changes.
They do not want a complete return to the old way. Judy
Thompson McKay warns us that we cannot give students *content*
divorced from our *feelings* about our religion. She feels this is *too*
conservative:

I feel very strongly that there is a need to return to content in
religious education, but I believe that means content as defined by
Webster—2.b) essential meaning; significance.

Many today have found that much of the content we were inundated
with is neither essential to their life or significant. The essence or
significance of the Catholic Church is the community. I don't feel
that I can say anything about community that has not been said
more eloquently by others. I'd merely state that a living community
has no need to indoctrinate.

The most important thing to keep in mind is that children operate on a feeling level 99 11/100% of the time. Bring them together; help them to feel good about themselves. This is not done by discussing the Sunday Mass "obligation" when the teacher knows a good percentage of the students sitting there didn't attend. What can that possibly do for the "education" of the child? Tell gospel stories; talk about what they mean to us. When children have acquired a sense of belonging they'll have a desire to discover their roots. (Judy Thompson McKay, "What Do We Really Want?" *The Alternative*, Feb., 1977, Vol. III, No, 3, p. 10)

Ms. McKay wants a religious education which is sensitive to the feelings which youth have. She does not want a religious education which simply pours content into them. Ms. Grieco is concerned that we are educating children to appreciate feelings of love and togetherness, but are not giving youth sufficient content. Ms. McKay notes that youth will not care about content until they care about the Church, and they will not care about the Church, until the Church cares about them.

Both positions are in the liberal camp. Conservative Catholics would say the problem is artificial. Simply return to the fundamentals outlined in the Catechism, and have children memorize this. Once they have this information, they will be able to apply it throughout life. They claim that religion is not a matter of feeling, but a response to God's grace. The Church has the answers revealed by God. These answers should be given in their totality. The student has only to learn the acquired wisdom of the Church. There is no need to "feel needed" or to "feel" anything at all. It is not a matter of emotion for them, but of commitment. It is a powerful point.

Questions about Religious Education

1. What is the liberal position about religious education?
2. What is the conservative position about religious education?
3. Have liberal Catholics modified their view in the last decade? Why?

4. What methods were you exposed to in the classroom?
5. Do you have an opinion about how religion should be taught in the classroom?
6. Do you think this present textbook will satisfy your needs?

CONTENTS

INTRODUCTION

Roots was a television phenomenon in the early part of 1977. It chronicled the family history of a modern black man. In his research he found that his family had African and Irish ancestry. He discovered both Moslems and Christians in his background. And he uncovered the fierce determination of his own people to survive in spite of harsh opposition. It is the story of every man and every family, and this is the reason why the televisied book had such a firm hold on American viewers.

We Catholics also have a rich heritage. Our Church is almost 2,000 years old. It has survived many fierce battles. It has its own collection of wise people and fools, saints and sinners, visionaries and reactionaries. It is a family of people. Its roots go back to Jesus of Nazareth preaching on the Galilean hillsides.

The television program *Roots* revealed how hungry many Americans were to go back to their own beginnings. They wanted to learn who they were, even if at times the learning was painful. No one likes to believe his roots include slave traders and whipping boys. No one likes to see how much evil and prejudice flows into his own soul.

Too many Catholic youth today are ignorant of their own roots. Over a decade ago, the Catechism was drilled into Catholic students. Willy-nilly, they learned something of the Church's doctrine and moral teaching, and also a bit of her history as well. However, in the past decade most Catholic children have been exposed to new formats. Few of these formats stressed content. The authors do not argue that these new formats were not needed. However, one unfortunate result has been clear to teachers of high school and college students in Catholic courses. Most Catholic children know little about their own Church's history. They have only the vaguest notion of her basic doctrine. They have not been taught how the Church's doctrine is the foundation for her moral teaching.

The older Catechism is not the answer. It would be inaccurate to teach Catholics that they live in a Church which has pat answers to all of the questions about life. There are disputes in the Church between reputable theologians and among Church authorities. We cannot act as if these disputes are not there. They are an integral part of the incredibly complex, beautiful and rich reality we call Catholicism. This work will not attempt to treat or solve all of the controversies in the Church today. However, the authors will attempt to introduce the readers to the Church's history, moral teaching and doctrine. It is hoped this will shed some light on the range of opinions in the Church, and also clarify authentic doctrine.

The Church has published a *General Catechetical Directory*. This Roman document has prepared the way for the future of religious education in the Church. It lays down some basic norms. The American bishops are also preparing a document. It will be the combined work of many theologians, teachers, parents, and others. It will eventually be called the *National Catechetical Directory*. It will lay the foundation for a series of textbooks and courses on Catholic teaching.

But what does the religious educator do in the meantime? Does the teacher gather together a wide assortment of paperbacks to create a course on fundamentals? Do the parents take out the old *St. Joseph's Catechism* and drill it into their children? "At least they'll have *something*!"

The authors have written this book to give more than "something." It is written with the hope that it will fill a real need in the classroom. So many teachers and students have asked for a book which would give the basics of Catholic teaching.

The authors have also included, as often as possible, two views on an issue. Some proponents are Catholic; others are not. The point is that the student lives in a Church filled with controversy. The book hopes to introduce him FIRST to Church

doctrine, THEN to Church morality, and FINALLY, to the controversies of most moral issues. This will give the student the tools
to make an informed moral decision in the light of the Catholic
tradition.

The following three chapters are an outline of traditional Catholic doctrine. The chapters treat first, of the ethics taught by Jesus of Nazareth; second, the history of the Church, which includes an outline of the moral teaching of the Church and its theological tradition over the centuries, with a special emphasis on the contemporary doctrinal teaching of Vatican II, and third, the final chapter is on the purpose of the Church. It is meant to give a simple explanation of why, in God's plan the Catholic Church exists in the contemporary world. All three chapters constitute an introduction to the theological doctrine of the Catholic Church. Rooted in the original teachings of Jesus, the Catholic Church has continued through the centuries to maintain His ethical doctrine. Even through different theologies and different councils, the Church has always kept to this single-minded purpose of continuing the ethical tradition begun by Jesus of Nazareth. The last chapter is intended to explain its *present* purpose; why the Church exists in the Twentieth Century. It is a continuation of the ethical tradition which began in Jesus, and even today its purpose is to help each of us to live a good moral life and to avoid falling into the trap of committing evil.

Chapter 1

THE ETHICS OF JESUS

It might seem strange to start our discussion with these three questions about ethics. After all, what difference does it make? Hopefully the answer will show the need for our ethics to be modelled on Jesus' ethics.

The first question is, what does the word ethics mean? It has been defined as a branch of philosophy that is concerned with what is morally good and bad, right and wrong. It can also mean a code of rules for moral behavior. At times it means a system of moral principles. In all three cases, the words ethic and moral have been used. In ordinary language, ethics and moral are interchangeable, that is a moral person is an ethical person.

Even though strictly speaking, ethics refers to a specific area of study and morality refers to a way of human conduct, it does not make any difference. When we speak of a person who is morally good, we are really saying that the person is ethically good. In fact, most people simply say that a person is good or bad. They usually mean that his or her actions are good or bad.

The second question is, do I or my friends have a code of ethics? Yes, you do. Everyone does. It does not mean that my ethics or my friend's ethics are good. They may be, but then again they may not be. It depends on one's relationship with God and with the neighbor. In other words, do my actions reflect the love of God and the love of neighbor.

Recall the case of Adolf Hitler. Hitler's position on genocide caused six million Jews and five million Christians to be exterminated because of religious hatred. There were two million

Germans put to death under Hitler's Euthanasia Act because of physical or mental deformity. Then, there was the case of Charles Manson in California. His murders were done in the name of God. The world was stunned by the tragic murders of President Kennedy, Martin Luther King and Senator Kennedy. The murderers of these men had a code of ethics but it was defective. These are famous cases. What about ordinary people, like you and me? Let us take your case. If you cheat in an examination, you steal what belongs rightfully to another student. However, you may rationalize your behavior, it does not make your actions right.

The third question is, what difference does it make if I have a good code of ethics? The answer to this question is crucial. Because if I do just as I like it is bound to affect others. We do not live in a vacuum but in an interaction situation. The English poet, John Donne, said in his writing, *Meditation 17* that no man is an island. It is true. If we think about it, two thirds of our day is spent talking, working and playing with one another. Therefore, my actions certainly do and will affect others.

Astute observers point out that the moral fiber of American Society has become weakened by the poor ethics of many people. In fact, they say, we resemble the final days of the great Roman Empire when its morality had become decadent. People in the streets are saying that the morality of American society is getting worse. Some authorities are saying that our western world is a moral disgrace. The reasons for this harsh judgment can be seen in the following facts.

Watergate—for the first time in our 200 year history, a President and Vice-President were forced to resign their offices. There were 36 men in different government positions who were convicted of unethical and illegal conduct. They lied and they cheated. They stole and they bribed. They abused and they threatened. The whole affair shook our country to its roots. It was a national disgrace and we have suffered for it. Public confidence is gone and it will be difficult to restore it. Not only did individuals suffer because of the actions of these men but a whole nation has suffered and is still suffering. It is very easy to tear something down but it is doubly hard to rebuild it.

Violent Crimes—In New York City, there are approximately

1500 murders a year. There are 700 reported cases of rape a year. There are thouands of robbery cases a year against the senior citizens of New York City alone.

Shoplifting—Statistics show that it is a $70 billion business. The odd thing about it, is that the people who are doing it are predominantly the white and black middle-class people. Business firms have to build into their budgets, a 10 to 15% expense for shoplifting.

Therefore, a good code of ethics can make a difference for the individual and society. The problem is, how can I be sure that my code of ethics is right? Is there any perfect code of ethics I can follow? Yes, there is. The teaching of Jesus.

Because of Watergate, violent crimes, theft, and widespread dishonesty, the need for the teaching of Jesus to be understood and accepted is becoming crystal clear. One might call it a Jesus revolution. Our world problems would be less complicated and frustrating if we allowed Jesus' ethics to guide us.

Who is Jesus?

Historically, Jesus was born in Bethlehem, Judah (present day Israel) in the first century. He was a Jew born of Jewish parents. When He was a young boy, He lived in a town called Nazareth. It was a small place with about two hundred people. Like Joseph, His foster father, He learned to be a carpenter. Like His fellow countrymen He lived under the hammer of the Roman power. Palestine was one of the many areas which were under the jurisdiction of Rome. In fact, most of Europe and the Mid-East was occupied by Roman soldiers.

As a young man, Jesus attended the synagogue in Nazareth where He learned the scriptures from the Rabbi. On the Sabbath, as a faithful Jew, He went to the Jewish services. There He prayed, meditated and discussed the meaning of the sacred scriptures. He spoke and read Hebrew and common Aramaic.

When he was about thirty years old, He started to preach and teach in many towns of Galilee. Soon, a number of people followed and listened to Him. The numbers grew daily. Within a short time,

His reputation spread. Some people called him a prophet. Others called him a Messiah. And others called Him a miracle worker. In any case, his followers believed He was truthful. They could trust Him because He was sent by God. Indeed, He was the long awaited Messiah. God had not forgotten His people and so He sent His Son. Jesus was His Son and He was the God-Man. How could it be? If man is capable of creating magnificent things such as heart-pacers, computers, laser beams, spacecrafts, cannot God create a special being, a God-Man?

What was His Message?

Jesus' central message is summarized in one idea, namely, love God and love thy neighbor. The Gospels which were written about 50-100 A.D., record it in this way:

A) Matthew 22:37-39, "You shall love the Lord your God with your whole heart, with your whole soul, and with all your mind. This is the greatest and the first commandment. The second is like to it: You shall love your neighbor as yourself."

B) Mark 12:30-31, "Therefore you shall love the Lord your God with all your heart, with all your soul, with all your mind, and with all your strength. This is the second, you shall love your neighbor as yourself."

C) Luke 10:26-27, "Jesus answered him: What is written in the Law? How do you read it? He replied: You shall love the Lord your God with all your heart, with all your soul, with all your strength, and with all your mind, and your neighbor as yourself."

All three gospel accounts are almost identical in their record of Jesus' message of the love of God and the love of neighbor. Each of these gospel writers were contemporaries of one another but lived in different parts of the world. For example, Matthew lived in Jerusalem; Mark lived in Rome and Luke lived in Greece. There is no mistake as to Jesus' wishes. Man must love God and neighbor.

However, one could ask the questions, Who is God? Who is the neighbor, and what is love? First, God has been described in many ways. Some define God as a supernatural being, others say He is energy, power, or knowledge. Obviously, God means someone greater than man. Christians call Him, the Father who is all powerful, all knowing and all present. Jesus spoke of Him as the loving Father.

Second, who is the neighbor? In the time of Jesus, it was the Egyptian, the Syrian, the Roman and the Greek. Today, it is the Black, the Cuban, the Puerto Rican, the White Man. It is the Jew, the Christian, the Moslem, the Atheist, and the Agnostic.

Third, what is love? Perhaps the word love has been the most abused and misused word in the English language. It has been defined as peace, joy or sex. St. Thomas Aquinas' (lq. 2a, a, 2, #1) definition is that a lover works for the good of the beloved as he works for his own. Love lives and lets live. It may shrink, wither, die, but it grows again. It understands, believes, shares, encourages and laughs. It recognizes the spiritual nature of another human being.

Therefore, we can say that Jesus' teaching on ethics is based on the love of God and the love of neighbor. This love is specified in the famous speech of Jesus which has been called the Sermon on the Mount.

In Matthew's gospel (5:1-12) we read:

> "When He (Jesus) saw the crowds He went up the mountainside. After He had sat down His disciples gathered around Him, and He began to teach them: How blest are the poor in spirit; the reign of God is theirs. Blest too are the sorrowing; they shall be consoled. Blest are the lowly; they shall inherit the land. Blest are they who hunger and thirst for holiness; they shall have their fill. Blest are they who show mercy; mercy shall be theirs. Blest are the single-hearted for they shall see God. Blest too the peacemakers; they shall be called the sons of God. Blest are those persecuted for holiness sake; the reign of God is theirs. Blest are you when they insult you and persecute you and utter every kind of slander against you because of me. Be glad and rejoice, for your reward is great in heaven; they persecuted the prophets before you in the very same way."

There is little doubt as to what Jesus meant. In reality, He is saying, here is the blueprint. Now read it and do it. He never said it would be easy and comfortable. It was not easy for the people of His time and it is not easy for our time. While dress and customs may change, yet human nature remains basically the same. There is in every person a little larceny, a little selfishness, a little envy. And in some cases, there is more than a little.

Once again, the choice stands . . . either the Ethics of Jesus or the ethics of others. Jesus' ethics have been around a long time roughly 2000 years. They are sound and solid.

Obviously, many people do not accept the ethics of Jesus. Why? There are two points of view about Jesus. Maybe, they will help to answer the question.

Comment

The fundamental basis for a Christian Ethics is falling in love with God and the neighbor. How does one fall in love? Obviously, it is not easy. We think it happens every day. The Christian has Jesus' Blueprint for Love. He showed us how it is done, namely giving His life for everyone who ever lived. That's real sacrifice. That is love. When one gives his life for a friend, it is the supreme act of love. It is selflessness and it is heroic. Fortunately, there are not many times when we are called to do it. Yet you and I are called to love. We are called to be kind, patient and understanding. These ideas are only part of love. Therefore, love is expressed in the way we act towards others. Our behavior has to be modeled on Jesus. If it is not, then it is not Christian.

Our society is filled with all sorts of ethical codes. How can we change these false, immature and devastating ways of behavior? It is up to the individual. Individuals make up society. If society is to change, it must start with the individual. The individual can and must change it. One can do it in three ways:

A) *by falling in love with themselves and others.* Psychologists say that one must love oneself before one can ever hope to love others. Love means one sees himself or herself and accepts the way he or she is. Likewise he sees others and tries to understand and accept others for themselves. Every human being is a beautiful person.

B) *by an inner turning to God.* The inner peace and serenity comes when one prays, listens and talks to God. Most people do not listen to others. Notice how some people have not heard a word you said when you have spoken to them.

C) *by conversion.* Very important! Unless one changes interiorly there cannot be a real change in a person. If there was only an exterior change it would be superficial. A permanent change comes from a true conversion. This conversion takes place when one allows human knowledge and divine assistance to enter into our deliberations.

Having explored the ethics of Jesus, let us summarize what has been said.

Summary

1. In ordinary languages the words, morality and ethics are used interchangeably.
2. A moral or ethical person is one who performs a good or bad act.
3. Everyone has some code of ethics.
4. Christian ethics are based on Jesus' Ethics.
5. The fundamental law of Jesus' Ethics is the love of God and love of the neighbor.
6. A poor code of ethics leads to many terrible situations such as Hitler's Euthanasia Act, the Kennedy and King murders and Watergate.
7. Jesus is the God-Man.
8. Jesus' central message is the love of God and the love of neighbor.
9. The gospels (written stories about Jesus) were written about 60-100 A.D.
10. Jesus specified the love of God and the love of neighbor in the Sermon on the Mount.
11. The choice remains for us . . . either the ethics of Jesus or the ethics of others.

It is time to ask some questions and see if we can expand our horizons.

Questions for Discussion:

1. How can Jesus' ethics change the world?
2. How does a Christian code of ethics differ from an Atheist's code of ethics?
3. Some say that morality is not essential to Christianity. Discuss.
4. How can a person love himself or herself?
5. How would you define God?
6. What is Jesus' relationship to God?
7. Is not the Sermon on the Mount an ideal rather than a practical way of behavior?

BIBLIOGRAPHY

Abbott, Walter ed. *The Documents of Vatican II*. Baltimore: Geoffrey Chapman, 1969.

Barclay, William. *The Mind of Jesus*. London: SCM Press LTD, 1968.

Ciuba, Edward. *Who Do You Say That I Am?* New York: Alba House, 1974.

Curran, Charles. *Blueprints for Moral Living*, Chicago, Illinois: Claretian Publications, 1974.

Finley, James; Pennock, Michael. *Christian Morality and You*. Notre Dame, Indiana: Ave Maria Press, 1976.

Greeley, Andrew M. *The Jesus Myth*. Garden City, New York: Doubleday and Company, Inc., 1971.

Hoffer, Eric. *The Ordeal of Change*. New York: Perennial Library, Harper and Row Publishers, 1967.

Kerns, Joseph. *How Does God Teach Us Morals?* New York: Paulist Press, 1969.

Lockyer, Herbert. *Everything Jesus Taught*. Vol. I. New York: Harper and Row Publishers, 1976.

Lohkamp, Nicholas. *What's Happening to Morality?* Cincinnati, Ohio: St. Anthony's Messenger, 1971.

Maslow, Abraham. *Religions, Values, and Peak Experiences*. New York: Penguin Books, 1976.

Rachels, James, ed. *Moral Problems*. New York: Harper and Row Publishers, 1971.

Sloyan, Gerard. *How Do I know I'm Doing Right?* Dayton, Ohio: George A. Pflaum Publishers, 1970.

We have looked at the moral teaching which Jesus began; now we turn to the history of the Church, which has tried for the last two thousand years to continue Jesus' ethical tradition. The Church has a varied and fascinating history. In that time, theologians have struggled with different theological definitions at different councils. Moral theologians have sought to articulate exactly what a Christian should or should not do, and this continuing dynamic interchange exists in our own century. Vatican II was, in many ways, the end and the fruit of all the long years of history before it. It is nothing new in the Church to have different theological traditions or different arguments about what is moral and what is not. This chapter is an attempt to give the student a clear understanding of the wide history of the Church, the different moral theologies which have existed in the Church, and the present doctrinal teaching of Vatican II.

Chapter 2

A BRIEF HISTORY OF THE CATHOLIC CHURCH

You have finished a chapter on the Ethics of Jesus. Jesus of Nazareth preached in the first century of the Christian era. How did His teachings come down to you? Why do people still hold fast to His principles? The answer is the Church: the community of men and women who believe in Jesus as Lord. They have preserved His moral principles up to our own day. Under the inspiration of the Holy Spirit, the Church wrote the Scriptures, preached the Word of God, and worshipped the Father.

You belong to a community which is a living part of human history. The influence of politics and society have deeply affected your Church. In the same way, the Church has had a profound influence on politics and society.

The world and the Church have not yet finished Jesus' work. None of us has reached the goal Christ set for us. No society, no believing community, is yet a perfect reflection of what it is called to become. A popular poster reads: "Be patient with me, God isn't finished with me yet." Be patient with the world and with the Church, God is not finished with them yet, either.

Christ began the Church, and Christ is the goal of the Church. As the Fathers of Vatican II taught:

> For God's Word, by whom all things were made, was Himself made flesh so that as perfect man He might save all men and sum up all things in Himself. The Lord is the goal of human history, the focal point of the longings of history and of civilization, the center of the human race, the joy of every heart and the answer to all its yearnings. He it is whom the Father raised from the dead, lifted on high, and

stationed at His right hand, making Him Judge of the living and the dead. Enlivened and united in His Spirit, we journey toward the consummation of human history, one which fully accords with the counsel of God's love: "To reestablish all things in Christ, both those in the heavens and those on the earth." (Ep 1:10) (Church in the Modern World #45)

The following is a brief history of the Church. It is really the family roots of the community to which you belong. Like any other family, the Church has had its successes and failures. It is not the story of a perfect people living in a perfect society. It is the story of real men and real women. They had faith in Jesus as Lord, and passed that faith on to us. We believe today because of them.

The limitations of space forced the authors to compress this history into a few highlights. The authors hope it will whet your appetite to learn more about your own family, the Church.

To help your understanding of the Church's history, we have divided this chapter into seven sections. The first five sections are chronological divisions of the Church's history. We have arbitrarily divided the 2,000 year history of our community of faith into five time zones: I. the Ancient Church, II. the Early Medieval Church, III. the Later Medieval Church, IV. the Early Modern Church, and V. the Modern Church. Each of these five sections has five further divisions: 1. An Historical Outline, with a list of significant Popes during that period, 2. A Survey of the Ecumenical Councils of that period, 3. A Survey of the Moral Doctrine of that period, 4. A Summary Statement, and 5. Discussion Questions. There are two additional sections: VI. a Summary of the Moral Doctrine of the Church from the Ancient Church to the Present, with appropriate discussion questions, and VII. a section on the Teachings of Vatican II, followed by a precise comment of the 16 documents, a summary statement, and suitable discussion questions.

The following outline will clarify the approach used in this chapter:

I. THE ANCIENT CHURCH, 1-600 A.D.
1. An Historical Outline, Significant Popes
2. The Ecumenical Councils

I. THE ANCIENT CHURCH, 1-600 A.D.

1. An Historical Outline

The First Century, 1-100 A.D.: Jesus preached in the Roman Province of Judea. His disciples and apostles made converts among the Jews and the Greeks. The New Testament was written in Greek.

The Second Century, 101-200 A.D.: Christians established an organized Church. Theology emerged as a union of biblical revelation and Greek philosophy. Roman officials executed the martyrs for not worshiping the pagan gods. The apologists wrote defenses of the Faith.

The Third Century, 201-300 A.D.: The Roman Pope permitted those who denied the Faith to return to the Church. It was a decisive moment in the development of the Sacrament of Reconciliation since penitents could now seek official forgiveness more than once for even the most serious sins.[1] A sect of Christians formed a separate Church and insisted that a Christian cannot deny the Faith during persecutions and then be readmitted.

The Fourth Century, 301-400 A.D.: Christianity became the official religion of the empire. The Arians and the Catholics debated over the nature of Christ. The empire—and the Church—divided into the Greek East and the Latin West.

The Fifth Century, 401-500 A.D.: The Germanic barbarians conquered the Western empire. The Nestorians and the Catholics debated the nature of Christ and of Mary. With no Western Roman Emperor, the Pope gained in prestige and power.

The Sixth Century, 501-600 A.D.: The Church expanded into the German countries and the British Isles. The Greek Emperor and the Roman Pope wrestled over who had the control of the doctrine and the administration of the Church.

Significant Popes of the Ancient Church

First Century: St. Peter (d. 64 A.D.) was martyred by the Emperor Nero.
Clement of Rome (90-100 A.D.) wrote to the Corinthians on Church order.

Third Century: Stephen (254-257 A.D.) defended his policy of readmitting apostates to the Church.

Fourth Century: Sylvester I (314-335 A.D.) the first pope to reign in an unpersecuted Church, yet one torn by internal debates.

Fifth Century: Pope Leo I (440-461 A.D.) one of the most powerful of the early Popes, intervened in the deliberations of the Council of Chalcedon.

Sixth Century: Vigilius (537-555 A.D.) struggled with the Greek emperor Justinian over control of the Church.

2. The Ancient Church: The Ecumenical Councils

A. Introduction.

A Council is a gathering of the bishops of the Church, called together by the Pope (in the ancient Church and in the East, the Emperor summoned a Council) in order to discuss questions of faith or morals or church discipline or guidance.

There are several types of councils: 1) A *general council* or *ecumenical council* consists of all the bishops of the Church, from all over the world, who have been summoned by the Pope. Their decrees become the law when the Pope announces them. 2) A *provincial council* is one which consists of bishops of a certain area; e.g., the northeastern part of the United States. 3) A *national council* is a gathering of the bishops of one country. 4) A *diocesan council* is a council composed of the bishop and clergy of a diocese; e.g., the Brooklyn Diocese.

The Roman Catholic Church has been in existence almost two thousand years. It was founded by Jesus Christ and it was Jesus who appointed Peter as its first leader (Pope). As the Church grew in the world, it encountered problems and it had to face them. From Peter to the present Pope John Paul II, each Pope has had the responsibility of Jesus' command, "All power is given to me in heaven and on earth. Go therefore, teach all nations, baptizing them in the name of the Father, and the Son, and the Holy Ghost. Teaching them to observe all things whatsoever I have commanded you; and behold I am with you all days even to the consummation of the world" (Mt 28:18-20).

Because of human problems and doctrinal controversies, the authorities of the Church have had to settle these matters. In its long history, the Church has had twenty-one general or ecumenical councils. However, it was not until the fourth century (325 A.D.) that the Church had its first general council.

Until the Fourth Century, "councils" were really groups of bishops of small areas who met to discuss pastoral practice, or to decide on the authenticity of the books of the Bible. A "General" or "Ecumenical" Council is supposed to have representatives from all Christian communities. This has always been an ideal not actually accomplished because doctrinal or political disputes often prevented some groups from being represented at the councils. There are twenty-one Councils recognized by the Roman Catholic Church. This means that the teachings of these councils are binding on Catholics unless the Pope vetoes the teaching. Almost all Christians recognize the teachings of the ancient councils as binding.

B. The Ancient Councils[2]

The Fourth Century: First Ecumenical Council: Nicea (325 A.D.) condemned the heresy of Arius, an Alexandrian priest, who denied the divinity of Jesus.

Second Ecumenical Council: Constantinople (381 A.D.) condemned Macedonius who denied the divinity of the Holy Spirit and Apollinarius, a bishop, who claimed that Jesus had a human body but no human mind.

Fifth Century: Third Ecumenical Council: *Ephesus* (431 A.D.) stated that Mary was the mother of the human and divine person of Jesus. Nestorius and his followers, who denied that Mary should be called "Mother of God," were condemned.

Fourth Ecumenical Council: *Chalcedon* (451 A.D.) emphasized that Jesus had a human and a divine nature.

Sixth Century: Fifth Ecumenical Council: *Constantinople II* (553 A.D.) denied the idea that human beings were pure spirits. It also condemned the "Three Chapters" of the Nestorians.

3. The Ancient Church: A Survey of Moral Doctrine

The First Century: 1-100 A.D.: In the earliest period of Christianity, preachers of the new religion (Christianity) used two forms, namely, proclamation and teaching. Proclamation (Kerygma) meant the news of Jesus' Life, Death and Resurrection. In contrast to the proclamation the teaching (Didache) meant the instructions for the Christian conduct of Life. Besides the New Testament there are three documents of this era that are particularly important: a) *Didache*—the earliest writing on Moral theology; a small manual on morals and church practices; b) *The Shepherd of Hermas*—a Christian writer's account of God's message; and c) Pope Clement's Letter to the Corinthians that urged them to restore a loving unity.

The Second Century (101-200 A.D.): In order to secure a more faithful adherence to the message of Jesus, one finds simple, sketchy summaries of moral instructions. a) St. Clement of Alexandria (150-215 A.D.) gave guides to the Christian Life in his works, *Protrepticus* and *Paedagogus* which gave a detailed description of the morality of a true Christian. b) Tertullian (160-, 225 A.D.) wrote several books such as *On Penance* and *On Idolatry* which taught that the Will of God was the First Pinciple of the Christian Moral Life.

The Third Century (201-300 A.D.): Christian writers wrote on profound questions such as Church Law, pagan philosophy, and the spiritual life of Christians. a) St. Irenaeus (d. 202) sometimes called "the First Christian Theologian" makes it clear that reflection and practical spirituality go together. b) Origen (d. 225) stressed man's ability to reason to understand the mysteries of God. c) St. Cyprian (d. 258) wrote on subjects of Christian morality such as patience, almsgiving, and virginity.

The Fourth Century (301-400 A.D.): When the Roman Empire was converted to Christianity in 321 A.D., there was a greater need to establish a Christian morality for a Christian society. a) St. Augustine (354-431 A.D.) may well be the greatest moral theologian of all times. His writings laid the foundations for the future moral systems. He said that charity is the most important principle of Christian morality. b) St. Cyril of Jerusalem (d. 386) wrote numerous sermons on Christian living. He is credited with writing the first catechism. c) St. Ambrose (d. 397) in his book *De Officiis* speaks about the supernatural life of the Christian. d) St. John Chrysostom (d. 406) wrote on subjects such as marriage, and priesthood.

The Fifth Century (401-500 A.D.): St. Gregory the Great (d. 604) wrote a work on the various Christian duties. His work is considered even today a classical work in moral theology.

The Sixth Century (501-600 A.D.): This century was generally unproductive in original writings on moral theology.

4. The Ancient Church: Summary Statement

The ancient Church started among Jews, and then spread

throughout the Roman Empire. Greek-speaking Christians created the early New Testament documents and the writings about the Faith. For the first four centuries the Church was a persecuted minority. Apologists wrote doctrinal defenses of the Church and tried to show to the pagan majority the "reasonableness of the Faith." Once the Church became the official religion of the empire, it suffered many internal debates. The Eastern Church concentrated on the questions about Jesus Christ and the Trinity. The Western Church was pragmatic, but interested in the issues of grace and sin. As the Germanic people weakened the power of the Western emperors, the Pope became the most powerful leader in the West. In the East, the Greek emperor had more control over Church affairs, and the Church leaders in the East usually supported the emperor rather than the Pope.

5. *The Ancient Church: Questions*

1. Why is Christian theology a union of Greek philosophy and Biblical Revelation?
2. Why did some early Christians refuse to accept the Sacrament of Reconciliation?
3. Why did the Pope emerge as a strong leader in the West?
4. What were some of the differences between the Church in the West and the Church in the East?
5. What did the early Church councils decide? Why did they concentrate on these issues about Christ and the Trinity?

II. THE EARLY MEDIEVAL CHURCH, 600-1054 A.D.

1. *An Historical Outline*

The Seventh Century (601-700 A.D.): The Pope took control of the civil and military administration of Rome. The Eastern Church debated Monothelitism, the doctrine that Christ had only one will. Mohammed preached the beginning of the Islamic faith.
The Eighth Century (701-800 A.D.): The Eastern Church

debated whether or not Christians can venerate images of the saints. Islam swept across the Middle East and North Africa. Major cities of the Greek Church were overrun. The Greek emperor and the Patriarch of Constantinople lost much of their power, and became more hostile to the claims of the Roman Pope. Pope Stephen III formed an alliance with the Frankish monarchy. In 800 A.D. the Pope crowned Charlemagne Emperor of the Holy Roman Empire.

The Ninth Century (801-900 A.D.): Charlemagne ruled a united France, Germany and North Italy. The Roman rite became the norm for these churches. British and Irish monks came to the Continent to teach the Christian tradition.

The Tenth Century (901-1000 A.D.): The papacy was very weak. Lay rulers controlled church administration. Clerics were more loyal to lay rulers than to Church officials. There was much absenteeism in dioceses and parishes. A married clergy often willed their income from parishes to their sons. A reform movement began in the Benedictine monastery at Cluny.

The Eleventh Century (1001-1054 A.D.): The monastic reform movement reached the papacy. The Pope regained control of church affairs. Zealous for papal authority, the Pope's legates in Constantinople excommunicated the Patriarch in 1054 A.D. This was the formal separation of Roman Catholicism and the Orthodox Churches.

Significant Popes of the Early Medieval Church

Sixth and Seventh Centuries: Gregory the Great (590-604 A.D.) reformed Church administration.

Ninth Century: Nicholaus I (858-867 A.D.) was one of the few popes at this time to insist on papal authority in his struggles with the Greek emperor and the Frankish kings.

2. The Early Medieval Church: The Ecumenical Councils

Seventh Century: The Sixth Ecumenical Council: Constantinople III, (680-681 A.D.): This council condemned Monothelitism, the doctrine that Christ had only one will. Monothelitism was an attempt to unite the factions in the Eastern Church, especially the Monophysites who taught Christ had only one nature.

Eighth Century: The Seventh Ecumenical Council: Nicea II, (787 A.D.) taught that Christians could venerate the images of the saints. The Moslems had conquered much of the East and condemned all forms of idolatry; there was much political pressure to conform to their practice.

Ninth Century: The Eighth Ecumenical Council: Constantinople IV, (869-879 A.D.): This council, under pressure from the Pope, condemned the Patriarch Photius' irregular elevation to the See of Constantinople. This action eventually caused the Greek schism.

3. The Early Medieval Church: A Survey of Moral Doctrine

The period from 600 to 1054 was considered to be a quiet transitional age for Moral theology. Great emphasis was placed on the writings and sermons of the men who had gone before them. Also the statements of the Popes, bishops and Councils were a guide for Christian formation. However, the only original and creative work during this period were the penitential books. These summaries of moral doctrines were a great aid to the priests who had to deal with the problems of their faithful. These books were predominantly concerned with the amount of penance for sins. In fact one of the books lists twenty varieties of murder and the appropriate penance for each one.

4. The Early Medieval Church: Summary Statement

The Pope and the Greek emperor continued their uneasy alliance. The Greek church suffered internal debates, and then was decimated by the rise of Islam. The Pope turned to the kings of the Franks for support and protection. For a brief period Charlemagne managed to unite most of Western Christendom. He reorganized Church order with the Roman ritual. Monks from the British Isles travelled extensively throughout the Continent. They helped set up monastic schools and introduced private confession.

The papacy became the tool of Roman nobility and was usually subject to the wishes of the Frankish monarchs. Priests and bishops were often the vassals of lay rulers, and more loyal to them than to Church officials. There were many absentee bishops and pastors. The income from these benefices could be given by married clergy to their sons. There were many abuses and many unworthy people in Church administration.

A reform movement began in the monastery of Cluny and then spread throughout the West. It reached the papacy in the middle of the eleventh century. Jealous of papal authority, the legates in Constantinople excommunicated the Greek patriarch. They drove the final wedge into the split between the Roman West and the Greek East.

5. The Early Medieval Church: Questions

1. Why was the Eastern Church unable to present a united front against the Islamic invasion?
2. Why did the Pope turn to the Frankish monarchs for military support?
3. What role did the British and Irish monks play on the Continent?
4. What were the abuses associated with lay control of the clergy and the married priests.?
5. How did the reform papacy create the final split between the Roman Catholics and the Eastern Orthodox?
6. Who introduced private Confessions?
7. What were the penitential books?

III. THE LATER MEDIEVAL CHURCH, 1054-1500 A.D.

1. An Historical Outline

The Eleventh Century (1054-1100 A.D.): Hildebrand, later Gregory VII, reformed the papacy. He stressed clerical celibacy, and greatly increased the Pope's control over Church affairs. He determined the Pope's right to excommunicate and depose a king or emperor. The First Crusade recaptures Jerusalem from the Moslems.

The Twelfth Century (1101-1200 A.D.): The Church in the West was strictly organized. The Church had canonical elections, clerical celibacy, official visitations, appeals to Rome, and the papal protection cf religious orders. This century saw the growth of monasteries, the building of cathedrals, and the illumination of manuscripts.

The Thirteenth Century (1201-1300 A.D.): Innocent III ruled at the peak of papal power. The Fourth Crusade turned away from the Moslems and sacked the Greek Christian capital Constantinople. The Franciscan and Dominican orders began. The great theologians of the period, especially Thomas Aquinas, synthesized Catholic theology and the Greek philosophy of Aristotle. The century ended with the Inquisition, which had the power to condemn heretics and hand them over to the state to be executed as traitors.

The Fourteenth Century (1301-1400 A.D.): The Pope moved to Avignon in France. There were many abuses in the central administration of the Church with the Pope out of Rome. The Great Western Schism had three popes claiming to rule the Church. The Briton John Wyclif warned of the need for reform.

The Fifteenth Century (1401-1500 A.D.): The Council of Constance ended the Great Western Schism. It condemned the Bohemian John Hus to death for heresy. The Council of Florence attempted to reunite the Western and Eastern Churches. The union was short-lived. The Moslems took Constantinople and the Eastern Empire was ended. The Pope struggled with Conciliarism, the doctrine that a General Council is superior to a Pope. The

Popes became wealthy Renaissance princes. Papal taxation was
resented by many.

Significant Popes of the Later Medieval Church

Eleventh Century: Gregory VII (1073-1085 A.D.) restored
papal authority, excommunicated the Holy Roman Emperor and
was exiled by him.

Twelfth Century: Innocent III (1198-1216 A.D.) was the most
powerful Pope of the Middle Ages. He interfered in many political
matters "for the good of the Church."

Thirteenth Century: Innocent IV (1243-1254 A.D.) increased
the papal tax; he excommunicated and deposed the Holy Roman
Emperor.

Fourteenth Century: John XXIII (1316-1334 A.D.) an anti
pope at Avignon is recognized as a financial and administrative
genius.

Fifteenth Century: Eugene IV (1431-1447 A.D.) strove to unite
with the Greek Church. He had constant battles with the doctrine
that a Council was superior to a Pope.

2. The Ecumenical Councils

The Twelfth Century: The Ninth Ecumenical Council:
Lateran I (1123 A.D.) confirmed the Concordat of Worms, which
settled disputes between the Pope and the Western Emperor on
questions about authority and control, and about the election of
bishops.

The Tenth Ecumenical Council: Lateran II (1139 A.D.) ended
the Western schism caused by the false Pope Anacletus II. It
condemned certain ideas, such as there are only two Sacraments
(Baptism and Eucharist), and also the rejection of the baptism of
infants.

The Eleventh Ecumenical Council: Lateran III (1179 A.D.)
confirmed the papal treaty with the Emperor. It ruled that a
majority of 2/3rd's of the Cardinals' votes were needed to elect a

Pope. It rejected the idea that only the New Testament and not the Old was inspired, and that there are two Gods.

The Thirteenth Century: The Twelfth Ecumenical Council: Lateran IV (1215 A.D.) condemned the sect, the Cathari. It defined the doctrine of transubstantiation, that is, that consecrated bread and wine changes into the Body and Blood of Christ even though the appearances remain the same. This Council obliged Catholics to go to Confession and Communion at least once a year.

The Thirteenth Ecumenical Council: Lyons I (1245 A.D.) confirmed the Pope's deposition of the Western Emperor. It organized a general Crusade.

The Fourteenth Ecumenical Council: Lyons II (1274 A.D.) created a short-lived reunion with the Greek Church. It set up a new crusade, and approved the new regulations for electing a Pope.

The Fourteenth Century: The Fifteenth Ecumenical Council: Vienne (1311-1312 A.D.) confirmed the abolition of the military order, the Knights Templar. It intervened in the quarrel between branches of the Franciscans about the vow of poverty.

The Fifteenth Century: The Sixteenth Ecumenical Council: Constance (1414-1418 A.D.) ended the Great Western Schism and elected Martin V the true Pope. It condemned the reformed teachings of John Wyclif and of John Hus, who taught that the Church is made up of people who are predestined. Hus was put to death as a heretic in 1415 A.D. It stated that a General Council was superior to a Pope and wanted councils held regularly. The Pope refused to accept this doctrine of "Conciliarism."

The Seventeenth Ecumenical Council: Basel-Ferrara-Florence (1431-1445 A.D.) Pope Eugene struggled to overcome Conciliarism. He secured another temporary union with the Greek Church.

3. The Later Medieval Church: A Survey of Moral Doctrine

From the stagnation of the moral theology of the early Medieval Church came a new era for Moral Theology. It was to be called the Golden Age of Moral Theology. Despite the rise of canonists (Church lawyers) who discussed moral problems within a juridical framework, it gave birth to men like St. Thomas Aquinas (1225-74) and St. Bonaventure (1221-74). Unfortunately, the canonists placed greater emphasis on Law rather than Love, as given by Jesus. In fact textbooks on Catholic moral theology, articles, instructions in the early part of the twentieth century echo the excessive stress on duty and obligation as given in the 12th and 13th centuries.

Another factor for the Golden Age of Moral Theology was the rise of the Universities and the formation of religious groups such as the Dominicans and Franciscans. The Universities, especially that of Paris, taught Theology as a subject. Eventually, the Dominicans with St. Thomas Aquinas and the Franciscans with St. Bonaventure explored many areas of moral conduct. Thomas' greatest contribution was his emphasis on the role of natural reason which helped man to understand his world. Reason with Faith, he said, will lead man to a good Christian morality. While Bonaventure stressed the role of Will and Love, Thomas stressed more the role of the intellect and knowledge in the understanding of the Faith. Because of Thomas' synthesis of theology, he is called the Father of Moral Theology. His books *Summa Theologiae* were followed as a guide in theology and were a foundation stone for today's Moral Theology.

The Golden Age of the 13th Century gave way to the 14th century, a century of crisis for Christianity, particularly because of the Great Western Schism. The Dominican and Franciscan schools lived on but without great men like Thomas and Bonaventure.

The 14th century was marked by William of Ockam's (d. 1359) Nominalism which emphasized the individual man and his individual acts. It became a moral system of individualism. It meant that the "good" is whatever God freely and even arbitrarily desires to be good. This moral system became a listing of "do's and dont's." It became an impersonal way of judging a person. Nominalism contributed to the legalism and obligationism in Catholic Moral Theology. By the 15th century, there was the beginning of the rejection of Nominalism and the restoration of the importance of human reason. Thomas Aquinas' greatest contribution was once more being recognized and applied as a guide for deciding what was right and wrong.

4. The Later Medieval Church: Summary Statement

During this period all of Western Europe was Christian. The papacy was reformed and became very powerful. Crusaders tried to take the Holy Land away from the Moslems. At first the Church succeeded in reform movements, but as the central administration grew in power and wealth, many abuses occurred. Theology reached its peak in the thirteenth century. The Dominicans and the Franciscans sparked a reform of the Church.

The papacy moved to the French court at Avignon and then fragmented into three competing Popes. A council settled the question but then defined a council as superior to a Pope.

The Eastern Church was part of many abortive attempts to reunite with Rome. Its political and military base evaporated with the fall of Constantinople, which had already been weakened by the Fourth Crusade's invasion.

The reformers John Hus and John Wyclif were ignored, and many abuses crept back into the Church. The Popes at the end of this era were Renaissance princes financed by an unpopular papal tax.

5. The Later Medieval Church: Questions

1. What did Gregory VII (also Hildebrand) do to restore papal prestige?
2. What was the purpose of the Crusades?
3. Why did the Eastern empire fall to the Moslems?
4. What is conciliarism and why did the later Popes try to end it?
5. Why was the papacy becoming unpopular at the end of this era?
6. What are the signs of the coming Reformation movement?
7. What was Thomas Aquinas' contribution to moral theology?
8. What was the difference between Bonaventure's teaching on moral theology and William of Ockam's?

IV. THE EARLY MODERN CHURCH, 1500-1789 A.D.

1. An Historical Outline

The Sixteenth Century (1501-1600 A.D.): Martin Luther ignited the Protestant Reformation. The Reform movement had four main branches: Lutheranism, Calvinism, Radicalism, and Anglicanism. The Council of Trent reformed the Catholic Church. The Jesuits were founded and spearheaded the Catholic reformation and the great missionary effort to the New World.

The Seventeenth Century (1601-1700 A.D.): Europe was ravaged by wars of religion. For the most part Catholicism triumphed in the lands originally belonging to the Roman Empire, and Protestantism in the lands which originally belonged to the Germanic and British tribes. Catholic missionaries brought Christianity to Canada, America, South America, India, China and Japan. The Catholic Church was troubled by Jansenism and Quietism. Jansenism emphasized man's unworthiness before God; Quietism taught a total passivity to the grace of God. Galileo was silenced.

The Eighteenth Century (1701-1800 A.D.): The Pope struggled with Febronianism, Gallicanism, and Josephinism. Febronianism tried to restore conciliarism into the Church. Gallicanism insisted on the French king's right to rule the Church in France. Josephinism involved the Hapsburg Emperors who wanted to intervene in Church affairs. The American Revolution succeeded in creating a democratic nation, where all religions are equal. Yet, many Protestant Americans suspected Catholics were tied up with monarchial governments in Europe. When the King of France was overthrown by revolution, violent anticlericalism was unleashed because the Church and clergy had been strongly identified with the monarchy. The papacy understandably did not support such violent revolutionary behavior.

For a while, the Bourbon monarchs succeeded in suppressing the Jesuits.

Significant Popes of the Early Modern Church

Sixteenth Century: Pius IV, (1559-1565 A.D.) confirmed the decrees of the Council of Trent.

Seventeenth Century: Urban VIII, (1623-1664 A.D.) ruled as Pope when the Inquisition condemned Galileo for teaching that the earth moves around the sun and also has a daily rotation. This scientific teaching implied that there were texts in the Bible which could not be taken literally.

Eighteenth Century: Pius VII, (1775-1799 A.D.) was taken prisoner by the French for being associated with the ancient monarchy.

2. The Early Modern Church: The Ecumenical Councils

The Sixteenth Century: The Eighteenth Ecumenical Council: Lateran V (1512-1517 A.D.) condemned the schismatic Council of Pisa. It settled questions about the human soul. It made some small attempts at reform, but really did not correct major abuses.

The Nineteenth Ecumenical Council: Trent (1545-1563 A.D.) made genuine reform. It condemned the erroneous teachings of Luther, Calvin, Zwingli, and other reformers, but left open the possibility of dialogue with the Reformers in the future on open issues. It restructured the Church. It gave official teachings about the Bible and Tradition, original sin and justification, the seven Sacraments, the Sacrifice of the Mass, and the cult of saints. In many ways it "froze" theology and liturgy.

3. The Early Modern Church: A Survey of Moral Doctrine

After the dryness of Nominalism came the famous 16th century in the Church History. The Protestant Reformation split the Christian Church. This disaster awakened Catholic moral theology to the need of the new times. This period witnessed the birth of moral theology as a distinct theological science. Moralists were interested in forming correct consciences of Christians and to teach confessors practical doctrinal principles to solve moral cases. Men like Francesco Suarez (1548-1617 A.D.) and Bartholomew Medina (d. 1560) introduced a new approach to solving moral problems. It was called probabilism. It meant that if one's conscience was in doubt about the Law, one could not be free to act until the doubt was resolved. Obviously, this approach to moral problems led to many difficulties. Thus other solutions arose. There was a system called Probabiliorism which said that you may follow the more probable opinion favoring freedom in resolving moral cases. Eventually this system led to the probabilissimus system which meant that one couldn't follow even the most probable opinion favoring freedom of conscience. One had to have absolute certainty before one could act. From these moral systems of "Probabilism" which went from a lax to a rigorous approach to solving moral problems, came the outstanding theologian, St. Alphonsus Liguori (1696-1787). He found a middle way between these two approaches.

Alphonsus' Moral system became known as Equiprobabilism. In reality, it meant that if one is in real doubt whether or not the Law binds, one could resolve the doubt in favor of freedom. One would not be bound by the Law in that case. Naturally, this system, like any system, is not perfect but it gave a practical, reasonable, humane way of handling moral cases.

4. The Early Modern Church: Summary Statement

The Renaissance papacy tolerated abuses which drove Martin Luther to break with the Church. Protected by the German rulers, he was able to spread Lutheranism. Luther taught justification by faith alone. He rejected the hierarchy, teaching that all the faithful were priests without distinction. Scripture was the rule of faith, but the individual, not the Church, was the interpreter. He reduced the sacraments to two: Baptism and the Eucharist. He denied the Mass was a sacrifice, but claimed it was a remembrance. He taught consubstantiation of the Eucharist, which meant Christ was present but not in the manner defined by a council.

Calvin went further and denied the validity of many Catholic practices and also the presence of Christ in the Eucharist. The Radicals went still further in denying the need for Church order. The radical Anabaptists taught that only an adult could be baptized. The Anglicans retained much of Catholic doctrine and practice, but made the English monarch head of the Church.

Lutheranism spread in North Germany and in Scandinavia. Calvinism started in Switzerland, and then spread throughout France, the Low Countries, and parts of Germany and England. John Knox brought it to Scotland. The Radicals were numerous in the Low Countries, Germany, Bohemia and Poland. They were often persecuted by both Protestants and Catholics. Anglicanism started in England and then spread throughout the British Empire.

The wars of religion exhausted Europe and drove many sincere religious people to the New World. With the advance of science, the intellectuals grew hostile to organized religion. The papacy struggled against a rising tide of nationalism, where heads of State also wanted to be heads of the Church. The American Revolution inspired the rising middle class in Europe to fight against the monarchies and Church authorities.

5. The Early Modern Church: Questions

1. How did Luther's teaching differ from the Council of Trent?
2. What were the four branches of the Reform Protestant movement?
3. Where did Catholic missionaries go during this time?
4. Why was the papacy uneasy about the effects of the American Revolution?
5. Define each of the following and show why it weakened the Pope's role in the Church: Febronianism, Gallicanism, and Josephinism.
6. Why is the Sixteenth Century the Golden Age for Moral Theology?
7. Define: a) Probabilism, b) Probabiliorism, c) Probabilissimus.
8. What did Alphonsus Liguori contribute to Moral Theology?

V. THE MODERN CHURCH, 1789-PRESENT

1. An Historical Outline

Eighteenth Century (1789-1800 A.D.): Napoleon turned France into another empire. He imprisoned the Pope.

Nineteenth Century (1801-1900 A.D.): After Napoleon was defeated, the Papacy supported the restoration of the monarchies. In the minds of many, the Church became associated with the conservative and the wealthy, while most of the people supported liberal and democratic ideas. The Jesuits were restored. There was a mass migration of poorer Catholics to America. They remained loyal to the Church, but enthusiastically supported the concept of democratic government and the separation of Church and State. The poverty of the working classes inspired the rise of Communism and Socialism. Both movements were atheistic and identified the Church with the oppression of the poor. The Pope lost control of the Papal States and all his temporal power. The Pope defined the Immaculate Conception of Mary. Vatican I taught that a Pope is infallible when teaching as head of Church in matters of faith and morals.

Twentieth Century (1901-present): Deprived of temporal power, the Popes became great spiritual leaders. A centralized Church flourishes, but faces persecution all over the world.

The First World War ends the power of monarchies. The Second World War ends colonialism. Totalitarian anti-Christian governments persecute the Church in Nazi Germany, Communist Russia, and Communist China.

The Ecumenical Movement struggles to reunite all Christian churches.

John XXIII and Vatican II lay the groundwork for modernizing the Catholic Church. Some conservative Catholics feel betrayed and want to return to the stricter traditions of Trent.

Significant Popes of the Modern Church

Nineteenth Century: Pius IX (1846-1878) tried to maintain

European monarchies, fought against liberal theology and liberal politics, which he felt would weaken papal power. He lost the Papal States and all temporal power, but was able to increase his spiritual authority by the teaching of Vatican I. The Church became very centralized after the Council.

Twentieth Century: Pius XII (1939-1958 A.D.) lead the Church during the Second World War. He was deeply respected for the intellectual acumen of his Papal encylicals.

John XXIII (1958-1963 A.D.) started to "open the Church out to the modern world." He summoned Vatican II, the first pastoral council, which attempted to modernize practice and liturgy, and also initiated dialogue with other Christians and other believers.

2. The Modern Church: The Ecumenical Councils

The Nineteenth Century: The Twentieth Ecumenical Council: Vatican I (1869-1870 A.D.) defined the primacy of the Pope and the infallibility of the Pope in matters of faith and doctrine.

The Twentieth Century: The Twenty-First Ecumenical Council: Vatican II (1962-1965 A.D.) a pastoral council which reexamined Church discipline, restored the vernacular language to the liturgy, revised the sacramental rites, stressed the importance of the laity, and opened dialogue with non-Catholics. Because of its influence on today's Church, this chapter has a special section devoted to its documents and teachings.

3. The Modern Church: A Survey of Moral Doctrine

Liguori's *Manual of Moral Theology* continued to be used in the following centuries even until our own times. It was the basic confessional Manual with some modifications for priests. Alphonsus' age of Rationalism gave way to Johann Sailer (1751-1832) and Johann Von Hircher (1788-1865) 19th century Age of Enlightenment. Sailer's *Moral Manual of Christian Morality* (1818) and Hircher's *Christian Moral Teaching as Realization of the Kingdom of God* (1834) spoke of the ideal Christian way of life.

These books were biblically oriented, however, they generally followed the moral principles laid down in Alphonsus' *Manual of Moral Theology*. Still it was Alphonsus' ideas that influenced the 19th and early 20th century moral thinkers.

It was not until the Second Vatican Council (1962-1965) that moral theology took a new approach. It opened a new era for moral theologians. It marked a new understanding of the nature of the Church. Naturally, it had to effect moral theology. Moral Theology today has a continuity with yesterday, but is open to the new knowledge and insights of the 20th century Man. The excessive stress on mortal and venial sins, on rules and regulations now gives way to Jesus' message of Love. The new moral theology is concerned with helping a person grow and develop as a son and daughter of God rather than condemning the faults of the person. It is a less negative approach to morality.

The moral theology of the post-Vatican II era is a theology based on a concrete, particular and individual thing and person rather than an abstraction, unchangeableness and certitude. Men like Bernard Haring, John Milhaven, Louis Monden, and others are creating a moral theology open to the data of sciences such as psychology, sociology and anthropology.

4. The Modern Church: Summary Statement

After the failure of Napoleon the papacy favored the restoration of monarchies. In Europe Catholicism would be associated with the ruling class and with wealth. The political conservatives remained pro-Catholic, but the liberals became more anti-Catholic and anti-monarchial. The opposite occurred in America, where poorer Catholics left Europe. American Catholics would be pro-Catholic but also accepted the principles of liberal democracy.

Karl Marx and Frederic Engels proposed an atheistic communist philosophy that formed the bases for the Russian Revolution.

After losing the Papal States, the Popes gained in spiritual authority and prestige. Church government became very centralized.

John XXIII saw the need for the Church to modernize, and summoned Vatican II. Conservative Catholics resent the changes, and want to return to the stricter Catholicism of the past.

Today the Catholic Church must face these three problems:

1) a secular First World indifferent to religion;
2) an atheistic Second World actively hostile to religion;
3) an impoverished Third World which wants a religion untainted by Western culture.

Also the Church is facing internal debates about the value of modernization. These debates concern every vital part of the Church: doctrine, liturgy, religious life, hierarchy, clergy, and laity. Many intelligent and sincere Catholics are confused and uncertain about the Church. They grew up in a more stable community, but now see a Church often divided on these key issues.

5. The Modern Church: Questions

1. How does European Catholicism differ from American Catholicism?
2. What role did the Papacy play in the European politics of the Nineteenth Century?
3. Why was the Papacy of the Nineteenth Century suspicious or hostile to the principles of liberal democracy?
4. What role did the Pope play in the Twentieth Century after the papacy had lost its temporal power?
5. What did Pope John XXIII and Vatican II attempt to do for the Catholic Church?
6. What are the problems facing the Catholic Church today from the outside and from within?
7. Do these issues have any impact on your personal future?
8. What were the contributions of Sailer and Von Hircher to Moral Theology?
9. What has happened to Moral Theology as a result of Vatican II?

VI. SUMMARY OF MORAL DOCTRINE FROM THE ANCIENT CHURCH TO THE PRESENT

1. The Ancient Church

In the first three centuries of the Ancient Church there was a great emphasis on the moral message of Jesus, namely Love. Jesus was the center of all moral teachings. These early writings show brief outlines of moral behavior. Most of the times, they were opinions on poverty, war, sex, slavery and sin. They were not long discussions.

However, as Christians integrated with the General Society, the next three centuries showed the beginnings of a real system of moral theology. Men like Ambrose, John Chrysostom, Cyril of Jerusalem, Gregory the Great and Augustine wrote many books on marriage, virginity, lying, patience, and so forth. However, it was Augustine's idea of Charity as the most important principle for moral theology which became the cornerstone for future Moral Manuals.

2. The Early Medieval Church

This period of Moral development was a stagnant, unproductive era. Most moral theologians relied on their predecessors. The only original and creative works were the Penitential Books of the seventh century. These works listed the types of sins and the corresponding penances for the offenses.

3. The Later Medieval Church

The twelfth century was a century of canonists (Church lawyers) who introduced into Moral Theology the legalistic approach. The ethic of Love was overshadowed by the ethic of Law. The scales were tipped in favor of Law. Moral decisions would be based heavier on Law than Love. Despite the canonists,

Thomas Aquinas stressed the role of natural reason as enlightened by God's grace in determining what was right and wrong, Aquinas' books *Summa Theologiae* became a landmark for Moral Theology. In one sense, he merits the term, "Father of Moral Theology" since he helped to systematize it. Even with the rise of the Nominalism of the 14th Century, Aquinas' teaching that God personally loves and cares for man influenced this era.

4. The Early Modern Church

The sixteenth century saw a new awakening for Catholic Moral Theology. It was an era marked by the term "Probabilism." Men like Suarez and Medina argued whether one could act when he had doubts. The idea of doubts broke down into just plain doubts, more doubts and great doubts.

This dilemma of Moral Theology was solved by the outstanding figure of Alphonsus Liguori of the 18th century. He proposed a middle way between the laxist's and rigorist's approach to moral problems. It was known as Equi-Probabilism which meant when one is in reasonable doubt, one may act. Liguori built on Aquinas' notion of reason, who had built on Augustine's earlier notion of Love.

5. The Modern Church

From the 17th century of Liguori to the present age of the Second Vatican Council, moral theology has been influenced by the notions of absolutism and unchangeableness of things and persons. However, the Second Vatican Council introduced a new era for moral theology. Because of man's new knowledge about himself and the world, moralists of today stress the total picture of Man in his relationship with God, other people, and himself. There is a stronger emphasis on Love than Law.

6. Comment: The Future of Moral Theology

One of the conclusions that came from the Second Vatican Council (1962-1965) was that it is a Pilgrim Church. What did it mean? Simply this. That it has not arrived at its destination but it is on its way. As it moves along the paths of events and ideas of history, it is constantly discovering and rediscovering its purpose and aim. Its course has to be adjusted time and time again. It cannot remain stagnant. It must remain open to the new knowledge which is being provided by sciences such as psychology, sociology, anthropology, biology, and so on. These sciences help man to understand himself better. And so they help him to grow and develop his potentialities.

Consequently, man is changing all the time. His moral life must be a response to God's love. Moral theology deals with God and human experience. When well done, moral theology is a great tool for knowing God's will and helping us reach our final destiny. Union with God is our ultimate aim.

Moral theology cannot rest on its laurels. Moral theology will never be perfect. Moral theology must remain vital. Moral theology must reflect the sensitivity, gentleness, kindness and lovingness of Jesus who is the center of every human being's existence.

Moral theology stresses the following:
1. the gospel message of Jesus' love
2. the maximum standards of good behavior
3. rapid social changes which have given new problems
4. the individual's responsibility to God and his fellow man
5. an integral and not merely moral vision of man's life
6. the biblical teaching on conversion (metanoia)
7. an open-ended morality

7. Questions for Discussion

1. What is Moral theology? What are Moral Systems?
2. What historical event caused the early systemization of moral theology in the Ancient Church. Why?

3. Why are Augustine, Aquinas and Liguori called the "Fathers of Moral Theology"?
4. Explain the notion of Probabilism and its effect on moral theology.
5. How did the Protestant Reformation of the 16th century impede the development of moral theology?
6. It has been said that the ancient Church's moral theology is similar to the modern Church's moral theology. Comment.
7. What positive effects did Vatican II have on present day moral theology?
8. What are the dangers of the "new morality" of love?

VII. THE MODERN CHURCH
THE TEACHINGS OF VATICAN II

1. Introduction

The time had come. The world needed a spirit of hope. The Church needed a new Pope. And so it happened that a short, robust, jovial man was elected the two hundred and sixty-first Pope of the Roman Catholic Church. Probably no one was more surprised than he when the cardinals selected him on October 9, 1958. On that day, thousands of people crowded St. Peter's Square in Rome asking the question, who will be the new Pope? In a loud, clear voice, a priest announced to the world that Cardinal Angelo Giuseppe Roncalli was the new Pope. And that he had selected as his title, John XXIII. Soon the world would refer affectionately to him as Pope John. The Church had a new Pope. The world had a new religious leader. At the age of 77, when most men have retired from their jobs, this man was about to begin a new career for himself and open a new era for the Church.

So it was that he announced on June 29, 1959 to the world:

> Bishops from every part of the world will gather here (Rome) to discuss serious religious topics. They will consider in particular the growth of the Catholic faith, the restoration of sound morals among

the Christian flocks, and appropriate adaptations of Church discipline to the needs and conditions of our times. This event will be a wonderful spectacle of truth, unity and charity.[3]

For two years, there were extensive preparations for what was to be called Vatican Council II. On October 11, 1962, Pope John XXIII formally opened the General Council. There were 2,908 Church leaders in St. Peter's Basilica who heard that the purpose of the Council was to "bring the Church up to date," (*aggiornamento*) and to work for its spiritual regeneration.

Before we survey the documents and teachings of Vatican II, we should recall two points, namely, certain terms or words commonly used, and the usual purposes and problems for which councils were called in the past.

A Council is a gathering of bishops of the Church, called together by the Pope, in order to discuss questions of faith and morals or church discipline or guidance.

First, the area of persons, the term Pope is a title given to the Bishop of Rome, who is the head of the Roman Catholic Church. A bishop is a priest who is in charge of a diocese (an area of land). A cardinal is the highest ranking title given by the Pope, usually to a bishop who is either administering a Church office or governing an important city.

Secondly, we have seen in the historical survey, there have been twenty-one Ecumenical Councils recognized by the Roman Catholic Church. Although all Christians usually hold the teaching of the Ancient Councils as universally binding, Orthodox and Protestant Christians do not acknowledge the authority of Councils which have met since their separation from Roman Catholicism.

It is interesting to note that Councils are not held every century and that Councils vary in length of time. What is important is that the Church looks at the particular problems of the day and does something about them. And so it was the case when Pope John decided to hold a General Council in 1962. Why? There are many reasons. Here are some:

1) to revitalize the Roman Catholic Church against today's deteriorating moral standards and militant atheism

2) to heal the wounds of schism and heresy among our non-Catholic brothers

3) to revise the seven sacraments so that they would be more meaningful

4) to restore the vernacular language to the Mass

5) to abolish certain excommunications which were important for their time

6) to portray the Church as the servant not the master of humanity

7) to reexamine old disciplines and regulations

8) to give lay people more responsibility in the Church

9) to utilize modern media

10) to decentralize Roman bureaucracy

11) to restore more authority to the local bishops.

Despite some opposition on the part of conservatives, Pope John formally opened the General Council in St. Peter's Basilica in Rome on October 11, 1962. There were four sessions of the Council. The first session was from October 11 to December 8, 1962; the second session was from September 29 to December 4, 1963; the third session was from September 11 to November 21, 1964; and the fourth session was from September 14 to December 8, 1965.

Unfortunately, Pope John died on June 3, 1963. It is generally recognized that the world lost a great man, a man of the people and a man of God. His successor, Pope Paul VI, continued the Council and presided over the other sessions. On December 8, 1965, he formally closed the Council. The only thing that remained was to implement the decrees of the Council.

In order to accomplish this task, Pope Paul established commissions to supervise the work and to interpret the texts that had been written. There were sixteen pieces of legislation. They were divided into the following categories.

2. The Documents of Vatican II

1. The 4 Constitutions:

The Dogmatic Constitution on the Church

The Dogmatic Constitution on Divine Revelation
The Constitution on the Sacred Liturgy
The Pastoral Constitution on the Church in the Modern
World

2. The 9 Decrees:

The Decree on the Bishops' Pastoral Office in the Church
The Decree on Ecumenism
The Decree on the Eastern Catholic Churches
The Decree on the Ministry and Life of Priests
The Decree on the Priestly Formation
The Decree on the Appropriate Renewal of the Religious
Life
The Decree on the Church's Missionary Activity
The Decree on the Apostolate of the Laity
The Decree on the Instruments of Social Communication

3. The 3 Declarations:

The Declaration of Religious Freedom
The Declaration on the Relationship of the Church to
Religious
The Declaration on Christian Education

Briefly this is what these sixteen documents say:

1. *The Dogmatic Constitution on the Church* is the most
important document. It set the theological basis for the other
documents. The basic points are:
   a. The Church is God's people, not necessarily to be
      identified with the ecclesiastical hierarchy.
   b. The center of the Church is Christ who is the light of all
      nations.
   c. All men are called to belong to the People of God, and make
      up the Body of Christ under one head.
   d. The Pope is the Vicar of Christ and the pastor of the whole
      Church.

e. The bishops are to have a greater role in the administration of the Church government.

f. The laity (lay people) are to have a greater role in the daily life of the Church.

2. *The Dogmatic Constitution on Divine Revelation* emphasized the vital part sacred scriptures (the Bible) play in the Church's life and liturgy. The basic points are:

a. The Church accepts the idea that revelation is a personal communication through the pages of history.

b. The Sacred Scriptures are to be understood in the customary and characteristic styles of feeling, speaking, and narrating which prevailed at the time of the writer.

c. The Church is the authentic interpreter of the scriptures and tradition.

3. *The Constitution on the Sacred Liturgy* permitted the use of the vernacular (local language) in place of Latin for the Mass and the Sacraments. The basic points are:

a. No person, even if he be a priest, may add, remove, or change anything in the liturgy on his own authority.

b. The Mass is the greatest liturgical act of worship to God.

c. The Sacred Liturgy is to be taught under its theological historical, spiritual, pastoral, and juridical aspects.

4. *The Pastoral Constitution on the Church in the Modern World* is the first ecumenical document to be addressed to all men, not just Roman Catholics. The basic points are:

a. The Church rejects atheism but respects and loves the atheistic person as a creature of God.

b. It condemned all forms of war as a means of settling international disputes, but affirms countries' rights of self defense.

c. It called all nations to organize and work to relieve the suffering of poor and starving peoples.

d. The Church has something to give to the world but has herself much to receive from it.

e. Marriage is not instituted solely for procreation, but also

for the mutual love of the spouses.
f. The Church must involve itself in the crisis of world growth, change of attitudes and cultural and social transformation.

5. *The Decree on the Bishop's Pastoral Office in the Church* discussed the collegiality of bishops. It directed the bishops to form national and regional conferences to meet local conditions and problems. The basic points are:
a. There is to be a synod of bishops to meet with the Pope periodically in Rome to act as an international senate or advisory board.
b. Bishops must be good pastors interested in their lay people and their priests.
c. Bishops must present Christian doctrine in a manner adapted to the needs of the times and guard against erroneous teachings that arise.
d. Religious and social research is to be fostered.

6. *The Decree on Ecumenism* pledges the Church to work for the unity of all Christianity, and encourages Roman Catholics to participate in the Ecumenical Movement. The decree permits Catholics to join non-Catholics in common prayer with the permission of the local bishops. The basic points are:
a. Non-Catholic Christian Communities are called Churches or ecclesiastical communities and no longer termed "sects" or heretical communities.
b. Catholics are to acknowledge and esteem the truly Christian accomplishments of our separated brothers.
c. The divisions among Christians prevent the Church from attaining the fullness of its goal.
d. Christ summons the Church to continual reformation as she exists in this world.
e. Catholics must be in dialogue with separated brothers who share the faith of Jesus Christ.
f. Baptism establishes a sacramental bond of unity among Christians.

7. *The Decree on the Eastern Catholic Churches* reasserted the equality of the Eastern Rite Catholic Churches with the Western Latin Rite. The decree established circumstances under which Catholics and Eastern Orthodox Church members could participate together in the sacraments and liturgy. The basic points are:

  a. The right of Eastern Catholic Churches to rule according to their own customs and rules providing they kept in mind their responsibility to the Pope who is head of the whole Church.

  b. The Church recognizes the right of difference while at the same time strives for unification.

8. *The Decree on the Ministry and life of Priests* reaffirmed the laws of celibacy for Roman Catholic priests, without modifying the Eastern Rite discipline allowing married and celibate clergy. The basic points are:

  a. Celibacy is not the essence of the priesthood.

  b. The priest is not surrounded by an aura of mystery but regarded as a real human being.

  c. The priest must be aware of the needs of the individual and the needs of the Church community.

  d. The celebration of the Eucharist must get special attention by the priest.

9. *The Decree on Priestly Formation* urges reforms in both the intellectual and spiritual training of a candidate for the priesthood. It gave more authority to the local bishops in their administration of seminaries. The basic points are:

  a. A candidate for the priesthood must be educated in the sociological and psychological studies as well as the theological areas.

  b. Biblical studies are very important and are the core of all theology.

10. *The Decree on the Appropriate Renewal of the Religious Life* speaks of modernizing the religious life of monks, priests, brothers and nuns. The basic points are:

MORALITY: HOW TO LIVE IT TODAY

50

a. The equal voting rights and complete equality of all brothers, monks and sisters, within their own communities.
b. Religious life must adapt itself to its present historical times, while not losing sight of its purpose and goals.
c. The supreme rule of a monastic foundation is not its own particular "rule and constitution," but Christ himself.

11. *The Decree on the Church's Missionary Activity* asks for greater cooperation and support between well established Churches and missionary Churches. The basic points are:
a. The missions are not a supplementary part of the Church.
b. The whole Church is a missionary and therefore should work to convert the pagan world.

12. *The Decree on the Apostolate of the Laity* urges the laity to use its capabilities in both religious and temporal matters. The basic points are:
a. The layman is taken seriously as a Christian by the official Church in his church and world role.
b. Women are especially asked to take an active part in the Church.
c. It establishes a closer link between laity and clergy.

13. *The Decree on the Instruments of Social Communication* urges its members to use every means of communication such as the press and motion pictures for moral purposes. The basic points are:
a. Man is directly influenced by the media.
b. The Church welcomes the latest means of technology for the work of Christ.
c. Catholics would encourage and patronize actors, writers, and news commentators who promote good morality and Christian ideas.

14. *The Declaration on Religious Freedom* states that freedom from coercion with regards to religious preference is an inherent right which belongs to every human being. This was a

dramatic change in the Church's historical position. However, it repeated the Church's claim to be the one true faith. The basic points are:

    a. Men are called to serve Jesus in truth and in spirit.

    b. Governments must create favorable conditions for education for all its citizens.

    c. Man must follow his informed conscience.

    d. In the use of all freedoms the moral principle of personal and social responsibility must be observed.

    15. *The Declaration on the Relationship of the Church to Non-Christian Religions* recognizes all men as the sons of the same creator. The basic points are:

    a. The Jews have no collective responsibility for the death of Christ.

    b. The Church is open to the religious experiences of all religions such as Hinduism, Buddhism, Islam and Judaism.

    c. The Church hopes that all religious groups will be able to exist in the world in a more harmonious manner.

    16. *The Declaration on Christian Education* gives the parents the right to choose freely the type of education they wish for their children. The basic points are:

    a. The physical, moral and intellectual abilities of children and young people must be helped with psychology, arts, sciences, and religious studies.

    b. The parent is the primary educator of the child.

    c. The state must protect the rights of all citizens and check on the ability of teachers.

    d. Catholic schools have a place in the field of education.

Today, these documents are being implemented throughout the Church. These documents reflect an awareness of the universality of the Church as well as each member's responsibility for the whole Church. However, not everyone believes that the Second Vatican Council was a good thing.

    Without trying to impose false labels, the term "liberal

Catholic" usually applies to someone pleased with Vatican II, while "conservative Catholic" usually applies to someone unhappy with it.

Comment

Prior to the Second Vatican Council (1962), the world was recovering from the horrors of the Second World War. The War had left its mark on everyone and everything. Six million Jews and five and a half million Christians had been murdered by the Nazi Germans. Likewise millions of Christians suffered at the hands of the Fascists in Italy. Europe was rebuilding her war-torn towns and cities. America was steeped in materialism. It has been said that the Red Cross had more influence on that society than the Catholic Church. The point can be argued, but it probably was true. The Church had distanced itself from the practical world. The forces of evil did not have to worry about a general Christian reaction because Christianity was no longer a way of life. The Church had become a powerless force. It had failed to communicate the gospel message.

No one was more aware of this than Pope John XXIII and his fellow bishops when they assembled in council at the Vatican in October of 1962. They were determined to make the Church visible and alive. It took a lot of courage and guts. They decided to reexamine old positions and reform what had to be done. And they did. Despite the loud cries of fear, anger, and threats from some of its members (laity and clergy), the Council fathers embarked on a new path in this new world of advanced technology and science. They showed that the message of Jesus is as relevant today as it was the first century. The Church would become a leader in the world and give sound direction towards solving its problems. No longer would it live in the shadows of hallways. It would walk in the sunshine, and in a sense it would be the sunshine.

When the Council, under the leadership of Pope Paul VI, completed its work in the winter of 1965 and implemented its decrees, it had accomplished the above mentioned aims. The

Church had come to the front and was ready to lead. Its greatest accomplishments were:

    a. It created a closer relationship with Orthodox and Protestant Christians, Jews and others.

    b. It shared responsibility with the laity.

    c. It internationalized the Roman offices.

    d. It respected the right of all men to follow their consciences.

    e. It restored the local language to the Mass and the Sacraments.

    f. It recognized the value of sciences such as psychology and sociology.

    g. It would use the latest means of communication to promote the Gospel message.

    h. It realized that it is a Pilgrim Church.

    i. It changed the attitude of the Church from a legal approach to a more human one.

To sum up, the Second Vatican Council formally opened on October 11, 1962 and was formally closed on December 8, 1965 by Pope Paul VI.

4. Summary

1. There are different kinds of Councils such as General (Ecumenical), National, Provincial, and Diocesan.

2. Pope John XXIII died on June 3, 1963.

3. Pope Paul VI opened the second session of the Vatican Council on September 29, 1963.

4. There were four sessions of the Council: 1) October 11-December 8, 1962; 2) September 29-December 8, 1963; 3) September 14-November 21, 1964; 4) September 14-December 8, 1965.

5. There have been 21 General (Ecumenical) Councils in the history of the Roman Catholic Church.

6. The First General (Ecumenical) Council was held in the fourth century.

7. A General (Ecumenical) Council means that all bishops of the world are summoned by the Pope to discuss, examine and reform Church problems.

8. There were sixteen documents issued by the Second Vatican Council.

9. The four constitutions of the Council are the Dogmatic Constitution on the Church, the Dogmatic Constitution on Divine Revelation, the Constitution on the Sacred Liturgy and the Pastoral Constitution on the Church in the Modern World.

10. The nine decrees of the Council are the Decree on the Bishops' Pastoral Office in the Church, the Decree on Ecumenism, the Decree on Eastern Catholic Churches, the Decree on the Ministry and Life of Priests, the Decree on Priestly Formation, the Decree on the Appropriate Renewal of Religious Life, the Decree on the Church's Missionary Activity, the Decree on the Apostolate of the Laity and the Decree on the Instruments of Social Communication.

11. The three declarations are the Declaration on Religious Freedom, the Declaration on the Relationship of the Church to Non-Christian Religions and the Declaration on Christian Education.

Now let us turn to a few discussion questions. Questions are stimulating because they help to clarify one's position and to apreciate another's point of view.

5. Questions for Discussion

1. Why do the decrees of a General (Ecumenical) Council become the law of the whole Church?

2. After a General (Ecumenical) Council, there is generally a schism in the Church. Discuss.

3. Do you think the conservative position is dangerous to the Church?

4. Pope John XXIII's death was deeply mourned by Catholics and Non-Catholics alike. Explain.

5. Why were the laity given a greater share of responsibility in the Church?
6. What is the difference among Orthodox Christians, Eastern Catholics and Protestants?
7. Why does the Church refer to herself as a "Pilgrim Church"?
8. Do you think that some Protestant Churches will come back to the Roman Catholic Church?
9. Does the English Mass make more sense than a Latin Mass?
10. How long will it take the Second Vatican Council documents to take root?

Footnotes

1. The bishops of Rome and North Africa affirmed the power of the Church to forgive the sins of apostasy, idolatry and murder. The sacrament of reconciliation had been an integral part of the New Testament community where people confessed publicly their sins to one another. The usual practice was to limit the act of forgiveness and reconciliation to once in a person's lifetime. The bishops recognized that the apostles were given special power to forgive and bind sins. Can you give the other position that was held?
2. The Council of Jerusalem met to decide if new converts had to become Jews before they could be accepted as Christians. Although it set the example for following councils, it is not considered an ecumenical council.
3. Francis Murphy. *The Encyclicals and other Messages of John XXIII*, *Washington, D.C.: TPS Press, 1964, 4-5.*

BIBLIOGRAPHY FOR HISTORICAL SURVEY

Biggs, Wilfred W. *Introduction to the History of the Christian Church*, St. Martin's Press, New York: St. Martin's Press, 1965.

Hughes, Philip. *A Popular History of the Catholic Church*, Garden City, N.Y.: Image Books, 1954.

Sarno, Ronald A. *The Cruel Caesars: Their impact on the Early Church*, Alba House, Canfield, Ohio: Alba House, 1976.

BIBLIOGRAPHY FOR SURVEY OF COUNCILS

Kung, Hans. *The Council, Reform and Reunion*, New York: Sheed and Ward, 61-147.

Murphy, John. *The General Councils of the Church*, Milwaukee: Bruce Publishers, 1959.

BIBLIOGRAPHY FOR SURVEY OF MORAL DOCTRINE

Abbott, Walter, ed., *The Documents of Vatican II*, Baltimore: Geoffrey Chapman, 1969.

Connolly, Rev. Donald. *The Documents of the Second Vatican Council*, Orlando, Florida: Reconciliation Press.

Curran, Charles E. *Christian Morality Today*, Notre Dame, Ind.: Fides Publishers, Inc., 1971.

Day, Rev. Edward. *The Catholic Church Story: Changing and Changeless*, Liguori, Missouri: Liguori Publications, 1975.

Hardon, Rev. John A., *The Catholic Catechism*, Garden City, N.Y.: Doubleday & Co. Inc., 1975.

Kung, Hans. *The Church*, New York: Sheed and Ward, 1967.

Milhaven, John. *Toward A New Catholic Morality*, Garden City, New York: Doubleday & Co. Inc., 1970.

Murphy, Rev. Francis X. *The Encyclicals and Other Messages of John XXIII*, Washington, D.C. TPS Press, 1964.

Regan, George. *New Trends in Moral Theology*, New York: Newman Press, 1971.

In the last chapter we studied the entire historical tradition of the Church, looking at the different centuries and the different movements which took place in the Catholic family. The Church continues today. It is neither separate nor distinct from the Church first begun by Jesus Christ. Its purpose has always remained the same: to help each and every Catholic to live a life rooted in the life and moral teaching of Jesus Christ. The Church has also constantly strived to create a community which would support this purpose.

Now we will consider the Church in the present day, armed with the precepts of Vatican II and the long historical tradition of the teachings of the Church and the Sacraments, all rooted in the ethical tradition of Jesus Christ. What is the Church's purpose today? In short, the Church's purpose is to help each one of us to live a life which is truly Christian.

Chapter 3

THE PURPOSE OF THE CHURCH

Everyone belongs to a group of some kind. Most of us belong to many groups. You belong to your family, a group of people. You have a set of friends, usually a group of your own age. You probably also belong to a group which does something you enjoy: dancing or skiing or going to movies or eating Big Macs or hanging out on street corners complaining that there is nothing to do.

What is a group? It is a number of people who get together *for a mutual purpose.* A group can be as temporary as five boys shooting basketballs for a summer afternoon or as permanent as the Roman Empire which lasted centuries. It can be as small as three girls discussing a date over a soda or as large as the Chinese nation, which is one-quarter of the world's population. A group is united by each member's personal decision to identify with it. In some way, the individual understands that the group has a purpose which is the same as his or her own. A group can have many different purposes: a classroom is a group which has the purpose of learning a subject (we hope!). A baseball team is a group which has the purpose of playing and winning ball games. It can have a secondary purpose as well: to entertain an audience of fans. The American Medical Association is a group of doctors, and the purpose of this organization is to promote the interest of physicians.

The larger the group and the more people who share the same purpose, the more effective it can be. There is a very great difference between a professional baseball team and a group of teenagers playing sandlot ball. One group has carefully selected its personnel. It has spent a large sum of money in training its players. It has a larger backup system if players get injured or leave the team. Even if the sandlot team wins a game and the professional team loses, everyone understands that the professional team has a greater commitment to the game. Put the two teams on the same field and who would win?

The Church is also a group. It is the people of God. In many ways it is one of the largest groups in the world. It is also one of the oldest groups in the world. How many groups can you name which has as many members as the Church? How many groups can you think of which are as old as the Church?

The Church is a group of people who share some of the same things. They share the same beliefs, hopes, and they have the same purpose. What is the purpose of the Church? The Church has many purposes but we can list some of the more important ones:

1. The Church continues Jesus' presence on earth. It tries to bring his ethical teaching into every day and every event.
2. The Church gives spiritual support and comfort to its members.
3. The Church helps its members to reach God through teaching, prayer, and worship.
4. The Church tries to improve the world—the material and the spiritual, both.
5. The Church offers worship to God.
6. The Church aids each of its members towards reaching their final destiny: heaven.
7. The Church offers each of its members mutual encouragement when others would try to frustrate the purpose of the Church by doing evil.
8. The Church struggles to change social structures so they reflect the Gospel message of Jesus.
9. The Church uses certain tools in achieving these purposes: prayer, liturgy, the sacraments, the Scripture, Tradition, Doctrine, etc. Its aim is also to maintain these tools so that it can continue to fulfill its purpose.
10. The Church is the body of Christ. As St. Paul says: "there

is neither Jew nor Greek, there is neither slave nor free, there is neither male nor female, for you are all one in Christ Jesus" (Galatians 3:28).

11. The Church is a sacrament (sacred sign). Through its seven visible signs, it gives unity, holiness, presence of Christ to all its members.

12. The Second Vatican Council called the Church the people of God.

In summary, the mutual purpose of the Church is to imitate Christ by doing what is good and fighting against what is evil.

If you have ever watched a group of people play ball, then you know there are many ways of belonging to a group. One player is full of skill and zeal. He is always calling out encouragement to the others. Another says nothing, but plays well. Still another is always calling out corrections to the other players but collapses in a tight spot. And yet another spends most of his time daydreaming about the shower or the date after the game. All of these people belong to the same group and share the same purpose. But each one belongs to the group in a different way.

This is the *type* of membership which one person has in a group. You can understand the type by the way in which that person relates to the mutual purpose of the group.

Let us look at this more closely:

1. The organization person. He accepts the purpose of the group with his heart and soul. He never questions anything about the group. He has no doubts about the group's purpose. As much as possible, he and the group are one.

2. The group-oriented person. He accepts most of the purposes of the group. He has some questions about the means which are used. Occasionally he will speak out against a particular problem. For the most part, he goes along. He can be relied on to support the group in general.

3. The person-oriented individual. He accepts some of the purposes of the group. He has a lot of questions about the means and some of the goals of the group. He is concerned that the group may overwhelm him at some point and ask him to do things against his inclination. He does not trust the group completely but

stays within it because it meets some of his personal needs.

4. The individualist. He accepts little of the group's purpose. He questions its goals, its means, its members. He is certain that the group is making too many demands on him as a person. He is not quite sure why he belongs to the group, but he is willing to stay as long as he is not hassled too much by others.

These four types exist in every group. Sometimes people will change drastically. We have all met the person full of enthusiasm who loses his zest when the going gets rough. Each of us is all of these different types at different times. It all depends on the group and what they are doing! If the same group of people are dancing and then playing football, the types will change. One person who is a lead dancer is not usually going to be a good quarterback. If the group changes or the group's purpose changes, then there is usually a shift in the types of membership. Have you ever been in a classroom (a group for learning) which has suddenly been given an unexpected recreation period (a group for playing)? Have you noticed how the enthusiasm level goes up? More people feel they can put more of themselves into this new purpose.

Let us look at the four types and at different groups. Study this chart carefully and decide what type of membership you would have in this group.

TYPES

I. ORGANIZATIONAL — Total Commitment

II. GROUP-ORIENTED — Commitment

III. PERSON ORIENTED — Some Commitment

IV. INDIVIDUALIST — Little Commitment

GROUP

Dance
Baseball Team
Religion Class

Car Thieves
Beer Party
U.S. Congress
March of Dimes Fund Drive
Catholic Church

The class might find it interesting to share what different people have put down. Every group has many different people with different interests and different abilities. Your class probably has excellent dancers, and stumblebums. There are probably natural athletes and those who do not know the difference between a strike and a ball. God has made us all different so it is natural that there would be quite a range of types in these different groups.

Each person changes during his lifetime. A person grows, meets new people, travels, develops interests and loses interests. You would probably have put down different answers last year. You would probably answer differently next year. If the class had had a chance to talk about each group and let certain people explain the value of what each group does, then it is also possible that your opinion would change.

For example, some people may not want to be involved in a March of Dimes Fund Drive. They would not like the work or time it would take. But another person might be very enthusiastic about the Drive and *convince others of the value of the group's purpose.*

In the Catholic Church we call this evangelizing. Pope Paul VI said, "the work of evangelization today must be considered with a broad and modern outlook: in works, in organization, and in the formation of missionaries." Obviously, then, evangelization is not merely preaching the gospel but also practicing it. The Church is concerned with building a just social and political world as well as a spiritual world.

This, then, is the purpose of the Church for each of you: it provides you with *a group which supports you in your effort to do good and avoid evil.* Many people, especially young people, do not see the need for group support—especially as a support for ethical behavior. "I can do it on my own." This attitude ignores two basic facts about our lives: 1) there are many groups putting pressure on us to do what is wrong; and 2) much of this pressure is subtle and we can easily be misled into believing that this pressure was really our own opinion.

Let us explain this more carefully. There are very few things you do entirely on your own. Despite the claim of many young people of being independent, rugged individuals, most of them are really conformists to the group. About the only thing you do on your own is breathe. If you eat an apple, you depend on a group: growers, pickers, truckers, warehouse workers, grocers, your parents who bought it. The act of eating an apple totally depends on the cooperation of others.

And the moral choices which you make: unconscious or conscious, totally depend on the input which you have received from others. Their influence can be very blatant, such as a television advertisement which implies that seduction is very chic. Their influence can be very subtle: such as the uneasy feeling that the group will not truly accept you unless you do smoke marijuana.

The devil goes stalking around like a roaring lion seeking whom he may devour (1 P 5:8). Thus St. Paul uses the symbol of a hunting lion to describe how pervasive is the pressure in this world to do evil.

If you say you do not need the Church to be good, you are really saying the following:

1. I am powerful enough as an individual to combat the world of evil.
2. I am stronger than any group pressure.
3. The world around is really not so bad, the power of evil is an exaggeration.

If the blind lead the blind, they both fall into the ditch. (Mt 15:14)

You will never understand the purpose of the Church unless you understand two basic truths:

1. You do not have sufficient resources in yourself to combat evil and do good. If you believe you do, you are deceiving yourself. The rugged individual cowboy who rides into town to right all the wrongs and then rides off into the sunset is a favorite American

myth. He is a myth because the truthful experience of most people is that you cannot correct an injustice by yourself. You need others. Even our cowboy hero had to learn the principles of democracy, the common law jurist system and how to shoot, *from a support group*.

2. The Church, for all its faults, is a support group for you. It provides an environment in which you are encouraged to do good and avoid evil. It sets up a counter-pressure against the group-pressure which is urging you to do what is wrong. In this way, the Church is the continuation of Jesus Christ; it is the support group, the environment, which provides you with the energy to follow the ethical teachings of Jesus. Without the Church, the moral teaching of Jesus would be no more. We have all met the sincere Christian individualist, the fundamentalist[2] who tells us he has no need for the Church; all he needs is the Bible and his own faith in Jesus. And then he quotes from the Scriptures, which would not even exist if a community of Christians had not preserved them just for him.

Now that we have looked at the purpose of the Church, let us study how an individual can belong to the Church. Remember what we said above about the different types of people and how they belong to a group? The Church is a support group. The purpose of the team is to do good and avoid evil. Everyone in the Church is playing the game in their own unique way. Each belongs to the Church in their own personal way. However, we can group people into general types—the four types we already mentioned.

By this time you may be getting a clearer idea of how you, yourself, belong to the group. Let us look at four writers and how they regard the support group, the Church, and also their own membership in it.

As each author explains his position, you may find that he is speaking your viewpoint or at least is close to your opinion.

As you read each author, see if you can answer the following questions about his opinion:

1. What does he say about the *purpose* of the Church?
2. What does he say the Church is *failing* to do?
3. How severe is his criticism of the Church: a) mild, b)

moderate, c) critical, d) very critical.
4. What type of commitment would you say this author has to
the Church: a) Type I-the institutional man, b) Type II-the
group-centered man, c) Type III-the person-oriented man,
or d) Type IV-the individualist?

The first writer is Jacques Maritain. He was a French
philosopher who was well known among Catholic intellectuals.
He was involved in a modern interpretation of the theology and
philosophy of St. Thomas Aquinas. As a philosopher, Maritain
was particularly concerned that his readers make a distinction
between the Church *in itself* and the *members* who made up the
Church. He believed that members of the Church could do evil
things but the Church itself is a good institution.

> In the first place the Church—the visible Church—is the place of
> *salvation:* all the saved are visibly or invisibly in her. . .
>
> In the second place, the Church—the visible Church—is *the
> universal sacrament of salvation*, and she is *herself present* not only
> in her members in an actual and visible manner but also, virtually
> and invisibly, in all other men by the sole fact that they are men
> come into the world after the sin of Adam and by the title, absolutely
> fundamental and universal elements of the Church. . .
>
> It is necessary to add now a third consideration or a third approach.
> The Church prays for the salvation of all men and in this sense she is
> *cause or agent of salvation*—not only for those who belong to her
> visibly but for the men of all the earth—according as she is dedicated
> to that co-redemption of love and of suffering through which Christ
> willed to unite to Himself, even in His redemptive sacrifice
> accomplished once and for all on the Cross, all those who have
> received his grace. As Pius XII says in the encyclical *Mystici
> Corporis*, Christ "requires the help of His members," not certainly
> by way of compliment but by way of participation, in order that His
> Passion may bear its fruits on earth.[3]

Mr. Maritain uses very precise theological and philosophical
terms. It may help you to understand his passage if some of these
terms were explained more fully. The *visible Church* are the
known members of the Roman Catholic Church. The *invisible
Church* are the good people who do not appear to belong to the

Church, but who really do because they are sons and daughters of God who lead good lives. A *universal sacrament of salvation* is the Church in the world, a grace given by God to men to help them to reach heaven. The *sin of Adam*[4] is original sin; every member of the human race has this sin and, therefore, needs the grace of Jesus' redemption in order to reach heaven. The Church therefore gives to all men, whether Catholic or not, the means to reach heaven, that is, the grace to do good and avoid evil. The Church is present in all who try to do good. Finally, the Church brings to all men the graces which Christ won for us on the Cross. The members of the Church do not *complement* Christ's grace, that is, they do not fill in something that is missing. They *participate* in the grace of the Cross, they "bring his grace" to the world which needs it.

Maritain sees the whole world affected by original sin. Therefore, every man needs the grace of Jesus Christ which was won on the Cross. The Church[5] is the means of bringing Jesus' grace to all men. The Church, through Christ, is the *source* of this grace. It is also the environment which encourages men to be good. The Church consists of all good men. The visible Church is an external sign of the good that is going on in all men who are doing the work of Jesus on earth. This is the true *Person* of the Church and it should not be confused with the *personnel* of the Church who are sometimes bad men and do evil things.

Questions:

1. How does Maritain see the Church?
2. What kind of criticism does he make of the Church?
3. Why does he quote a papal encyclical to make his point? What does this tell you of his view of Church authority?
4. What type of commitment would you say he has to the Church?

The second writer is Hans Kung, the German theologian who had a great influence at Vatican II. He has written both scholarly works and popular ones, and has spoken on both the Continent and in the United States. The following excerpt was written by him as an answer to Catholics who claimed that the Roman Catholic Church was a "perfect society" and did not need reform. It was written at a time when many Catholics identified reforming the Church with Protestants who had left the Church.

> It would be a very odd sort of Christian who could survey his Church from the outside with detached indifference or from the inside with cozy contentment. He would certainly not be what St. Paul sees as a living, feeling, participating member of the body of Christ. There is such a thing among both clergy and laity as false pride in the Church, a false enthusiasm for the Church. It is the product (when not due to excusable ignorance) of a far from excusable superficial, illusory, often even frivolously presumptuous assessment of the situation of the Church in the world. Anyone who has never, as a member of the Church, suffered on account of his Church, has never known her as she really is and never loved her.[6]

Dr. Kung has always been sensitive to the Lutherans of Germany and has always written in such a way as to appeal to them. One of the points of his book was to point out to Catholics the reforms which Luther had said were needed in the Church and to indicate in many places that Luther was right. Lutherans appeal to the authority of the Scriptures so why would Kung quote St. Paul rather than a papal encyclical? Kung's writings have been unpopular with some scholars but his books have been popular with many Catholics, including the clergy.

1. What does Dr. Kung have to say about the cost of belonging to the Church?
2. From this excerpt, do you think that Dr. Kung has written criticism of the Roman Catholic Church?
3. What kind of membership would you say Dr. Kung has in the Church?
4. What would Dr. Kung have to say to Mr. Maritain about his view of the Church?

The third author is Mr. Steve Clark. He is a convert to Catholicism. Mr. Clark is a national leader of the Catholic Charismatic Renewal and has spoken all over the United States on the lay prayer movement. The movement did not start with Church officials but with lay Catholics. Even though many clergy and religious belong to the Catholic charismatic movement, it can honestly be said to be the first lay-inspired reform movement to stay within the official Church. The open atmosphere created by Vatican II has made this possible.

Mr Clark writes:

> The diocese today is no longer a local grouping. It is a regional grouping. It cannot function like a local Christian community. It cannot be a body. It cannot meet the daily needs of the Christian people. That is not to say that the diocesan (regional) groupings are not important. They are especially important today when people are more interdependent over a larger area and when more resources are needed to do certain basic things. What kind of structure the Church should have in a larger area is an important question. But for the purposes of this book, it is important only to see that a diocese is not basic Christian community even though canonically it may be "the local Church."

Mr. Clark notes the present structure of the Church: it is made up of a geographical area, headed by a bishop. This is needed to make an official local Church. It then has all the means and personnel to do the job of making people good. However, it cannot do its job because it is too large and too impersonal. Mr. Clark goes on to explain that Catholics need small support groups, communities which they join voluntarily. These smaller support groups in which each person knows everyone else can have the power to change lives for the better. Without them the Church would remain an institutional organization with little impact on the daily lives of its members.

It is the task of a basic Christian community, as seen by Mr. Clark, to create an environment in which a person can do good. He does not see the present local Church creating such an environment.

1. Does Mr. Clark believe that bishops and priests are necessary?
2. What does he see the local Church *not* doing for its people?

3. What kind of a member do you believe he is within the Church?
4. How would you describe his criticism of the Church: mild, moderate, critical, very critical?

The last author is Fr. Andrew Greeley, a well-known priest-sociologist, who also writes a syndicated column in many American newspapers. In the following text, he sees the Church as composed of two parts: the first part is the "mystical tradition" which can be defined as facilitating a genuine "religious experience" either for one or several members of the Church. The other part is the "organization" i.e., institutional men and women (the clergy) who run the daily operation of the Church.

His term "apologetic Catholicism" refers to the Church in those times when the organizational concerns were more important than the "mystical." He is quite careful to point out that institutional clergymen never deny the worth of the mystical, but they also never really foster it either. It is sufficient for these institutional people to rely on the written Scriptures, the seven sacraments, the clerical hierarchy, and the canon law codes.

Fr. Greeley believes that some Church officials—particularly those involved in the liturgical reform of Vatican II—never quite met the actual need of the people. The people needed a "mystical" liturgy, one which would have promoted a "religious experience." But instead, the Church officials gave the people an un-adorned prayer service and a discussion group. The liturgical reform, he claims, did not meet the religious needs of the people, because the organizational officials who were involved in the change did not have the vision or the courage to create such a dramatic form of worship, capable of producing a mystical experience.

He also notes that it is very difficult for the Church's organizational members to cope with the religious fervor of its saints and mystics. Organizational people by temperament protect their own interests. But mystics and saints proclaim—often quite forcibly—that the organization has failed to live up to its own ideals. It is very difficult to discern what spirits—good or bad—are moving such dramatic people. Are they voices of the Holy Spirit? Or are they fighting the system out of some neurotic need to be noticed? Or are they led by evil-spirits who wish to ruin the work of the Church on earth? Are they paving the way for genuine reform as Jesus did when he toppled over the money-changers' tables? Or are they just wrecking things to create havoc? Since it is so difficult to discern such a weighty matter, the temptation is for Church officials to come down heavy on the side of the institution. According to Fr. Greeley, the organization wins, the mystic loses. Obviously this does not always happen in the Catholic Church, which has a long history of victories and losses between organizational members and mystical members. (Some would say brilliant compromises). Fr. Greeley argues that unfortunately, too often the institutional interests win out over the expense of the mystical.

> In point of fact, however, the present mystical revival, I think, makes sense only if one sees it as an attempt to recover precisely that form of knowledge and that level of consciousness which was much more readily available to our prescientific ancestors than to our modern selves. If this perspective is correct, then it would follow that what the Catholic liturgy should have become was not a low church prayer service or a discussion group but a religious experience, which for some could have served as a prelude to ecstasy. The liturgical scholars and the Vatican bureaucrats who engineered the reform of the liturgy might reply that very few in our Sunday congregations are capable of religious experience. To which the only appropriate answer would be that this is a terrible judgment both of our times and of our church.

> In apologetic Catholicism there was a good deal of ambivalence about mystical experience. On the one hand, it was clear that our great saints were mystics and that our spirituality was set in a context of preparation for mystical experience. On the other hand, mystics do not make good assistant pastors or second-grade teachers, and they are notoriously difficult to deal with. Furthermore, tense and neurotic religious and clergymen could easily imagine themselves mystics and work a great deal of havoc on the order and discipline of community life. So a happy compromise was arranged in which lip service was paid to the idea of mystical contemplation, but in practice we were adjured to be wary of religious experience, make our daily meditation, keep the rules, and obey our superiors. Mysticism, in other words, was a nice thing, but since we had the gospels and the sacraments and the Pope and the bishops the code of canon law, we really didn't need it.

In one sense there was some truth in this position. The goal of the
Christian life is not ecstasy but loving service.[8]

But, Fr. Greeley would continue, without the mystical, the
Church members lose the spiritual zest which fuels the loving
service. Apostles do not run on organizational charts, but on the
love for God. If they create an organization, its primary purpose is
to serve God, not institutional men. If organizational members
neglect this, then, as Fr. Greeley notes, we have the crisis in
confidence which troubles so many contemporary Catholics. They
want "more" but they are not quite sure what that "more" is.
Unfortunately, he adds, the response of the institutional Church is
to react like a bureaucracy, and interpret this need as a need for
"more organization."

1. What is Fr. Greeley's view of the Church as an organization?
2. What does he mean by "mystical" tradition? Does this
   compare or contrast with Maritain's view of *Person* and
   Personnel in the Church?
3. What type of criticism is he leveling against the Church?
4. What type of membership does he have in the Church?

Comment

You have read four Catholic authors, all of whom in one way
or another have expressed dissatisfaction with the Catholic
Church. Have you ever heard of similar critiques? Have any of your
teachers or relatives ever expressed opinions like these writers?

What about you? Are all of these arguments just words, or are
these writers touching a vital nerve in your body? Do you think that
these criticisms are meaningless theological debates? Or are these
Catholics speaking out of a deep love and concern for the Church?

Would any of these authors have written similar themes in the
last century? How does the Ethics of Jesus come into play here? Is it
His Church? Does He care about what type of membership we have
in His Body?

Only you can answer these questions. You are the only one who *knows the purpose of the Church for your soul.* Does the suffering of the present Church bother you at all? Are you the player who looks at the bleachers and sighs for the time when the game is over and you can get out of the heat and pain? Or are you the player who is deeply concerned and wants to play the game to win? The game we are talking about is eternal salvation.

Summary

The Catholic Church is a support group. Its purpose is to make it possible for its members to live good lives and to avoid evil as Jesus Christ taught. There are four types of members in the Church: the institutional person who accepts the Church fully; the group center person who thinks more of the Church than of his own needs; the person-oriented individual who thinks more of personal needs than of the group, and the individualist who has a very deep concern for himself and has little regard for the needs of the group. Each of these four types contribute in their own way to helping the Church fulfill its purpose.

Footnotes

1. Jack Wintz, "Evangelization," *Catholic Update*, Cinn., Ohio, Mar. 1975, 1-2.
2. Although Fundamentalists often see truth as an individual assent to the literal meaning of scripture, they recognize the fact that the Spirit has preserved the scriptures in the Church, and the fellowship of believers.
3. Jacques Maritain, *On the Church of Christ: The Person of the Church and Her Personnel*, trans, Joseph W. Evans, Notre Dame, Indiana: University of Notre Dame, 1973, 133.
4. In this context, it is more accurate to understand Adam not as a historical person but a figurative person representing all people.
5. For Maritain, the Church as an institution can be defective. But it is needed. It is flawless as the sacrament (sign) of salvation, the visible place of salvation, the cause, the agent of salvation, and the *Mystical Body* of Christ.
6. Hans Kung, *The Council and Reform*, trans. Cecily Hastings, New York: Sheed and Ward, 1961, 54-55.
7. Steve Clark, *Building Christian Communities: Strategy for Renewing the Church*, Notre Dame, Indiana: Ave Maria Press, 1972, 66-67.
8. Andrew M. Greeley, *The New Agenda*, Garden City, New York: Image Books, 1975, 197-198.

BIBLIOGRAPHY

Clark, Steve. *Building Christian Communities: Strategy for Renewing the Church*, Notre Dame, Indiana: Ave Marie Press, 1972.

Greeley, Andrew M. *The New Agenda*, Garden City, New York: Image Books, 1975, 197-198.

Hebblethwaite, Peter. *Theology of the Church*, Notre Dame, Indiana: Fides Publishers, Inc., 1969, No. 8.

Kung, Hans. *The Church*, trans. Ray and Rosaleen Ockenden, New York: Sheed and Ward, 1961.

————, *The Council Reunion and Reform*, trans. Cecily Hastings, New York: Sheed and Ward, 1961.

Maritain, Jacques. *On the Church of Christ: The Person of the Church and Her Personnel*, trans. Joseph W. Evans, Notre Dame, Indiana: University of Notre Dame, 1973.

Peters, Edward, ed. *The Constitution on the Church of Vatican Council II*, Glen Rock, New Jersey: Deus Books, Paulist Press, 1965.

We have studied the doctrinal tradition of the Catholic Church, even as it exists in today's contemporary world. Now we will focus on Catholic morality. Morality is the teaching of ethical behavior. Catholic morality is rooted in Catholic doctrine. The following chapters have as their purpose, an introduction to the different value systems which exist in the contemporary world, the meaning of an informed conscience, which must select from those different value systems, and lastly, the different sources of morality, all of which strive to be the foundation for the behavior of modern people.

Chapter 4

VALUE SYSTEMS: VARIOUS VIEWS

Who needs values? What good are values? Why are there values? Do we not live in a valueless society? No doubt these questions have bothered you at one time or another.

Perhaps these questions come from a disease of our time called valuelessness. It has been described as immorality, emptiness and hopelessness. A major television station presented a program called "New York—A Sin City, Another Sodom and Gomorrah." It illustrated how people use and abuse other human beings for their own profit and gain. What about the statistics which show the highest rate of suicides among our youth? Suicide implies hopelessness. Pornography is a multibillion dollar business. The Fashion and Cosmetic industries spend billions of dollars stressing the, "Body Beautiful." In our American society, it is a liability to grow old. Old age is not respected or cherished. It is only tolerated. There are numerous magazine articles about public funds, pension plans and trust funds that have been misappropriated or embezzled. Our daily newspapers report the stories of thieves, rapists and killers who walk our city streets. Is it any wonder that people without Christian values seem to be winning the battle of good over evil?

Many sociologists, psychiatrists and religious educators believe that our society has reached a very dangerous point of moral collapse. The traditional values of honesty and goodness seem to be replaced with treachery and connivance. Despite our sociological and technological advances, we have not attained worldwide brotherhood and peace. Failure and hopelessness will continue until Christian values take root. That is the cure for this disease.

At this point, it would be helpful to examine five questions: 1) What do we mean by world "value"? 2) What types of value exist? 3) How are values formed? 4) How can values be clarified? 5) Do we need values?

1. *The Meaning of Value*

First of all everyone has values. But what do we mean when we use the word "values"? It is a difficult question to answer. Clyde Kluckholm says, "A value is a conception, explicit or implicit, distinctive of an individual or characteristic of a group, of the desirable which influences the selection from available modes, means and ends of action."[1] There are three ideas in this definition. Values are abstractions which come from human experience. Second, values are desirable because of a person's physical, personal, emotional or psychological need. Third, values are selected on the basis of business, social, religious, educational or recreational needs.

Cornelius Van der Poel says, "value refers to the understanding of a certain good for an individual or society which is considered worthy of realization."[2] For example, it is considered to be a value to speak decently and gently. To speak decently and gently is a value at all times but what decent and gentle speech means varies from generation to generation or from culture to culture.

Brian Hall, Michael Kenny and Maury Smith define value, "something that is freely chosen from alternatives and is acted upon, that which the individual celebrates as being part of the creative integration in development as a person."[3] In this definition, there are three key words: Free, Choice, Personal.

Others have defined a value as a principle, a standard, or a quality considered worthwhile or desirable. However a person's value is conditioned by many conscious and unconscious psychic motives as well as numerous environmental, cultural and religious factors.

These definitions are samples. There are other definitions which are more technical and elaborate. They would not serve our purpose. So we will omit them. Simply then, *a value is something or someone who is considered good or worthy and is desirable or useful.* A value creates a force upon a person. A value pulls a person to act in a certain way. For example, school marks are a value for most students because a high index will open more job opportunities. They will, therefore, do certain things and avoid certain things to get high grades.

Having defined what a value is, let us examine the second question. What types of value exist? We have said that every person or group of people have values. The musician values his instrument and protects it. A union values its members and will bargain to protect their rights.

2. *Types of Values*

There are many types of values such as personal, political, religious, moral, economic, human or Christian values. Rarely do these types exist isolated from one another. Generally, they are interdependent and interconnected. For example, a person values money. Money is an economic-personal value even though at times it can be solely an economic or personal value. For clarity, each value-type will be discussed.

First, personal values are clothes, friends, money, health, drugs, driving, drinking or privacy. Other personal values might be pleasure, beauty, fun, happiness, etc. For instance, clothes are a value. A few years ago, only women were interested in clothing fashions and styles. Today that is not true. Men's fashions are on an equal par with women's fashions. Men are very conscious of colors, styles and fabrics. Men and women alike are searching to be distinct and unique even in the area of clothing.

Second, political values are virtually held by all. Government and Freedom are typical of these values. These pages of history remind us what men's political values have done for the world. In 1917, Lenin's Marxism overthrew the Czar Nicholas II Russian Government. Because the Hungarian people valued their freedom, they revolted against their Russian occupation. During the October days of 1956, thousands of Hungarians died for their freedom. In a German prison in 1944, a Lutheran minister, Dietrich Bonhoeffer, died because he opposed Nazi Atheism. On November 22, 1963, President John F. Kennedy was assassinated. Finally, an assassin's bullet killed Martin Luther King Jr., a prominent civil rights leader, on June 22, 1968.

Third, religious values have influenced millions of people. People like Confucius, Buddha, Mohammed, and Luther taught values such as love, God, salvation, prayer and forgiveness. Jesus taught a few hundred people of his time that man must love God and his neighbor. Jesus said that they must have a personal relationship with Him. They would have a common life, a common Father, and a common love. Jesus called for prayer, forgiveness, honesty, love, respect, etc. A Christian has these ideas spelled out in the Ten Commandments of Jesus. The first three commandments speak of God, the other seven of man. These commandments tell us that it is wrong to steal, to kill, to lust, to be disrespectful, and so forth. These laws are general and cannot be applied to specific situations. They are like the boundary lines of a baseball field. The specific application of the laws (commandments) is done by our conscience. For example, we know that we must love our parents. But how do we love our parents? What do we do, not do, say, not say? Our conscience applies the general laws to specific situations. Our conscience is guided by Jesus' command to love God and our neighbor. From His time until our own, millions of lives of men and women have been affected by Jesus' value of love.

Fourth, moral values such as sex and responsibility are fiery topics in any discussion group. We hear slogans such as "Sex will make you free," "Free love for everyone," "Sex is here to stay," and "Down with authority—up with freedom." Everyday thousands of men and women are sexually exploited. Some are willing. Some are coerced. In these cases, sex is brutalized instead of sanctified. In these cases, responsibility is damaged. A selfish person thinks predominantly of himself. He uses people as things. Without responsibility, a person cannot bridge the chasm between himself and others.

Fifth, economic values can either control or benefit individuals and nations. For instance, money buys food, clothes, houses, vacations, cars, etc. That is good. These items give us happiness. On the other hand, money can be used to buy power. In itself, there is nothing wrong with power. Too often, however, it is used for the wrong reasons. It can manipulate, dominate and destroy people. The damage can be physical, emotional, psychological and even physiological. It is said that power corrupts. Without a proper set of values, it does.

Sixth, there are human values. We will consider two basic human values, namely, self-realization and self determination. What do they mean? Self-realization means that a person recognizes within himself three areas: existentialism, personalism and humanism. By existentialism we mean that he exists with other human beings in time and space. He is an individual who is distinct and unique in the plan of God. By personalism, we mean that he is a corporal-spiritual being. Because of his relationship with God, he has a soul as well as a body. Therefore, he has another life after this one. He is made in the image and likeness of his creator. Humanism means that he recognizes that he is limited by physiological, biological, biochemical, psychological, sociological, educational and religious factors. By his existentialism, personalism, and humanism, he realizes who he is. The question, "what can he do?" will be answered by an analysis of his other basic human value, self determination. It means a conscious and knowledgeable direction of his life. Knowledge of himself, others and the world will equip him to act. Naturally, the poorer the knowledge the poorer will be his action. While knowledge can impede his direction, yet force and fear are his most formidable enemies. The latter exercises tremendous influence over a person and, therefore, limits his freedom to action. For example, if force and fear are over-exaggerated or imaginary, one's direction will be stopped, altered or changed. This could present the complete and total development of his full potentiality. In that case, the person suffers and so does the world.

Up to this point, we have looked at the main value types that exist. We have seen how man can build a personal value system, a political value system, a religious value system, a moral value system, an economic value system and lastly, a human value system. All these systems are generally interdependent and interconnected. Is there another value system which is more important, more practical and more stable? It is a Catholic Christian Value system. Is it that the Catholic Christian Value system is better than a Protestant Christian Value system? No that is not the point. The words Catholic and Protestant simply mean the traditional heritage from which a Christian has come. In this case, Catholics and Protestants have Jesus as the source for their Value System. Catholics have a supplementary source, namely the Church, with its 20 centuries of living experience. Therefore, let us focus on a Catholic Christian Value system which can affect other value systems. This value system does not stand separate or independent from other value systems mentioned. It is entwined, interwoven, interconnected and interlaced throughout the personal, political, religious, moral, economic and human values. It is the cohesive element in any value system. It is the major ingredient for any value system. At the base of a Catholic Christian value system is Jesus' message which is summarized in his Sermon on the Mount (Mt 5:3-12)—"How blest are the poor in spirit; the reign of God is theirs. Blest too are the sorrowing; they shall be consoled. Blest are the lowly; they shall inherit the land. Blest are they who hunger and thirst for holiness; they shall have their fill. Blest are they who show mercy; mercy shall be theirs. Blest are the single-hearted for they shall see God. Blest too the peacemakers; they shall be called the sons of God. Blest are those persecuted for holiness' sake; the reign of God is theirs. Blest are you when they insult you and persecute you and utter every kind of slander against you because of me. Be glad and rejoice, for your reward is great in heaven; they persecuted the prophets before you in the very same way." For example, money is an economic value. It can be an economic Christian value. How? One day Jesus was asked about the Roman coin. When they brought one, he said to them, "Whose head is this and whose inscription is it?" "Caesar's," they told him. At that Jesus said to them, "Give to Caesar what is Caesar's but give to God what is God's " (Mark 12:16-17). Obviously, money can have a material and spiritual value. The Catholic Christian can use it to pay bills but also to relieve the hardships of the poor. The Catholic Christian's Value system sees each person as the child of God and the brother and sister of Jesus. And so there is a spiritual nature to his value system.

3. Value-Formation

In this section, our attention will be focused on Value-Formation. What is it? How can it be accomplished? Christian Value-Formation is a lifelong process of growing which gets its strength from Jesus' Sermon on the Mount. Whether the values which are formed are good, bad or indifferent depends on two factors: influences and experiences. First, let us consider the influence factor. It depends on a person's internal influence such as intellectual and emotional capabilities. It depends on his open-mindedness which permits the reception of relevent information which may modify existing values. It depends on the Church's awareness of its role as a Pilgrim Church. It depends on parents who have a deep reverence and respect for the Godliness reflected in their children. It depends on teachers who can communicate kindly, gently and truthfully the message of Jesus. It depends on the community whose values reflect the wonder and beauty of people and things. These influences are only a few of the many which help to formulate our values. Notice how these influences are corelated in some way such as parent-child, teacher-student, person-person relationships. For example, if a teacher is a bigot then he conveys his value of discrimination. Obviously, it is a poor value. A student may accept his teacher's value as his own because he admires the teacher. In reality, the teacher should have adopted the Christian value of brotherly love. There is no question that we are greatly influenced by people's values. Sometimes these values are good, sometimes they are bad. It is the Catholic Christian who can help formulate a value system for himself and others which reflects the lovingness, the kindness, the gentleness of Jesus' value system.

Second, there is the experience factor which affects our value formation process. Like good influences, good experiences are needed in value formation. There are four types of experiences which will help a Catholic value formation process.

First, the liturgical experience is an act of worshiping God and sanctifying man by the community (Church). Liturgy is more than ritual. Liturgy is more than rubrics. Liturgy is an interchange experience between God and people. Liturgy means:

> that in the liturgical assembly you have an adequate reflection of what the Christian community is all about. All the elements which are necessary to make some community to be Church are found in the gathering of Christians for worship: the presence of the community, the proclamation of the gospel, the ministry of the Church and the celebration of the sacred banquet of the Lord. In this sense the liturgy reflects the Church.[4]

It is a dynamic experience. It is an invigorating experience. It is an awakening experience. It puts us into contact with the living Christ and His values.

Here are two aspects of the liturgy. First there is prayer. Simply, it is a communication process between the person and God. It can be public or private; it can be silent or vocal; it can be with or without formulas. Whatever way is chosen, there is an awareness of the individual's worth and God's concern.

Then there is music. There is no doubt that music creates an atmosphere. We have experienced it when we have dined. It adds something to the event that is taking place. Some say it creates a mood. Whether it creates an atmosphere or a mood, it does affect our senses. If you are listening to music then the ears alone are affected. But should you be playing a musical instrument, then the ears, eyes, hands are affected. Music demands our concentration and attention to the words and ideas being played or sung. A songwriter conveys his values through his songs. The listener picks them up through the musical experience of a Rock and Roll concert, a Metropolitan Opera performance or a church recital.

Second, the Bible experience tells us about the dreams, ambitions, hopes, sorrows, joys, frustrations, anxieties and reflections of men and women who lived in the 4000 year history of the Judeo-Christian period of history. For the Catholic Christian, these people are his ancestors. They have something to say to him. Some of their experiences formed their values. Perhaps, the Catholic Christian can relate to those experiences filled with timeless values. For example, the story about the Maccabean brothers who suffered and died rather than renounce their God. Their experiences have influenced man's fight for the value of religious freedom.

Third, the learning experience of each person is extremely valuable. He listens, talks, examines, searches and reflects on his daily situations. From these encounters, he evaluates and choses his values. For example, John wants to join the Olympic Swimming team. In order to qualify for the team, he has to swim five hours a day. In the beginning, he was faithful to this schedule but after three months, he swam for two hours a day. Needless to say, he failed to make the Olympic team. This learning experience made him value the daily five hour swimming program if he wanted to reach his goal.

Fourth, the human experience is an awareness that man lives in society. The English poet, John Donne in his writing, Meditation 17, said that no man is an island. He cannot live as if there were no other people around him. Man is a social being who relates to other human beings. He gives and he receives. Depending on these human experiences, he can develop his fullest capabilities as God intended. For example, some men and women who were in the Nazi concentration camps performed heroic acts of love and mercy despite personal dangers.

In conclusion, man's value formation process is influenced by many factors, is experienced in various ways and is finally accomplished by reflection and assimilation.

4. *Value Clarification*

In this section we will consider Value Clarification. Probably this task is the most difficult. Man can distinguish the various types of values and can even formulate a value system but he finds value clarification an almost hopeless and useless effort. While it is difficult to accomplish it, it can be done. Determination is needed.

Let him use his human inventiveness and resourcefulness. His blueprint for this task is Jesus' Sermon on the Mount. It is the measuring stick by which all values can be appraised. Yet how do we clarify these values? There are three basic steps which will enable a person to clarify his values. They are choice, value and action.

What is meant by choice? Psychologists tell us that no one is completely free. We will not argue the point because it is basically true. However, man is relatively free. He is the master of his actions. This is not to say that force, fear and coersion does not play a part in his choosing a value. What we are saying is that he should be aware of his choices. That he has alternatives. From these alternatives, he must make a choice. It is hoped that he will select those values that correspond to Christian values. At the same time, once he has made the choice, he must also be aware of the consequences of that choice.

What is meant by value? Having made the selection of a value, then he must be happy with it. His happiness should stem from the fact that he likes it and wants it. Also, his happiness should enable him to mention it to others. He should want to share it. If he cannot do this, then maybe he really does not cherish it.

Finally what is meant by action? This step should naturally follow from the previous two steps. Once a value is selected, valued, then it should be used. It should be put into action. And it should be used frequently not just occasionally.

All three steps are necessary in this value clarification process. One without the other will jeopardize the entire process and will result in chaos.

5. Do We Need Values?

Up to this point, we have spoken about what values mean, what type of values exist, how values are formed, how we can clarify our values. Now we turn to the final question, "Why do we need values?" Perhaps this question sounds superfluous. Not really. It is an important question. Because if we are not convinced of the need for Christian values, then the non-Christian values will dominate and cripple our society. And we have seen what that has done for our times. Too many people have confused, misguided, misdirected and even evil values today. They have slowed down the Christianization process. They have misread Jesus' blueprint.

Comment

A final comment on the subject of values is that everyone has values. The child values toys. The teenager values his car. The golfer values his golf clubs. As a person matures, it is hoped that he will move from material values to spiritual values such as love, God, friendship. Furthermore, it is hoped that the Catholic Christian will adopt these spiritual values as given by Jesus and his Church. These values should become the foundation stones on which other values are built. A Catholic Christian's value system will be firm and solid because it will be built on the teachings of Jesus. What can these Christian values do for us? They can do three things: learn, grow and change. From these values we can learn that God is our Father, Jesus is our brother and all men and women are our brothers and sisters. From these values we can grow in our experiences whether they be religious or social, whether they be good or bad. It is like the child who touches the hot coffee pot on the table and burns his finger. He quickly learns that there are hot and cold coffee pots. He grows from this experience in that he must be more careful when he touches a coffee pot. From these values we can change because we were hurt or because we became depressed or because we realized that we can change. One final point— Values shape motives, motives shape decisions, decisions make a person responsible for action.

Summary

1. The non-Christian values seem to be dominant in today's world.

2. Everyone has values.

3. A value is something or someone who is considered good or worthy and is desirable or useful.

4. There are types of values such as personal, political, religious, moral, economic, human and Christian values.

5. All value systems are interdependent and interconnected.

6. A Catholic Christian's Value system has its source in Jesus and the Church.

7. A Catholic Christian's Value system is not separate or independent but it is entwined, interconnected, interwoven and interlaced throughout all value systems.

8. The Value-Formation Process is influenced by people and certain experiences.

9. The person, parent, teacher, community, church, influence the Value-Formation Process.

10. The liturgical, Bible, learning and human experiences influence the Value-Formation Process.

11. Jesus' Sermon on the Mount is the blueprint for a Catholic Christian's Value System.

12. Value-Clarification takes place in three steps: Choice, Value, Action.

13. Catholic Christian Values are needed otherwise the non-Christian values will dominate and cripple our society.

Questions for Discussion

1. Give some examples of a valueless society.

2. What are some conscious and unconscious psychic motives behind a person's value system?

3. How do Kluckholm, Van der Poel and Hall, Kenny, Smith's, value definitions differ?

4. Give some examples of moral, economic, and human values.

5. What does a corporal-spiritual being mean to you?

6. What is the difference between a Catholic and Protestant Christian Value Stystem?

7. Why is Jesus' Sermon on the Mount the basis for a Christian Value System?
8. List your values and your priorities.
9. Give examples that illustrate the three steps of the Value-Formation Process.

Footnotes

1. Talbcott Parsons and Edward Shils, etc., *Toward a General Theory of Action*, Cambridge, Harvard University Press, 1954, 356.
2. Cornelius J. Van der Poel, *The Search for Human Values*, New York, Paulist Press, 1971, 74.
3. Brian Hall, Michael Kenney, Maury Smith, *Value Clarification as A Learning Process*, New York Paulist Press, 1973, II.
4. John P Mossi, ed., *Modern Liturgy Handbook*, New York Paulist Press, 1976, 24.

BIBLIOGRAPHY

Finley, James and Pennock. *Jesus and You*, Notre Dame, Indiana: Ave Maria Press, 1977.

Goldman, Ronald. *Religious Thinking From Childhood to Adolescence*, New York: The Seabury Press, 1968.

Hall, Brian P. *Value Clarification*, New York: Paulist Press, 1973.

Maslow, Abraham. *Religious Values and Peak Experiences*, New York: Penguin Books, 1970.

Nelson, E. Ellis. *Where Faith Begins*, Richard, Virginia: John Knox Press, 1971.

Van der Poel, Cornelius. *The Search for Human Values*, New York: Paulist Press, 1971.

Westerhoff, John J. III. *Values for Tomorrow's Children*, Philadelphia: Pilgrim Press, 1970.

Yankelovich, Daniel. *The New Morality, A Profile of American Youth in the 70's*, New York: McGraw-Hill Book Company, 1974.

In the previous chapter we have considered the different value systems which exist in the modern world. Obviously, some are clearly Christian values and others are not. Part of modern life is to choose from these value systems and select the one which is appropriate for our own personal moral code. This moral selection is made by our conscience, which should be informed by Catholic teaching.

Chapter 5
CONSCIENCE: THE MEANING OF AN INFORMED CONSCIENCE

Introduction

There are many different names for conscience. Some people call it "the unwritten law." Others call it "the still small voice." People understand that "conscience" signifies man's ability to judge right from wrong. This meaning comes out in the popular expression, "My conscience is bothering me." The person who says this is telling us something about himself. He is saying that he is aware that he has done something wrong. It can also mean that he has failed to do something good which he believed he should have done. The traditional terms for these two situations are 1) "sins of commission" and 2) "sins of omission."

What Consciense is Not: The Super-Ego

Today "conscience" is very often confused with the super-ego. Although there are some similarities, *the super-ego is not conscience*. Since so many people confuse the two, it would help to explain what the super-ego is, and how it is different than moral conscience. The super-ego is a term used by psychologists. Psychologists say that we have three separate functions in our mind: 1) the super-ego, 2) the ego, and 3) the id. The super-ego is an unconscious function in the mind. It makes us feel guilty when we have done something which we believe we should not have done.

However, this super-ego makes us feel guilty *no matter how serious or minor the* wrong-doing is. Such guilt feelings can arise for simple fault as well as for a very serious matter. The id is the unconscious drive for self-pleasure. The super-ego is the function which makes us feel guilty for wanting this pleasure.

The ego is the conscious function in our mind. Its task is to balance the two other conscious functions. It selects what we will be aware of. It also decides what we will keep unconscious. It also decides what we will do and not do. The uncontrolled id is the drive of a selfish person who is concerned only for his own pleasure. He is normally unconcerned about anyone else. The uncontrolled super-ego is the drive in an uptight person who is afraid to do anything pleasurable at all. A sane person is one who can balance pleasure (id) and responsibility (super-ego). He lives a fruitful life. A mentally disturbed person usually cannot control either the id or the super-ego. This model of the three functions of the mind has become very popular. So today people often act as if conscience and super-ego are the same. They are not.

The super-ego is an *unconscious* part of the mind. It is the storehouse of all the things we were forbidden to do in our childhood. It is like the attic of an old house. Instead of old furniture, it is filled with all the "don'ts" and "can'ts" which were drummed into us as children. It erupts into our consciousness like a spring coiled in on itself. It plagues us with fear and anxiety. It does this whenever our mind suspects that we are doing something which other prople might disapprove of. It is irrational. It can plague us with guilt feelings for the simplest errors. For people with sick minds, the super-ego can be a curse. For healthy people, it helps them to act in a mature way.

Definition: What Moral Conscience Is

A moral conscience is a *conscious, spiritual, human* power. It makes a person aware of what is right and what is wrong. It depends for its power on the *spiritual* ability of a *human* person to *understand, create,* and *sustain personal* and *community relationships.* It warns a person when he has broken such a relationship. It causes feelings of remorse and guilt when a relationship is broken. It brings feelings of satisfaction and achievement when a broken relationship is restored.

Some examples will help to understand the definition of a moral conscience. Keep in mind that we are discussing a *conscious, spiritual power* and not an *unconscious psychological drive.*

Example 1: A man does not send a gift to his mother on her birthday. How does he feel about this? Why?

Example 2: A woman prepares her husband's favorite dinner after he has been away for a long time on a business trip. How does she feel about this? Why?

Example 3: A busy salesman gives up meeting a customer and making a certain sale so that he will have the time to vote in a city election. Does he have mixed feelings about this choice? How does he feel about the decision he has made? Why did he do it? Why choose a community relationship over a personal one? Would he have made the same decision if his wife had been ill in the hospital?

Teaching From Scripture About Moral Conscience

Most of the Bible is concerned with moral conscience. The Scriptures tell how people obey or disobey their moral conscience. Both the Old and the New Testaments stress the importance of having a good conscience before the face of God.

The following Scriptural passage is from the *Book of Proverbs.* The writer acts as if he were a kindly teacher talking to a favorite student. The teacher considers the pupil his son. He is teaching the student the value of living with a *good moral conscience.*

He tells him that a good person will enjoy a long and healthy life. A good conscience is a gift of Wisdom, which is itself a special gift of God. The good person walks the "straight and narrow path of virtue."

The instruction to be a good person is like a special charm with the power to keep the holder alive and well.

People who choose evil walk another path. The student must avoid it. Evil people plot evil things. Even the meals they have are filled with fighting and evil deeds. They are like men walking in a dark night who stumble on hidden traps. Good men walk a straight path lit by the Sun, (a symbol of the Truth of God).

The teaching of a virtuous teacher is like good food. It brings health and well-being to the whole person. The "heart" is an ancient word for the modern idea "conscience." A person with a good conscience does not lie, and is honest in business dealings.

The person who chooses to do good is like someone who stays on the "straight and narrow path." He does not let temptation to do evil sway him away from his true direction.

Hear my son, and receive my words,
  and the years of your life shall be many.
On the way of wisdom I direct you,
  I lead you on straightforward paths.
When you walk, your step will not be impeded,
  and should you run, you will not stumble.

Hold fast to instruction, never let her go;
  keep her for she is your life.

The path of the wicked enter not,
  walk not on the way of evil men;
Shun it, cross it not,
  turn aside from it, and pass on.
For they cannot rest until they have done evil;
  to have made no one stumble steals away their sleep.
For they eat the bread of wickedness
  and drink the wine of violence.
The way of the wicked is like darkness;
  they know not on what they stumble.

But the path of the just is like shining light,
  that grows in brilliance till perfect day.

My son, to my words be attentive,
  to my sayings incline your ear;
Let them not slip out of your sight,
  keep them within your heart;
For they are life to those who find them,
  to man's whole being they are health.

With closest custody, guard your heart,
  for in it are the sources of life.

Put away from you dishonest talk,
    deceitful speech put far from you.
Let your eyes look straight ahead
    and your glance be directly forward.

Survey the path for your feet,
    and let all your ways be sure.
Turn neither to the right nor the left,
    keep your foot far from evil.

(Proverbs IV:10-27)

A Christian Moral Conscience

Almost everyone in the world, no matter what their religion, would accept the teaching of Proverbs on moral conscience. They would accept that it is a conscious power of the human person. Its purpose is to inform us if we have broken or sustained a relationship. This relationship can be with 1) the self, 2) another person, 3) the community, or 4) God. The moral conscience reminds us that we do certain conscious actions, for which we are personally responsible. If a moral conscience causes guilt feelings, it arises from something specific. We have broken a relationship. Unlike the super-ego, it is never vague and uncertain, but clear and distinct.

A good number of these people would also accept the Ten Commandments as an excellent guide for good moral behavior. Even the ancient Jewish writers presented the Ten Commandments as binding on all men because *they proclaimed the universal moral law.* This law was recognized by the conscience of all good men.

How then does a Christian conscience differ from that of another religion? There is a basic difference. A Christian understands that every personal relationship involves the Person Jesus Christ.

The Christian believes that the Jesus of history, now risen and in glory with God the Father, is deeply concerned about the moral choices which he makes in this world. To choose to do good is to follow the teachings of Jesus. To choose to do good, for the Christian, nourishes and sustains his personal relationship with his Savior. To do evil is to break that relationship. If a non-believer refuses to support a sick parent, he has broken the relationship between child and parent. If a Christian does the same thing, he has also broken his relationship with Christ. That is why the saints say that for a Christian to do such an evil thing, *the person has denied the faith.* For the Christian faith understands that faith in Christ leads to Christ-like deeds. If it does not, it is not faith but a sham.

Jesus' teachings were first presented in the chapter "The Ethics of Jesus." His teachings are ideals about good and evil. They are recorded in the New Testament. The Catholic Church continues to teach His ideals in the world. Catholics believe that the Church helps them to continue their personal relationship with Jesus. The Church also teaches that the Ten Commandments and other rules aid Catholics in developing their moral conscience.

Catholics also believe that Jesus is now risen from the dead. He is in heaven. They can have a personal relationship with Him. Through the Church's Sacraments and personal prayer, they can sustain and nourish this relationship. The healthier the relationship, the better they can keep their moral conscience.

The Church's liturgy provides Catholics with the Biblical teachings of Jesus and other saints about a good moral life. Personal reading of the Bible also helps to nourish this life of virtue.

Catholics also believe that Jesus Christ is the Judge of all men. He is judging at the present. He sees and understands all our deeds, and all our thoughts. Through the Holy Spirit He sends us gifts of grace to aid us in living a good life. He is always aware of the choices we are making, and He is always judging us. He never breaks the personal relationship with us.

At death, Jesus will be the Judge of each person. He is the one who decides whether the person has earned eternal life with Him or not. At the end of the world, Jesus will judge all men of all ages, living and dead. He is the universal Judge. A Christian moral conscience is one that tries to live each day as if *the person were standing before the Judgment Seat of Christ.* A Christian is one who strives to keep his personal relationship with Christ alive and well. A good Christian, who follows the teachings of the Jesus of history, is not afraid to face the risen Christ of Judgment.

Let us summarize the things which make a Christian moral conscience different. A Christian moral conscience has all of the following elements:

1. It accepts the Ten Commandments as a basic moral guide.
2. It believes in following the ethical teachings in the Bible, especially those which emphasize love of God and love of neighbor.
3. It believes in a personal relationship with Jesus Christ.
4. It accepts the ethical teachings of Jesus as its ideals.
5. It believes that Jesus Christ is judging its choices now, and
6. It believes that Jesus Christ will be the final Judge of its destiny in the next world.

Jesus' famous story of the Prodigal Son is an excellent summary of what we have been saying about a Christian moral conscience. In the story, a young man demands that his father give him his inheritance immediately. He then goes off and uses his father's hard-earned money to live a life directly opposite to the values he had been taught by his family. He breaks the relationship with his father. He lives a life of selfish pleasure (the uncontrolled id). He ends up starving on a pig farm. This degradation becomes a means of grace for him. He admits that he has broken a personal relationship. He admits his own responsibility for his problem. He admits that he has also broken his relationship with God. He vows to heal the broken relationship with his father. He is even willing to accept a menial job on his father's farm rather than the rights of a son and heir. He returns to seek reconciliation, abandoning the life of evil. The father, who is a symbol God the Father, runs with joy to accept his son back. He is forgiven and reconciled. His return is cause for celebration; he has come back to a good moral conscience. He is like a lost person who has been found, like a dead man who has been raised to a new life. Jesus teaches in this story that he is always waiting to reestablish a relationship which has been broken by sin.

THE PRODIGAL SON

Jesus said to them: "A man had two sons. The younger of them said to his father, 'Father, give me the share of the estate that is coming to me.' So the father divided up the property. Some days later this younger son collected all his belongings and went off to a distant land, where he squandered his money on dissolute living.

After he had spent everything, a great famine broke out in that country and he was in dire need. So he attached himself to one of the propertied class of the place, who sent him to his own farm to take care of the pigs. He longed to fill his belly with the husks that were fodder for the pigs, but no one made a move to give him anything.

Coming to his senses at last, he said, 'How many hired hands at my father's place have more than enough to eat, while here I am starving! I will break away and return to my father, and say to him, "Father, I have sinned against God and against you; I no longer deserve to be called your son. Treat me like one of your hired hands."

With that he set off for his father's house. While he was still a long way off, his father caught sight of him and was deeply moved. He ran out to meet him, threw his arms around his neck and kissed him. The son said to him, 'Father, I have sinned against God and against you; I no longer deserve to be called your son.' The father said to his servants: 'Quick! Bring out the finest robe and put it on him, put a ring on his finger and shoes on his feet. Take the fatted calf and kill it. Let us eat and celebrate, because this son of mine was dead and has come back to life. He was lost and is found.'

Then the celebration began." (Lk 15:11-24)

America today is filled with prodigal children. Many youth have run away from their families and live lives as wicked and as empty as the Prodigal Son. Some even wander into relationships with very evil cult figures. Susan Atkins was such a person. She was part of Charles Manson's "family," and was convicted of murdering Sharon Tate and other people in the State of California. Some pathological criminals cannot comprehend a feeling of guilt. They have so dulled their moral conscience that they have no guilt feelings at all. When they are brought to court for a violent crime, they will insist either 1) they did not do it, or 2) the victim forced them to do it. Sometimes they even try to convince themselves that the victims wanted them to mistreat them. This pattern of behavior is common with violent criminals. Unlike the Prodigal Son, they cannot admit to themselves or others the responsibility for their evil deeds.

Susan Atkins: A Modern Prodigal Returns to the Father

The court records indicate that Charles Manson was such a figure. He and the three women tried with him for mass murder made a mockery of their trial. They did everything to disrupt the court proceedings. At the end of it all, one of the women, Susan Atkins,[1] found herself sitting in a California jail awaiting death in the gas chamber.

Susan had lived a life of evil: drugs, sex, ritual murder, and her senses were so dulled she could barely feel anything at all. Her body had been ravaged by her life of passion:

> Even my body was deteriorating badly. I had had gonorrhea (VD) so many times that the prison medical authorities wanted me to have a hysterectomy. But I refused. And my teeth were getting uglier and uglier, and painful, too. I had taken so many drugs that my entire mouth was rotting away. I had to have tons of dental work.

Even when sentenced to death, all she could do was concentrate on her loneliness. She could not feel guilt, or anger, or fear; she had no personal relationship at all:

> I had betrayed humanity. I had betrayed my colleagues, and I had betrayed myself. There was no one left. My alienation was complete.

Cut off from human and community relationships, Susan Atkins waited for the gas chamber. A Roman Catholic chaplain gave her a Bible. People came to visit her, urging her to give her life over to Jesus. Like the Prodigal Son, she found herself in a pig sty. Unlike him, she could not admit her responsibility for being there. She did not believe that anyone (including God) could care for her at all. She did not believe that anyone could restore the human relationships which she had broken. In a stupor, she waited for her execution. For the Prodigal Son, the fact that his father's servants ate better than he did was the grace which penetrated his moral conscience and got him on his feet and on his journey to the Father. For Susan Atkins, it was the announcement that the California Supreme Court had abolished the death penalty in her State.

> The news announcer's voice penetrated my consciousness. "From

the state capital, this story: The California Supreme Court has voted six to one to abolish the death penalty in the state. Citing cruel and unusual punishment. . ." That's as much as I heard before the words repeated in my mind: "voted to abolish the death penalty in the state. . ."

Almost unconsciously, I felt myself slipping off my bed twoards the floor. I was on my knees. And the tears came. In seconds, sobs were rising from deep in my chest, and I was weeping audibly, not loudly, but openly. And for the first time since my mother's death, I spoke to God. I remember distinctly; I called him "God," not "Father," or "Lord." It was only two short sentences: "Thanks, God. I want to thank you for letting me live—and all the others, too."

The news broke into her heart. For a brief moment she could understand that she did have a personal relationship with God. But she could go no further than that. After this experience, much later, she was holding the Bible which the priest had given her:

One day, I turned the brown leather Bible over in my hands. The people were corrupt and violent. They had turned their backs on God.

At another time, the girl finally understood what her moral conscience needed:

After several minutes of silence in the dark a new sentence formed on my lips—an entirely new spoken idea for me. "I want to be forgiven," I said, barely audibly. The thought burned me, refusing to leave.

This was a long and tortuous path for Susan Atkins. It took much longer for her than it did for the Prodigal Son. It was harder for her because her culture did not help her in the same way as the Prodigal was helped. Susan had to accept many things about herself before she could ask for forgiveness: 1) that she had a personal relationship with God. All her companions had denied this. 2) that there were things that were wrong and things that were good. Again, her companions had denied this. 3) that drugs cause confusion in the mind, not clearness of thought. Again, her companions denied this. 4) that she had obligations to herself, others, the community, and God. She lived a life which denied all of these relationships. 5) that she could be forgiven. It is very hard to admit responsibility of guilt if you are convinced you cannot be forgiven.

After Susan Atkins admitted her need for forgiveness, her life changed. She tells of a vision of Christ which she had. This vision may have come from her imagination, or from prayer, or from a special gift of God. It is not the point of this book to claim it was legitimate or imaginary. It was a moment of grace for her, and a time when her moral conscience accepted the fact that God forgave her for her sins.

In this vision, Christ told her:

> Susan, I am really here. I'm really coming to your heart to stay. Right now you are being born again and you will live with me in heaven through all eternity, forever and ever. This is really happening. It is not a dream. You are now a child of God. You are washed clean and your sins have all been forgiven.

> I was distinctly aware that I inhaled deeply and then, just as fully, exhaled. There was no more guilt! It was gone. Completely gone! The bitterness, too. Instantly gone! How could this be?

> For the first time in my memory I felt clean, fully clean, inside and out. In 26 years I had never been so happy.[2]

Comment—An Informed Conscience

Susan Atkins' earlier life is a clear indication of what can happen to someone who refuses to accept any moral guidance for their conscience. So far this chapter has studied 1) the super-ego, 2) the moral conscience, and 3) the Christian moral conscience. The last thing to be studied is an *informed* Christian moral conscience.

Our conscience is the deepest part of our personality. It is the thing which most belongs to us and is most responsible for making us the type of person we are. It does not belong to the Government, or the Church, or our parents. It belongs to *us*.

The greatest freedom we have, especially in America, is that we can live as our conscience tells us to live. This does not mean that we can do whatever we want to do. Charles Manson's conscience told him to have sex with whomever he pleased, to steal money which did not belong to him, to take whatever drug he wanted, and to kill people who had never done him any harm. Such a person cannot be allowed to live free in society. His conscience is so deviant from the community that the community is forced to lock him up like an animal to protect itself.

On the other hand, no society has the power to take away those freedoms which are the God-given rights of men. If a man decides to worship as a Catholic, or as a Jew, or as a Moslem, he is exercising a freedom of moral conscience. He is not destroying the rights of his neighbors. A society which locks such people up is inherently corrupt.

So it must be understood that there are limits to the freedom which our conscience has. These limits are set up by the tradition of the moral law which we find in the Bible. Society can also add others to preserve good order.

Summary

These are the basic elements of an *informed* conscience, for a Christian. When a moral choice is to be made, the following requirements are necessary:

1. The person respects the ethical teachings of Jesus about the choice.
2. The person uses the moral tradition in the Bible as a guide.
3. The person learns the Church's traditional teaching on the matter.
4. The person respects the traditions and customs and laws of the community in which he lives.
5. The person uses these tools in making a decision. The decision is always the personal responsibility of the person who made it.

Sometimes the matter will be clear. If a person has the urge to kill someone in cold blood, there is a long ethical and legal tradition to advise him against doing it. If, however, he is a soldier fighting in a war, and some authorities believe the war is just and some believe it is not, the moral choice is not so easy.

The purpose of the following chapters is to provide you with guidelines. These guidelines will help you to understand how to inform your conscience, so that you can make moral choices in the future. The guidelines are the tools given to you by your Church. The tools help to *inform* your conscience. Sometimes they may be so clear that they will really *decide* for you. At other times, it will not be as clear, and you will have to make the decision with little to go on. But the final decision is always your personal choice. An informed conscience is not a dictator flashing do and don't signs, but a wise teacher, guiding you on the path of virtue.

> *But the path of the just is like shining light,*
> *that grows in brilliance to perfect day.*
>
> (Proverbs IV: 19)

FOOTNOTES

1. "A Killer Finds Christ: Convicted Manson Murderess Susan Atkins now lives for Jesus," *Daily News*, Friday, September 23, 1977, page 43. From Susan Atkins: *Child of Satan - Child of God* by Susan Atkins as told to Bob Slosser, Copyright 1977 by Logos International. All rights reserved. Used by permission.
2. *Ibid.*

BIBLIOGRAPHY

Atkins, Susan. *Child of Satan - Child of God,* Logos International, c. 1977.

Bier, William C., ed. *Conscience, Its Freedom and Limitations,* New York: Fordham Press, 1971.

Harrington, Jeremy, ed. *Conscience in Today's World,* Cinn., Ohio: St. Anthony Messenger Press, 1970.

Janssens, Louis. *Freedom of Conscience and Religious Freedom,* Staten Island, New York: Alba House, 1967.

Smyth, Kevin, trans. *A New Catechism,* New York: The Seabury Press, 1969.

Springer, Robert H. *Conscience and the Behavioral Sciences,* Washington and Cleveland: Corpus Books, 1968.

Stevens, Edward. *Making Moral Decisions,* New York: Paulist Press Deus Books, 1969.

We have explored the meaning of a conscience which has been informed by the traditional teaching of the Catholic Church. This conscience, once formed by the Catholic Church, must then look at all the different sources of morality which come into that conscience and help to determine the decisions it will make. The sources of morality are personal, family, social, governmental and ecclesiastical. Each of these is a very powerful, very influential source. The following chapter explores each source, how it effects the individual conscience, and how each of us can relate and make decisions based on the source and the way in which that source is urging us to do good or to do evil.

Chapter 6

THE SOURCES OF MORALITY:
SELF, PARENTS, FRIENDS, CHURCH, GOVERNMENT, MEDIA

In the previous chapter we have studied different types of values. We have looked at personal, political, religious, moral, economic, human and Christian values. Where did these collections of values come from? All of these types of values come to us from sources of morality. Just as there are different types of values, there are also different sources of morality. A source of morality can be either an individual or a group. A source of morality can be small and weak, like a frightened child pleading for protection. It can be very large and very powerful, such as the United Nations' *Declaration on Human Rights*. A Source of morality urges our conscience to act for the good and not for evil. A source of morality is *abused* when it is used to urge us to choose evil instead of good.

In the process of growing up and becoming a responsible person, an individual "owns" or "claims" certain values as belonging to him or her. The value is no longer "from the outside" but is "within the heart." In a very real sense, the person has become the source of values. This dynamic interchange between the individual and the outside continues our whole life. In this chapter we will study the different sources of morality. Each of these calls out to us for personal acceptance. Each source urges each of us to claim its values as our own. We will also study the means each source uses to try to influence our personal set of values. It is vitally important to realize that a source can *abuse* its trust and can be used for urging us to evil instead of good.

A. Different Sources of Morality

Let us first define a source of morality. *A source of morality is either a person or a group which guides our activity by establishing certain values as norms for behavior.* There are different sources of morality. These sources are 1) personal, 2) familial, 3) social, 4) spiritual, 5) political, and 6) cultural.

1. Personal Sources of Morality

The self is a source of morality. The sum of experiences, the attitude of mind towards life, the history of moral decisions which were made in the past, all together define a person's character. Others are aware of this character. So they can say of an individual: "That is an honest man." or "She is a loving woman." or "He's a crook and you can't trust him with money." Every person's character is a personal and unique source of morality.

The other person in our life is also a source of morality. Any other person that we are close to, whether we like them or not, has an effect on our own character. Even a close friend has a "power" over us and over our choices. Their character becomes a continual source of morality determining our character. Such an individual can urge us to behave in a certain way, urging us either to good or evil. The closer the person is to us, the more we love that person (or fear, or hate), the more powerful is their influence on our character.

2. Familial Sources of Morality

The family, especially the mother and father of a child, provide "the primary environment for the teaching of values." These experiences become one's familial heritage. They are a very powerful source of morality. It is very hard for someone who has been raised in a good, moral family to adopt totally bad values. It is also hard, on the other hand, for someone from a very selfish and fragmented family to be a kind and a considerate person. The familial source of morality has always been considered the most powerful in shaping a person's character. This does not mean that a person is totally determined by his family and not free to choose his own character. What it does mean is that it takes incredible drive and energy to change from the personality which was first molded by the family unit. Other members of the immediate family also influence our character.

3. Social Sources of Morality

Groups also mold our character. This includes any group which has influence on our selection of values. Such groups would be relatives, neighbors, friends, co-workers, other students, etc. All of them form a social force which acts as a source of morality. This social force urges us to conform to its values. Teenagers are especially vulnerable to pressure to conform in order to be acceptable to the group.

4. Spiritual Sources of Morality

As we explained in the chapter on the Purpose of the Church, the Catholic community of faith, consciously strives to create a spiritual source of morality for us. The Community of faith includes all believers, clergy, religious, laity, the Church in the past, and the Church in the future. The Church's teachings, Sacred Scripture, the Liturgy and the Sacraments all form spititual sources of morality.

5. Political Sources of Morality

The Government consists of local, State, and national branches. In America it is divided into three functions: the executive, the legislative, and the judiciary. The executive branch enforces the laws of the country, the legislative branch writes the laws, and the judiciary decides whether or not the law has been violated. The executive power also includes the police and the military. All of this is a political source of morality.

Executive Government officials include: the President, Governors, Mayors, County Executives, and their appointed subordinates, such as the Commissioners in a city. The police, soldiers, investigative agencies are all part of the Executive Branch. Legislative officials include State Assemblymen, State Senators, U.S. Congressmen, and U.S. Senators. They also have legislative aides to help them to write the laws. Judiciary officials include the Supreme Court of the United States, Federal Courts, States Courts, County Courts, and local magistrates. The Bench has judicial aides to help them carry out the obligations of the judiciary.

The government—in all of its branches, whether local or national—is responsible for the good order of society. This includes the management of civil and criminal law. The purpose of public law is to make all of us aware of the values which the community holds as proper for the good order of society. In general, criminal law defends us against immoral behavior, and civil law defends us against illegal behavior, which may or may not involve the moral law. (For example, traffic violations are set up in an arbitrary fashion. A red light does not *have* to mean stop but it is a convention. Murder, on the other hand, is both illegal *and* immoral. Furthermore, even though traffic patterns are arbitrary and part of the civil code, the willful violation of them can lead to a serious accident, kill an innocent party, and make the violator subject to the criminal code.)

6. Cultural Sources of Morality

Art has always been a source of morality. It has been used to inspire, teach and instruct. The most powerful art forms today are the media, especially the electronic means of communication. Movies, newspapers, books, phonographs, magazines, radio, television, live entertainment, etc.—all contribute to a modern source of morality. These media influence very many people over a wide range of geographical areas. Propagandists consider them the most powerful opinion shapers of all time. It is very, very difficult to hold values which are contradicted by the values of the media, or, on the other hand, to contradict values which are supported by the media.

Obviously, each source of morality mentioned above: personal, familial, social, spiritual, political, and cultural, can be abused. It can be used to encourage evil behavior. Hitler controlled the media in Nazi Germany. He determined what news the German people heard and what they did not. This was his way of controlling their behavior. His attitude, which was grimly borne out in experience, was that if the Big Lie was told often enough and loud enough it would be accepted as true.

Work Exercise on Sources of Morality

Consider each of the following sources of morality and discuss whether it is aiding a good value or a bad one:

1. (Personal): A personal decision to read the Bible for fifteen minutes each day. A friend who abuses drugs.
2. (Familial). An alcoholic father who beats his child for a minor offense. A mother who teaches her child how to pray.
3. (Social). A class decision to help a missionary build a church. A ball team deciding how to break an opponent's arm in a match.
4. (Spiritual). The Pope writing an encyclical on world order and peace. A pastor lying to his congregation about the financial status of the parish.
5. (Political). A President ordering the FBI to investigate the sex life of one of his opponents. A judge sentencing a murderer to life imprisonment.
6. (Cultural). A television commercial aimed at convincing you that you need an expensive medicine you cannot afford. A marathon radio show to raise money for a cancer ward.

B. The Means Used by the Sources of Morality

Introduction

The different sources of morality use different means to encourage good behavior. These means can range from the very mild to the very serious. They can range from a mother scolding her child for not cleaning his room all the way to the ultimate means, when the State executes a condemned criminal for a serious offense. The first means is the withdrawal of parental approval. This can be quite painful for a young child, but in the long run is really a small penalty. The child can recover from the loss by regaining his mother's approval. The taking of life, however, is much more serious. There is no recovery after this means is used.

So the sources of morality have a wide range of means. They range from minor means to major means. All of these means share in the same goal. These means are techniques of discipline which encourage moral behavior and discourage immoral behavior. This leads to our second definition in this chapter: *the different means used by sources of morality are ethical tools which encourage us to do good and avoid evil.* We will now study these means as used by the different sources of morality.

1. *The Ethical Means of Personal Sources of Morality*

I) The personal self uses certain tools as ethical means. These are:
  a. Imitation
  b. Education
  c. Courage
  d. Decision-making

Imitation is using another person as a model for behavior.

Education is using the classroom or books or other learning tools as a guide for moral behavior.

Courage is the ability to make a moral choice, even if it is in opposition to other people who have a power over the self.

Decision-making is the ability to make free and independent choices about moral questions. As the individual matures, more and more decision-making is done independent of others. Each decision is part of the overall pattern which determines a person's eventual character.

II) The relationship we have with one other person also has certain tools which become ethical means.

The significant relationships with one other person are:

    a. True friendship
    b. True love
    c. False friendship
    d. False love

True friendship is between you and one other person and this relationship encourages good moral behavior.

True love is between you and one other person of the opposite sex and encourages good moral behavior.

False friendship is between you and one other person and discourages good moral behavior and encourages evil behavior.

False love is between you and one other person of the opposite sex and it discourages good moral behavior and encourages immoral behavior.

2. *Ethical Means of the Familial Sources of Morality*

In early age, a child is encouraged to do good behavior by a mechanism of reward and punishment. The child does not choose good for its own sake. For the most part, good behavior is based on the child looking to the parents for example and this is the only guide the child has on how to behave. As the child grows older and develops in wisdom and discernment, the child can now choose what to imitate and what not to imitate. Parents, like any other group of people are neither completely good nor completely bad. Therefore, it is important to learn how and what those behavior patterns are which should be imitated and those which should not be imitated. The family has the ability to create tremendous pressure on the child and this forms a very strong means of preserving morality. When it is abused, it can cause a great deal of confusion in the child's moral development and can lead to immoral behavior.

3. The Ethical Means of Social Sources of Morality

Just as the family creates a pressure on the individual, so small groups can also create pressure on the individual. The greatest pressure is one of acceptance or rejection. Therefore social pressure uses the ethical means of deciding what behavior patterns will make the individual "one of us." The following questions will clarify exactly how this social pressure works. Who influences your behavior for good? Who influences your behavior for evil? Where in your choices of life are you strong? Where in your choices of life are you weak? Who has a "power," over you? The answers to these questions will help you determine who is responsible for molding your character. Usually a group can only have a social pressure over you if you let it have such power over you. Usually a group can only do this if you want to belong to its membership. If you have no desire to be part of a particular group, it is very difficult for that group to control or influence your behavior. The following questions will help to clarify this. What are the values of your closest associates? What does this tell you about who you are as a person? Does your social group encourage concern for others? Does your social group encourage drugs and sex? Does your social group encourage responsibility or irresponsibility?

Introduction to Moral Institutions

The most powerful group pressures on an individual are institutions. They can form the conscience of a whole nation. They can establish values which are accepted by very large numbers of people. They create an entire "milieu" in which each of us lives almost unconsciously, as fish do in a sea. Fish do not recognize their environment that they do not think of themselves as animals that live in water. In the same way, when we live in a moral climate, we do not even see it as a moral climate, we just accept it as the environment in which we are. This "milieu" sets a moral climate by which a whole people lives out its code of ethics. Accepting certain values or rejecting them, is part of this moral code. The most powerful social groups which are the institutional sources of morality in the contemporary world are: the Church, a spiritual source of morality; the Government, a political source of morality; and the electronic media, a cultural source of morality.

Let us look at these three institutions and the ethical means which they use more closely.

4. The Ethical Means of the Spiritual Source of Morality

The Catholic Church uses as one of its tools of encouraging ethical behavior the examples of the Saints. Saints vary in history according to age and sex, political and religious allegiance, and there are many strong personality differences among the saints. Some people have the misconception that all saints are very pious and live very far removed from the everyday world. All the saints in the Catholic Church have had an extreme range of occupations, ages and abilities. St. Joan of Arc was a teenage girl who led the French Army against the invading British troops. She has now become the Patron Saint of France. St. Thomas More was a shrewd lawyer who used his legal skills to help the government of Henry VIII. When Henry VIII broke from the Church, Thomas More was forced to use his legal skills to oppose the King and was eventually executed for treason. Both of these courageous people are presented to us as examples of heroic sanctity. When the Church declares someone a Saint, it declares that they are examples of good behavior and of a correct Christian moral life. The Church does not expect us to imitate the particular personality or skill of the saint, but to look to the saint as a moral guide.

The Church also uses its regular teaching authority as an ethical tool for developing knowledge and application of ethics. The Fathers of Vatican II taught in the Council Documents the Church's role in the teaching of ethical behavior. In the *Decree on Religious Freedom,* we read the following:

In the formation of their consciences, the Christian faithful ought carefully to attend to the sacred and certain doctrine of the Church. The Church is, by the will of Christ, the teacher of the truth. It is her duty to give utterance to, and authoritatively to teach, that Truth which is Christ Himself, and also to declare and confirm by her authority those principles of the moral order which have their origin in human nature itself. Furthermore, let Christians walk in wisdom in the face of those outside, "in the Holy Spirit, in unaffected love, in the word of truth" (2 Cor 6:6-7). Let them be about their task of spreading the light of life with all confidence and apostolic courage, even to the shedding of their blood.

(Decree on Religious Freedom #14)

A third ethical tool of the Catholic Church is the contemporary community of faith which creates a moral climate for encouraging good behavior. The Church also teaches that the political community has an obligation to preserve the moral order. This can be seen from St. Paul's teaching in Romans 13 about civil order of society:

Let everyone obey the authorities that are over him, for there is no authority except from God, and all authority that exists is established by God. As a consequence, the man who opposes authority rebels against the ordinance of God; those who resist thus shall draw condemnation down upon themselves. Rulers cause no fear when a man does what is right but only when his conduct is evil. Do you wish to be free from the fear of authority? Do what is right and you will gain its approval, for the ruler is God's servant to work for your good. Only if you do wrong ought you to be afraid. It is not without purpose that the ruler carries the sword; he is God's servant, to inflict his avenging wrath upon the wrongdoer. You must obey, then, not only to escape punishment but also for conscience's sake. You pay taxes for the same reason, magistrates being God's ministers who devote themselves to his service with unremitting care. Pay each one his due: taxes to whom taxes are due; toll to whom toll is due; respect and honor to everyone who deserves them. (Rom. 13:1-7).

This Scriptural teaching will prepare us now to consider the political sources of morality.

5. *Ethical Means of Political Sources of Morality*

The three principal means that governments have for acting

as sources of morality are a) the examples of national heroes, b) Civil Law and Criminal Law, c) active citizenship.

a) The Example of National Heroes. Every country puts forward certain people as heroes to be imitated. In America, George Washington, the first president, is considered a national hero. He is venerated for his ability to lead a military victory at the time when the American colonies were fighting for their independence from Britian. The sixteenth President of the United States, Abraham Lincoln, is universally admired for his ability to preserve the Union during the Civil War, and also for his teachings on the immorality of slavery. He is a special hero to the Black people because he emancipated them from slavery in America.

b) Both the Civil law and the Criminal law are tools which are used by the political society to encourage good behavior. Abuses in this system are always possible and it is the role of the good citizen to preserve the legal system within his country so that it can be used to maintain good behavior. It is also recognized by the Church that the State has the right to punish those people who violate either the Civil or the Criminal Code. St. Paul taught that the Christian has the obligation to obey the just laws of his country.

c) Active citizenship is extremely important for preserving the Civil law and the Criminal law. It has been noted by some historians that because good Christians refused to be involved in the political life of Germany in the early thirties, it was possible for the Nazi Party to take over control of the government. They argue that if Christians had had more input into the political system that it would have been far more difficult for the racist nationalistic party to gain control of Germany. Active citizenship means voting, serving on juries, paying taxes, urging good legislation, following court decisions, letting one's view be known to those in authority, being willing to run for election in office, being willing to serve on Civil Councils and also monitoring the Criminal Justice and Civil law Court system. The good order of society is ruined when good people refuse to be involved in any of these political or legal activities. It helps to strengthen society the more that good Christians are involved in these activities. For example, here are some questions that you can ask about the Criminal Justice system as it now exists in your particular county or state: Is it a racist system? Does it punish only those who are poor or belong to minorities? Recently, in New York State a nursing home operator who had cheated the federal government out of millions of dollars was given a four month sentence. This white collar criminal was given a far lesser penalty than someone from a minority group who would steal a few hundred dollars from someone's purse. Is this just? What does this reflect on our society that only the powerless or those that belong to minorities are those who are jailed for evil behavior?

6. *The Ethical Tools of the Cultural Sources of Morality*

The most powerful means for creating a moral climate today is the electronic media. Most people argue that it is not living up to its obligation to encourage good moral behavior but rather is causing a deterioration of morality in our culture. The following excerpts are from John Gardner's recent book *Moral Fiction*.[1] These excerpts are basically involved with his analysis of what is wrong with the print media. But everything he says can certainly be said also of the electronic media. Mr. Gardner is complaining that most contemporary authors do not have a clear moral vision in their books. They do not give their readers a moral viewpoint, but rather simply report on what is going on in contemporary culture:

> Too often we find in contemporary fiction not true morality, which requires sympathy and responsible judgment, but a fierce code that under closer inspection turns out to be a parochial group's manners and habitual prejudices elevated to the status of ethical imperatives, axioms for which bigotry or hate, not love is the premise.

> If we are unable to distinguish between true morality—life-affirming, just, and compassionate behavior—and trivial moral fashion, we begin to doubt morality itself.

Mr. Gardner goes on to say that in today's society media has opted for two choices: either the contemporary artist celebrates fashionable moral values and ignores those which are out of fashion or the artist simply holds up a mirror to the immoral behavior which is occurring in the society as a whole.

In such a society, the careless thinker can slide into the persuasion that the celebration of true morality has ceased to be the serious writer's function and may even be pernicious. If the writer, so persuaded, is a decent human being, he or she tends to adopt one of two humane and praiseworthy, but in the long run unfruitful, programs. Either the writer celebrates important but passing concerns, such as social justice for particular minorities (dates and thus trivial once the goal has been achieved), or the writer serves only as historian, holding up a mirror to his age but not changing it, simply imitating, as Pound said, "its accelerated grimace."

But in comparison with the true artist's celebration of the permanently moral, both programs are nevertheless secondary and can only produce art that with the passing of its age must lose force.

Mr. Gardner's observations can be said to be true today of movies, television, phonograph records and other forms of electronic media. He continues to delineate the responsibility of the novelist to use literature as an ethical tool.

We read literature in the hope of experiencing our highest, most selfless emotion either to reach a sublime communication with the maker of the work, sharing his affirmations as lovers do, or to find characters we love as we do real people. Ultimately, in fact, plot exists only to give the characters means of finding and revealing themselves, and setting, only to give them a place to stand. As for "thought," it is simply what the characters say or would say if they were wiser and had our distance from their story. In art, morality and love are inextricably bound: We affirm what is good—for the characters in particular and for humanity in general—because we care. The artist who has no strong feeling about his characters—the artist who can feel passionate only about his words or idea—has no urgent reason to think hard about the characters' problems, the "themes" in his fiction. He imitates human gesture in the movements of his puppets, but he does not worry as a father worries about the behavior of his son; and the result is a fictional universe one would not want one's loved ones forced to inhabit.

Mr. Gardner notes that today's contemporary writers (and all involved in media production) have not developed any compassion for their characters nor a will enthused with love for what is morally good.

Without will—the artist's conscious determination to take his characters and their problems, seriously—no artist can achieve real compassion. And without compassion—without real and deep love for his "subjects" (the people he writes about and, by extension, all human beings)—no artist can summon the will to make true art; he will be satisfied, instead, with clever language or with cynical jokes and too easy, dire solutions like those common in contemporary fiction.

Mr. Gardner expresses his opinion that the moral sickness in art represents a loss of faith in the form which parallels the loss of faith that many people have had with traditional religion.

The sickness goes deeper, to an almost total loss of faith in—or perhaps understanding of—how true art works. True art, by specific technical means now commonly forgotten, clarifies life, establishes models of human action, casts nets toward the future, carefully judges our right and wrong directions, celebrates and mourns. It does not rant. It does not sneer or giggle in the face of death. It invents prayers and weapons. It designs visions worth trying to make fact.

Mr. Gardner's observation about pure art can also be said of true ethics and true religion. Mr. Gardner concludes by seeing a parallel between art and Fascism, the political system of total control.

Art is in one sense Fascist: It claims, on good authority, that some things are healthy for individuals and for society and that some things are not. Unlike the Fascist in uniform, the artist never forces anyone to do anything. He merely makes his case the strongest case possible. He lights up the darkness with a lightning flash, protects his friends the gods—that is, values—and all humanity without exception, and then moves on.

Comment

A source of morality can be from inside the self or from outside. The interior source of morality is the spiritual nature of each person. God made us with a soul. This soul has two special powers: the intellect and the will. The intellect seeks truth. It has the power to understand and comprehend what is good. The will seeks the good. It has the power to decide to act for the good. Free choice is the spiritual power to accept or reject what is true and good.

The exterior source of morality is any significant other, i.e., a person or a group which has the power to influence us for good or evil. An insignificant other, whether a person or group, has no power over us. A primary group is one in which we know the members personally. This can be our family, relations, friends, co-workers, fellow students, etc. Primary groups have a great deal of power over the moral climate in which we live. They are very forceful sources of morality. Functional groups are usually made up of large numbers of people whom we do not know personally. Yet they have a power over us because they can create a moral climate for a whole society of people. Such institutional sources of morality are the Church, the government and the media. Institutional sources of morality also strive to create a primary relationship with us by having local representatives whom we do know personally. The local cop on the beat or the priest in the parish are representatives that we know personally but they both represent larger institutional sources of morality. Media are powerful sources of morality because they create an artificial primary relationship *immediately* with large numbers of people who are geographically distant from one another. No other source can do that. A TV celebrity who extols pre-marital sex can actually be present in our living-room telling us his opinion. It is an *artificial* primary relationship however, because it is not face-to-face. Even though we see and hear him, we have no way of responding to him. He is molding our character, but we have no influence over his character. That is why the media at times can be more powerful than the government and the Church. As powerful as they are, we can still "talk back" to the local representative.

Summary

A source of morality is either a person or group which guides our activity by establishing certain values or norms for behavior. The different means used by sources of morality are ethical tools which encourage us to do good and to avoid evil. Our spiritual nature is an interior source of morality. An exterior source of morality is a significant other which has a power over us to create a moral climate.

The sources of morality are: 1) self, 2) familial, 3) social, 4) spiritual, 5) political, and 6) cultural. The first three are primary social groups, and the second three are institutional sources of morality. No exterior group has a power over us unless we claim or own its moral attitude as our own.

In today's world the media are a very powerful source of morality and can easily be abused to encourage evil behavior.

Questions

1. How is the self a source of morality?
2. How can love and friendship be a source of morality? When are they not used properly?
3. How does a primary group create pressure on us to act in a certain way?
4. What are the ethical tools of the Government?
5. What are the ethical tools of the Church?
6. Why are media as a source of morality more powerful than a spiritual source of morality in today's world?
7. Explain how the institutional sources of morality differ from the primary sources.
8. How does media create an "artificial" primary relationship?

Footnotes

1. Excerpted from *ON MORAL FICTION* by John Gardner, (C) 1978 by John Gardner, Basic Books, Inc. Publishers, New York.

BIBLIOGRAPHY

Brown, Raymond E. *Biblical Reflections on Crises Facing the Church,* New York: Paulist Press, 1975.

Duska, Ronald and Whelan, Mariellen. *Moral Development,* New York: Paulist Press, 1975.

Farrell, Melvin. *Theology for Parents and Teachers,* Milwaukee, Wisconsin: HI-Time Publishers, Inc. 1972.

Jersild, Paul and Johnson, Dale, ed., *Moral Issues and Christian Response,* New York: Holt, Rinehart and Winston, Inc., 1971.

Milhaven, John G. *Toward a New Catholic Morality,* Garden City, New York: Doubleday and Company, Inc., 1970.

Specific Moral Issues

Chapters 4, 5 and 6 were explorations of Catholic morality. In each of these chapters, we looked at the different value systems, how a conscience is formed by the teaching of the Church, and the different sources which urge us to behave in a certain way. In the following chapters, from 7 until 13, we will explore specific moral issues in the contemporary world. Each of these issues is something which is very important and something which has a profound influence on our life today. It is hoped that the background on Catholic doctrine and Catholic morality has prepared the student to look at these specific moral issues with the tools of traditional teachings on doctrine and morality.

The first chapter in the section on Specific Moral Issues has to do with the worth of the individual. Contemporary society has put tremendous pressures on each individual to behave in a certain way. It is unfortunately very common that many people do not decide how they will behave. This is not the authentic Christian tradition, which teaches that each individual is responsible for his own moral actions and must make a free and independent moral choice on whether to do good or to do evil. The Chapter explores some specific examples of persons who have strived to maintain their independent moral conscience at a time when other forces in the Church or society were pushing them to act in a way contrary to their own conscience.

Chapter 7

THE WORTH OF THE INDIVIDUAL:
The Power of the State vs. the Value of the Individual Freedom of Conscience

Both the State and the Church contribute to a moral atmosphere of the people. Yet, each individual has an independent moral conscience. Most times the moral conscience of the individual is at one with the moral atmosphere established by the larger group. What happens when one individual believes that his unique moral conscience is right and the rest of the group is wrong? This is a classic dilemma, one explored in all the great literature of the world. In Catholic teaching, individual conscience is *the* supreme judge of what is right and wrong. However, this supreme judge must be informed by the traditional teaching of the Church and the inspiration of the Holy Spirit. The Fathers of Vatican II taught about the supremacy of the individual conscience:

> On his part man perceives and acknowledges the imperatives of the divine law through the mediation of conscience. In all his activity a man is bound to follow his conscience faithfully, in order that he may come to God, for whom he was created. It follows that he is not to be forced to act in a manner contrary to his conscience. Nor, on the other hand, is he to be restrained from acting in accordance with his conscience, especially in matters religious.
> For, of its very nature, the exercise of religion consists before all else in those internal, voluntary, and free acts whereby man sets the course of his life directly toward God. No merely human power can either command or prohibit acts of this kind.
>
> *(Declaration on Religious Freedom, #3)*

St. Paul taught that when Christ rose from the dead, He created a new freedom, a freedom which had its pinnacle in the individual moral conscience: "Now we have been released from the law—for we have died to what bound us—and we serve in the new spirit, not the antiquated letter." (Rm 7:6)

It is never easy to adequately describe a moment when the individual conscience must go against the institutional Church or the Government or a large group of people. The social pressures to conform are great. The reasons by which a person understands that he should contradict the values of those around him are often nebulous. However, there are times when there are clear-cut matters in which the individual must stand over against society. We will use this chapter to study those moments, and individuals who have been examples of such freedom of conscience.

In 1977 the Nobel Peace Prize was given, not to an individual, but to Amnesty International. Amnesty International strives to free prisoners in countries all over the world who are in prison solely for their political beliefs. Amnesty International also documents the brutal tortures frequently meted out to those who disagree with the politicians in power. Idi Amin, in Uganda, has become a sorry example to the world of a totalitarian leader who will brook no opposition from his own people. There is documented evidence that many of his own citizens have been killed only because they oppose his political regime. Sadly, the list is very, very long of political tyrants who have used their power to intimidate, crush and destroy those who oppose them. The freedom and liberty enjoyed by Americans is a rare occurrence in a world full of totalitarian tyrants. Yet, the Gospel of Jesus Christ clearly trumpets the value of the individual moral conscience and the great value of human freedom.

Rather than an abstract treatment of freedom of conscience, let us study concrete examples. This will help you to comprehend the concept clearly.

1. *Jesus Christ and the Roman Empire*

When Jesus appeared before Pontius Pilate, the Roman

Governor of Judea, he charged Him with treason. The charge stemmed from the fact that Jesus was being taken as the Jewish Messiah. The word "Messiah" meant "king" and the Romans allowed no one to have this title unless they were approved by Rome. Jesus, however, claimed that his kingship was not one of political and military authority, but rather a spiritual one over the souls of free men. The legal representative of Rome was very threatened by Jesus's teaching, because in its essence it meant that man was free and independent of totalitarian political regimes. Therefore, one of the reasons why Jesus Christ was crucified by the Roman political power was that he was seen as a clear threat to the empire's totalitarian control of its people. This does not mean that Jesus was involved in raising a political and military revolution. What it does mean is that the politicians of His day clearly understood that he was an apostle of individual freedom and that such an apostle must be destroyed by men who are owned by others. Tyrants cannot brook the voice of freedom and independence. Such a voice shatters the corrupt power which they have built for themselves.

The Trial Before Pilate

At daybreak they brought Jesus from Caiaphas to the praetorium. They did not enter the praetorium themselves, for they had to avoid ritual impurity if they were to eat the Passover supper. Pilate came out to them. "What accusation do you bring against this man?" he demanded. "If he were not a criminal," they retorted, "we would certainly not have handed him over to you." At this Pilate said, "Why do you not take him and pass judgment on him according to your law?" "We may not put anyone to death," the Jews answered. (This was to fulfill what Jesus had said indicating the sort of death he had to die).

Pilate went back into the praetorium and summoned Jesus. "Are you the King of the Jews?" he asked him. Jesus answered, "Are you saying this on your own, or have others been telling you about me?" "I am no Jew!" Pilate retorted. "It is your own people and the chief priests who have handed you over to me. What have you done?" Jesus answered:

"My kingdom does not belong to this world.
If my kingdom were of this world,

> my subjects would be fighting
> to save me from being handed over to
>   the Jews.
> As it is, my kingdom is not here."
>
> At this Pilate said to him, "So, then,
> you are a king?" Jesus replied:
>
> "It is you who say I am a king.
> The reason I was born,
> the reason why I came into the world,
> is to testify to the truth.
> Anyone committed to the truth hears
>   my voice."

"Truth!" said Pilate, "What does that mean?"
(John: Chapter 18, verses 28-38.)

Pilate is the voice of political realism. He cannot understand what a free and independent person is. His whole political future depends on his blind allegiance to the Roman Emperor and when he faces an independent man with the freedom of one of the children of God, he is completely and utterly baffled. Jesus says that his authority is from God, and his authority is over the hearts and minds of men. Jesus clearly teaches that he had no intention of raising sedition against Rome. He says that if he were a political and military leader, he would have a gathering of worldly followers who would have prevented him from being taken. But he has no such followers. His followers are men and women of the spirit and they have no power in the worldly sense of that word. Pilate turns away from Jesus and turns back to the real world, the world that Pilate understands. The world that Jesus represents is one of spirit and truth and Pilate cannot comprehend it. In Christ's world, free men and free women do not have to be coerced. In Christ's world, people live freely according to their conscience and God's law. In Christ's world people are not forced to believe or act by violence or threats of violence but are stimulated to act out of love.

2. *Joan of Arc and the English-French Church*

Joan of Arc was a teenage girl who lead the French armies against the invading British. She turned back the British invasion and enabled the legitimate king of France to be crowned. When the war was over, the English and the French made an agreement. They wanted to discredit Joan by having her burned at the stake. They put Joan through a mock trial. Her own nation and her own nation's people turned away from her. Church authorities were brought in. She was accused of wearing men's clothing; she was accused of being an evil person. None of these charges were true. Joan was accused because she had freed her people from a great military invasion in her own nation. Some say her "little voices" were the voice of conscience, the Voice of God telling the people that they were free and independent. But the trial was another voice, the voice of fear; the voice that said only the state can control the minds and hearts of people. Unfortunately, some Church officials went along with this, and Joan was burned at the stake for treason and heresy. Years later, Joan was vindicated of all charges and Church officials made her a saint. The French nation, which had once abandoned her, made her the patron of their country.

3. *St. Thomas More and Henry VIII of England*

Robert Bolt has a famous play called "The Man for All Seasons" and it has also been made into a very well-known movie. It tells the story of St. Thomas More, Chancellor of England, and a bosom friend of Henry VIII. As long as England remained Catholic and Henry VIII was a Catholic king, Thomas More was respected and given many honors by his own country. When Henry VIII decided to divorce his first wife and break with the Roman Catholic Church, he set himself up as the head of the English Church. Thomas More could not in conscience agree with this decision, but he felt it prudent not to speak out. Silently he withdrew from public life and kept his opinions and thoughts to himself. But his refusal to participate in Henry VIII's government was a powerful indictment of Henry and his Parliament. One of the characters in the play, when he speaks of More's silence, explains the power that More had over the Continental Europe of the day. "That man's silence is bellowing all over Europe!" he exclaimed. The decision was made to try Thomas More. He was arrested for treason and put through a mock trial, to "prove" that a man who had been loyal to the king of England all of his life was, in reality, a traitor. The purpose of the trial was to discredit St. Thomas More and to make him appear to be an evil man. True to his conscience, Thomas More never once broke. He refused to swear an oath of allegiance to the succession of the King's and Anne Boleyn's child. He was beheaded by the English Government. The Catholic Church declared Thomas More a saint and martyr. He is a genuine example of courage in the face of institutional immorality.

4. *Galileo and the Catholic Church's Hierarchy*

Galileo Galilei was an Italian astronomer who taught in the early part of the 17th Century. He was the first man to see the moons of Jupiter and the craters on the moon. He conclusively proved, by visual means, that Copernicus's theory was correct. Copernicus, a century earlier, had taught that the Earth revolved around the Sun and had a daily rotation. This shattered the philosophical and theological pre-suppositions of Renaissance European Christianity, which depended upon the earth's being stationary, in the center of the Universe surrounded by rotating heavens. It was taught that Jesus had descended, as the Incarnate Son, through these concentric spheres, until He reached the earth. Man was considered the center of the Universe and the drama of redemption had been worked out on this earthly sphere because it was the very heart of all that was created. Obviously, none of this teaching was essential to Christianity. But many people saw the ideas of astronomy linked intimately with those of philosophy and theology. They were afraid that men like Giordano Bruno, who also believed in the Copernican theory of the earth, would wind up denying the teachings of the Church and the value of Sacred Scripture. This was a real problem for Renaissance Catholics also, because the Protestant Reformation had denied so many of the teachings of the Church and had weakened many people's belief in Scripture and Church authority. Galileo found himself in the midst of,—not only an astronomical argument,—but also a theological, political and philosophical debate. In 1616 Galileo was requested by the official Church authorities to teach his theory only as an hypothesis, not as a proven fact. He agreed to do so. In 1633, Galileo was brought to trial by Church authorities, for teaching in textbooks that the revolution of the earth around the sun was not a theory, but a proven fact! He was forced to recant his teachings and to accept the traditional view that the earth stood still and the sun revolved around it. All of his textbooks were put on the index. This is a sad chapter in the Church's history. It shows Church officials afraid to deal with new ideas and it is also extremely embarrassing because Galileo was eventually proven right and the officials of the Church were proven wrong. Galileo himself is not an heroic man. He recanted ideas he knew in his heart were true. He himself admitted that he was not a hero. He was not about to be martyred for the Copernican theory. However, his story is a sad example of how power can be abused. The Church was founded to teach theological truths. God never gave it the ability to teach scientific truths. If the Church officials of his day had recognized that they did not know scientific truths, they would not have put themselves in the embarrassing position of declaring something false which God knew was true.

The Issue of Freedom in the Modern Church

A contemporary view of conscience is presented by John Deedy, a Catholic Theologian.[2] He says:

> "The Catholic understanding is that all authority derives ultimately from God—civil authority, parental or familial authority, and, most particularly, ecclesiastical authority. The Catholic Church is the church, if not of, then, founded by Jesus Christ, God and Second Person of the Trinity. The church's claims on authority go back to him and the New Testament, where, explicitly and implicitly, these claims are spelled out. It should be noted, however, that authority in

the New Testament is conceived in a manner that is democratic
rather than absolute; likewise, it belongs to the whole church rather
than to particular officers. At the same time, authority in the New
Testament does not coerce or compel . . . love of ideas, or institutions or things has so often displaced or superseded love of persons
as to disorient concepts of authority up and down the range of
human sensibilities . . . when authority is any of these things, it
violates personal freedom and very probably personal conscience as
well."

Deedy's position is that Christian conscience has always developed
in community. Therefore, a person should make his/her own
judgments with responsible freedom. This freedom should not be
driven by coercion but by a sense of christian love.

Individual Examples of Freedom in Civic Society

There are many individuals who have raised their voice
against totalitarian regimes. These are people who are true examples of freedom of spirit and hope. Even though they lose their
reputation, their families or their friends, they still stay true to
what they believe is the correct thing to do. They may be politicians or churchmen or philosophers, but in each case they stood
for a principle which eventually the rest of the community saw as
valid.

a) Solzhenitsyn in Russia

In the book "The Gulag Archipelago" Alexander Solzhenitsyn tells the story of the Stalin labor camps in Russia. Detail by
detail he shows how the Soviet Russians have denied freedom to
their own people. They have arrested people and taken them to
labor camps, citizens who had never done anything against the
laws of their country. They have created a police state in which
people can be charged with treason with very little evidence. They
have taken many of their own intellectuals who depart from the
current political orthodoxy and locked them up in mental institutions because they dared to differ from the official position.

b) Mahatma Ghandi and British India

One of the best known examples in the 20th Century of the freedom of the individual against an oppressive political regime is Mahatma Ghandi. Ghandi was an Indian who was educated in Britain and returned to his own native country. There he was appalled by the colonial government of the British and decided to free his people. He decided to lead a moral crusade rather than a military one. Rather than fight the occupying power with an army, Ghandi decided to do a series of spiritual activities to free his people. These included prayers, vigils, fasting and mass demonstrations. One of his most popular techniques ("The Hatar") was to close down all the shops in an area so that no business would be transacted. Another was to go on long hunger strikes. A third was to be arrested and jailed for civil disobedience. Each of these events caused the occupying power to arrest him and punish him in a way that became excessive. Gradually Ghandi built up a world opinion which was morally revolted by the colonial occupation of India. He succeeded in freeing his people from the British government. He himself based many of his teachings on the non-violent disobedience of the American Henry Thoreau.

c) Henry Thoreau and the United States

The author of *Walden,* Henry Thoreau, was a New Englander who withdrew from everyday life to live as a peaceful hermit near a pond in Walden, Massachusetts. There he wrote and reflected about the beauty of nature and getting away from the hectic ratrace of everyday life in America. He wrote a pamphlet *On Civil Disobedience.* When the local town passed a tax which Thoreau believed unjust, he refused to pay it and was jailed for his disobedience. When his friend, Ralph Waldo Emerson, came to visit him he called out to Henry and said, "Henry, what are you doing in there?" He called out to Emerson, "Emerson, what are you doing *out* there?" Thoreau taught that a person should be willing to disobey unjust laws and suffer arrest and imprisonment if necessary.

d) Martin Luther King, Jr. and Institutional Racism in the United States

Another follower of Thoreau and Ghandi was the black minister, Martin Luther King, Jr. Upset by the institutional racism in America, Martin Luther King, Jr. knew that he could not lead people into violent revolution. He knew that he lived in a large white society that could easily crush a black revolution. His solution was to do the non-violent oppostion of Henry Thoreau and Ghandi. He organized boycotts, sitins and demonstrations. He was the one who orchestrated the March on Washington in 1963, in which thousands of black people came to Washington to change the institutional racism of the United States. Martin Luther King, Jr. was one of the voices instrumental in creating the Civil Rights Act of the United States. He was also considered one of the black leaders who prevented widespread violence and encouraged non-violent demonstrations. While organizing a garbagemen's strike in Memphis, Tennessee, King was assassinated. His death left a great void for Black people in America. He was a recipient of the Nobel Peace Prize. There is an unsung hero in the story of Martin Luther King, Jr. He is Federal Judge, Frank Johnson. One of the first things that King did was to lead a bus boycott in Montgomery, Alabama. This is what brought him into national prominence and it was Judge Johnson that found King's case just and broke the Jim Crow laws in the Deep South. Judge Johnson has paid a terrible price for making judicial decisions which favored what was just rather than unjust.

> The lasting image of Federal Judge Frank Johnson that comes from the manuscript pages of the book Robert F. Kennedy Jr. is writing about him is not one of a stern jurist ordering the police of Selma to allow a civil-rights march. It is one of Johnson, with armed U.S. marshals watching, playing golf at Maxwell Air Force base, walking on the green, alone. Marshals have been guarding the fifty-nine-year-old judge for twenty-two years, since he gave Martin Luther King, Jr. his first victory, ruling that a black woman named Rosa Parks could sit anywhere she wanted to on a Montgomery bus. That and a hundred locally unpopular decisions like it did not cost Frank Johnson any money. But it twice may have cost him appointment to the United States Supreme Court because of the

livid opposition of the Alabama congressional delegation, and it may have cost him much more. His only son, Johnny, who was harassed in classrooms and on the street all through school, once said:"You have no idea what it's been like being Frank Johnson's son... There has always been something to keep us on edge." A year after he said that, Johnny Johnson committed suicide in his father's guarded home.

Johnson does not like to talk about himself, but his friends explain him by pointing to a three-word answer he once gave when asked about principle: "Follow the law." He is a Republican and had never been involved in civil rights or anything like it when he was appointed a federal district court judge by President Eisenhower in 1955. He dealt with the cases that inevitably filled his docket in troubled times—eliminating the Alabama poll tax, abolishing the red-neck power of justices of the peace, reapportioning the state legislature, integrating the state police. And they hated him for it.[3]

Judge Johnson is another example of a man who believes that individual moral principles are more important than the values of the group or the society in which he finds himself.

Self-Integrity Vs. Selfishness

To be a person of self-integrity is to be someone who is a morally good person. The examples noted above are all of individuals who refused to buckle under a system. They refused to let the law of the Church or the State lead them astray: Even though in an environment diametrically opposed to what they believed in, they did not succumb. They kept their own integrity and stayed with the truth, even when it cost some their lives. It is important to understand that in each case the institution involved, which is supposed to preserve the moral law, instead, worked against it. Individuals had to be certain that what they were doing was good even when many of the people whom they loved and respected were trying to get them to act and believe in another way. The selfish person is the person who only looks out for his own interests... Whether or not something is morally wrong, whether or not society approves of it, makes no difference. The only thing that is important is that he always get his own way and that his own

children into the world is a sacred responsibility and cannot be lightly dispensed with. Young children need careful parenting and need to be taught the moral teachings of the Church. Lesbian relationships or promiscuous relationships are detrimental for men or women. They also prevent the establishment and growth of families. This aspect of Women's Liberation cannot be accepted as true freedom, but rather as a false one.

Comment

The purpose of the spiritual institution of the Church and the purpose of the political institution of the State is to preserve and enhance the moral order. There are times when the individual, rather than being helped by these institutions, is, instead, hindered in his own need for moral reinforcement from the larger group. These are the times when an individual must stand over against the group and proclaim values which the institution is either ignoring or suppressing. There are examples of individuals who have stood for the value of the individual moral conscience in opposition to the larger group. These people have opposed injustices in both the State and in the Church. The Catholic Church teaches that the individual moral conscience, informed by the traditional teaching of the Church and inspired by the Holy Spirit, is the supreme judge of all moral actions.

Summary

Both the Church and the State are responsible for establishing a moral atmosphere.
1. At times the individual moral conscience must go against the State and the Church.
2. Individual moral conscience is the most important element in moral decisions.
3. One of the reasons Jesus Christ was condemned to death by the Roman Empire was that he extolled freedom of conscience over against a totalitarian, political regime.

4. St. Joan of Arc was condemned as a heretic, even though she had done nothing wrong. She is a representative of freedom of conscience before Church authority which was abusing its power.

5. St. Thomas More maintained his integrity and was martyred by Henry VIII of England, who wanted More to approve his second marriage.

6. Galileo Galilei was condemned by Church officials for teaching the Copernican Theory of astronomy. This is an example of official Church authorities abusing their teaching power.

7. Sometimes an individual must stand up for a moral principle, even in a totalitarian regime. This is very difficult and may actually be a form of martyrdom. Some modern examples of individual freedom of conscience in the face of totalitarian or universal opposition have been Solzhenitsyn, Ghandi, Thoreau, King, Jr., and Judge Frank Johnson.

8. Self-integrity is a value which should be chosen over selfishness. At times this is very difficult and costly.

9. The Women's Liberation Movement strives to maintain the worth of individual women. Some exponents of the movement have values which are anti-Christian and cannot be accepted by the Church.

Questions for Discussion

1. Explain the Church's teaching on the value and worth of the individual moral conscience.

2. Give instances of State governments which have oppressed the individual moral conscience and examples of those persons who have fought such an oppression.

3. What is non-violent Civil Disobedience and who are some of the persons who have employed it?

4. Give examples when the institutional Church has oppressed the individual moral conscience.

5. Explain the Vatican II's teaching on the individual moral conscience.
6. Discuss the viewpoint of John Deedy. Is his observation valid or is he overstating his case?
7. What elements of the Women's Liberation Movement can Catholics accept and what elements are against traditional Church teaching?

Footnotes

1. The Church officials did enter into a scientific discussion and were proved wrong. Galileo, however, himself quoted scripture to prove that his discovery was not anti-revelation and by quoting scripture left the purely scientific realm and entered the religious. Galileo's discovery meant that some passages of scripture could not be taken literally, and at the time of the Catholic-Protestant pole in the Bible, Catholic officials believed Galileo was undermining it in the word of the Bible.
2. John Deedy, *What a Modern Catholic Believes about Conscience, Freedom and Authority*, Chicago, Illinois: The Thomas More Press, 1972, 10-11.
3. Richard Reeves, "The Last Angry Men," *Esquire*, Mar. 1, 1978, 42-43. First published in Esquire Magazine.

BIBLIOGRAPHY

Bolt, Robert. *A Man for all Seasons*, New York: Random Press, 1966.

Brodrick, James. *Galileo: The Man, His Work, His Misfortunes*, London, 1964.

Deedy, John. *What a Modern Catholic Believes about Conscience, Freedom and Authority*, Chicago, Illinois: The Thomas More Press, 1972.

Flood, Edmund. *Jesus and His Contemporaries*, New York: Paulist-Newman, 1976.

Kennedy, Jr., Robert F. *Judge Frank M. Johnson, Jr.*, East Rutherford, New Jersey, Putnam, 1978.

King, Jr., Martin Luther. *Why We Can't Wait*, New York: Mentor Books.

Polak, H.S. et. al. *Mahatma Ghandi,* Thompson, Conn., Inter Culture.

Sarno, Ronald A. "A Sixteenth Century War of Ideas, Science Vs. the Church," *The Annals of Science,* London, England, Vol. 25, No. 3, September 1969.

Shaw, George Bernard. *Saint Joan,* Baltimore, Maryland: Penguin, 1951.

Solzhenitzyn, Alexander. *The Gulag Archipelago,* New York: Harper and Row, 1977.

Thoreau, Henry. *The Best of Walden and Civil Disobedience,* Englewood Cliffs, New Jersey: Scholastic Book Service, 1973.

Wahlberg, Rachel Conrad. *Jesus According to a Woman,* New York: Paulist, 1978.

We have explored different incidents in which people have demonstrated that their conscience could be independent and free of evil influences from those around them. Marriage, of course, is a state of life most of the readers will choose for themselves. Marriage is also the source of human life and is the "domestic church" that first introduced us to the teachings of Jesus and his Church. Marriage is one of the most important institutions in contemporary society. Marriage, of course, is under tremendous pressures in modern society. The rapidly changing culture in which we live has made it extremely difficult to live a married life that corresponds to the teachings of Jesus and His Church. This chapter will present the Church's understanding of marriage as a sacrament and explore some of the contemporary problems, such as the soaring divorce rate, that Christians have to deal with.

Chapter 8

MARRIAGE:
Marriage, Remarriage, Divorce, Open Marriage

Ninety percent of the people will marry at some time of their lives. Statistics show that eighty percent of today's first marriages are permanent and successful. The other twenty percent have failed. Why? There are many reasons. However, these head the list, namely: 1. the unwillingness or inability to love one another maturely, selflessly and completely; 2. a breakdown of social supports for all permanent commitments. 3. a misuse of personal freedom; 4. a misconstrued version of women's liberation that stresses a freedom based on power rather than self giving; 5. an unwillingness on the part of some husbands to allow their wives to reach their potential as adults; 6. A hedonistic approach to sex; 7. The sensationalism of the media that undermines traditional marital values.

A stable, loving relationship is possible in a Catholic marriage. There is no magic formula for establishing and sustaining a Catholic marriage. But there are some practical insights which might help.

Let us examine five questions. What is a Catholic Marriage? What are the qualities for a stable, loving relationship in Catholic Marriages? What is the Rite of a Catholic Marriage? What about Divorce and Remarriage in the Catholic Church? What about Open Marriages as a substitute for Traditional Marriages?

1. *Catholic Marriages*

Every marriage is the union of the two unique persons who are loving people, develop and enrich their abilities and who are aware of each other's needs for privacy and independence. They commit themselves totally to each other so that they might grow in mutual understanding, and appreciating their God-given human personalities. As the bishops of the Second Vatican Council said:

> A man and woman . . . by the marriage covenant of the conjugal love "are no longer two, but one flesh" (Mt. 19:6) render mutual help and service to each other through an intimate union of their persons and their actions. Through this intimate union they experience the meaning of their oneness and attain to it the growing perfection day by day. As a mutual gift of two persons, this intimate union, as well as the good of the children, imposes total fidelity on the spouses and argues for an unbreakable oneness between them. (*Constitution on the Church in the Modern World*, art. 48).

Every marriage is a covenant and not a contract. A contract involves things such as pledges, rules and penalties. In the biblical sense, a covenant is an agreement between people. It is a friendship agreement. It is an open-ended commitment. It is a dynamic not a static alliance. Each marriage is a covenant involving the efforts of God, husband and wife. This idea was expressed on the Second Vatican Council:

> For as the God of Old made Himself present to His People through a covenant of love and fidelity, so now the Savior of men and the Spouse of the Church comes into the lives of the married Christians through the Sacrament of Matrimony. He abides with them thereafter so that, just as He loved the Church and handed himself over on her behalf, the spouses may love each other with perpetual fidelity through mutual self-bestowal. (*Constitution on the Church in the Modern World*, art. 48).

Every marriage is a Sacramental sign of Jesus. Jesus communicated by signs to man. For example, Jesus took the blind man's hand and led him outside the village. Putting spittle on his eyes he laid his hands on him and asked, "Can you see anything?" The man opened his eyes and said, "I can see people but they look like walking trees." Then a second time Jesus laid hands on his eyes, and he saw perfectly; his sight was restored and he could see everything clearly. (Mk 8:23-25).

During Jesus' lifetime, He cared for the sick, listened to the disturbed, forgave the sinner. His signs of love are examples for the husband and wife's relationship with one another. The Second Vatican Council expressed it this way:

> Let the spouses themselves, made to the image of the living God and enjoying the authentic dignity of persons, be joined to one another in equal affection, harmony of mind, and the work of mutual sanctification. Thus they will follow Christ who is the principle of life. Thus, too, by the joys and sacrifices of their vocation and through their faithful love, married people will become witnesses of the mystery of love which the Lord revealed to the world by His dying and His rising up to life again. (*Constitution on the Church in the Modern World*, art. 52).

Every marriage is a community of love. The problem is, what is love? It has been defined a thousand different ways. Perhaps the best definition is that it is the giving of self. Ann Landers expressed it this way:

> Love is tender, patient, considerate, and hopeful. Love can be a man's strength, his desire to succeed, his need to be needed. Love can be a woman's central motivation for living, for giving and forgiving. Love is a oneness, an emptiness filled. To love is to be alive in the fullest, most meaningful sense of the word. For loving is living. Love lives and it lets live. It is not given to smothering and possessiveness. Love is a beginning of purpose, a quieting of restlessness, an establishing of confidence. Love can be lighthearted and full of fun. It can be deadly serious and heartbreaking. Love can wither, but it grows again. Love may shrink but it expands again. Love may die but is reborn. Love is joy and laughter, tears and grief, growing and learning. Love sees, understands, believes, trusts and sustains. Without it we are nothing. Love makes us cardcarrying members of the human race.[2]

The greatest love of all is between a man and a woman. Through sex, they express the love they are building. Sex is part of the total picture of love. It is important and it must not be abused. It must be nurtured and cultivated, so that it may grow into the beautiful thing that it is. It is God-given and it is beautiful. The Bishops of the Second Vatican Council stated:

> This love is an eminently human one since it is directed from one person to another through an affection of the will. It involves the good of the whole person. Therefore it can enrich the expressions of body and mind with a unique dignity, ennobling these expressions as special ingredients and signs of the friendship distinctive of marriage. This love the Lord has judged worthy of special gifts, healing, perfecting and exalting gifts of grace and of charity... This love is uniquely expressed and perfected through the marital act. The actions within marriage by which the couple are united immediately and chastely are noble and worthy ones. Expressed in a manner which is truly human, these actions signify and promote the mutual self giving by which spouses enrich each other with a joyful and a thankful will. (*Constitution on the Church in the Modern World*, art. 49).

Because of increasing pressures of new values in our society, Catholics must examine what marriage means in light of what has been said. A Catholic Marriage is anchored on the commandment of Jesus "This is my commandment, that you love one another as I have loved you" (Jn 15:12). He came to dramatize love and to show us how to love. And the Church is the visible organization of people who share, inspire, and transform the vision of Jesus.

2. Qualities for a Stable, Loving Relationship

Let us turn to our second question, what are the qualities for a stable, loving relationship in a Catholic Marriage? There is no magic number but there are four basic qualities which we will examine. Without them, a marriage is certain to fail.

First, there must be communication. By communication, we mean a meaningful conversation about your personal feelings. However, there is a right way and wrong way to do it. Be sure to beware of your voice: choose a suitable time to talk; be gentle and loving as possible; keep your temper; be prepared to listen; be prepared to hear unpleasant things.

Second, there must be honesty. One cannot build a good

relationship on lies—No problem is ever solved by pretending that it doesn't exist. We are human which means that we are imperfect. The problem is that we hate to admit it. From our early childhood days, we learned to become defensive. We did not want to be punished. So we hid our faults. It is difficult to reverse the process. Yet we can take courage from the fact that Jesus said that the truth will make us free.

Third, there must be commitment. Today we hear a lot about this word. It is important because no one grows without it. Many couples in the United States today have a double-ring ceremony. Both give a ring to each other. It is an external sign of their internal commitment to love and honor until death. The giving-receiving which characterizes every marriage symbolizes how Jesus deals with us.

Fourth, there must be permanence. It is an essential ingredient in any successful marriage. Many say that it is impossible, because of the different life styles of our society. There is no doubt that it is more difficult today but it is not impossible. With Jesus, all things are possible. The old marriage ritual summarized rather well the total picture of married life:

> This union then is most serious, because it will bind you together for a life in a relationship so close and so intimate that it will profoundly influence your whole future. That future with its hopes and disappointments, its pleasures and its pains, its joys and its sorrows, is hidden from your eyes. You know that these elements are mingled in every life and are to be expected in your own. And so, now knowing what is before you, you take each other for better or for worse, richer or for poorer, in sickness and in health, until death.

What disappointments, pains, joys, or sorrows await a married couple are unknown. What is certain is that they are part of life. They can face and accept if there is love. It is love that will make the marriage endure forever. St. Paul in his letter to the Corinthians said:

> Love is patient, love is kind. Love is not jealous, it does not put on airs, it is not snobbish. Love is never rude, it is not self-seeking, it is not prone to anger; neither does it brood over injuries. Love does not rejoice in what is wrong but rejoices with the truth. There is no limit

to love's forbearance, to its trust, its hope, its power to endure. (1 Cor 13:4-7).

3. Rite of a Catholic Marriage

Our third question is what is the rite of a Catholic marriage? Anthropologists tell us that man has always celebrated a serious event of his life with a religious ceremony. These sacred rites show the importance and dignity of the event. In this case, the Sacrament of Matrimony.

Because the theology of the Second Vatican Council considers Christian marriage as an "intimate partnership," a "conjugal covenant," it encourages couples to take a more active role in their marriage ceremony. The marriage ceremony is no longer a stereotyped ritual. A couple has many options such as choosing their scripture readings, writing their marrige vows, and selecting their blessing of the rings. Each ceremony is unique and personal.

The rite[3] itself reflects six ideas: 1) a serious concern for the spiritual and human enrichment of one's partner; 2) the awareness of the love of God, of neighbor, of oneself; 3) faith and trust in God and in the spouse; 4) acceptance of the power to create; 5) the importance of mutual respect and support; 6) the value of conjugal love.

There are two rites for celebrating a marriage, namely the rite for celebrating marriage during Mass and the rite for celebrating marriage outside of Mass.

Rite for Celebrating Marriage During Mass

Entrance Rite

The priest, attendants, witnesses, parents of the bride, parents of the groom and others may take part in the procession. An entrance hymn is sung.

Liturgy of the Word

The Mass begins. Depending on preference, there may be three scripture readings, one of them from the Old Testament. After the gospel, the priest gives a homily.

Rite of Marriage

At this time, there is the exchanging of vows and the blessing of the rings.

Liturgy of the Eucharist

The order of the Mass is followed with the following changes. During the offertory, the water and wine may be brought to the altar by either the bride and groom, by parents or members of the wedding.

After the Lord's Prayer, the Nuptial Blessing is given. Immediately after the blessing, the priest will give some sign of peace to the couple (e.g. a hand-shake). They are invited to exchange a sign with each other, such as an embrace or a kiss, then to extend a sign of peace to their parents and others.

Communion

The newly married couple has the option of receiving Holy Communion under both species (bread and wine).

Final Blessing

Before blessing the people at the end of Mass, the priest blesses the bride and groom.

Rite for Celebrating Marriage outside Mass

While the couple is encouraged to have a Nuptial Mass, they do have the option to have a ceremony without the Mass. The procedure would follow this order: 1) Entrance Rite; 2) Liturgy of the Word; 3) Rite of Marriage; 4) Nuptial Blessing; 5) Holy Communion (consecrated bread only); 6) Final Blessing.

Ever since the Second Vatican Council, the marriage rite is very flexible. The bride and groom have many options. They should study the choices and choose whatever is more suitable to their taste. In this way, their wedding day will be a most memorable day. A final note is that local customs and circumstances must be considered when you are deciding on the day, time, flowers, music, photography and other matters.

Interfaith Marriages

We have discussed the marriage rite between two Catholics. But what about Catholics who marry Protestants, Jews or Orthodox Christians?

Because of mass communication, mingling of populations, and a softening of religious prejudices, there are more Interfaith marriages today. Notice we have not called them, Mixed Marriages. Why? Even though the latter term is still used, it is dying out. Mixed marriages refer to differences. Interfaith marriages emphasize faith traditions. While there are real differences the couple is encouraged to respect, understand and build a common spiritual relationship.

The bishops of the Second Vatican Council recognized the need to change the Church Law on Mixed Marriages. The recommendations of the Council have been put into effect. They can be summarized:

1) A Catholic must receive what is called a dispensation, that is, a permission to marry. It is easily obtained by the priest who handles the paperwork.

2) The Catholic is asked to promise, "with God's help I intend to continue living my faith . . . and will do all in my power to share that faith with our children by having them baptized and reared as Catholics." The Catholic may make this promise either in writing or orally. The Non-Catholic partner is no longer required to make any formal promises to raise the children in the Catholic faith.

3) It is possible with permission, that an interfaith marriage take place in a Protestant Church, an Orthodox Christian Church, or a synagogue. Under very special circumstances it is possible to

have the ceremony take place in a secular place.

4) There cannot be two religious ceremonies.

5) Several Clergymen (priest, minister or rabbi) can participate in the marriage ceremony. One may accept the couple's marriage vows while the other may say additional prayers, give a blessing and/or give a homily.

6) The Interfaith marriage may be celebrated with or without a Nuptial Mass. Because interfaith communion is not yet accepted by the Catholic Church for doctrinal reasons, a marriage ceremony seems to be preferred.

The interfaith marriages are celebrated in the spirit of the wishes of the Second Vatican Council which said:

> Let the spouses themselves, made to the image of the livng God and enjoying the authentic dignity of persons be joined to one another in equal affection, harmony of mind, and work of mutual sanctification. Thus they will follow Christ who is the principle of life. Thus, too, by the joys and sacrifices of their vocation and through their faithful love, married people will become witnesses of the mystery of that love which the Lord revealed to the world by his dying and his rising up to life again. (*Constitution of the Church in the Modern World*, art. 52).

Unfortunately, we cannot say that all marriages are permanent and successful. This point leads us to our fourth question, what about Divorce and Remarriage in the Catholic Church?

4. *Divorce and Remarriage*

A. Divorce—"Divorce has become an American bad habit, indulgence in which seldom secures either happiness or emotional freedom."[4] Either the writer was a prophet or just followed the trend of the ever increasing high divorce rate. Surely, if in 1948 divorce was considered a bad problem, today it might be called a major dilemma.

In the United States the civil courts have the power to dissolve marriages. A divorce means the complete termination of an existing marriage. The grounds for a civil divorce vary from state to state. Generally, the reasons for divorce are: desertion, habitual drunkenness, adultery, violent temper, extreme cruelty and others.

Unlike the civil courts, the Catholic Church does not recognize the right of the state to dissolve a valid, sacramental marriage. The Church's position stems from five New Testament passages. Before commenting on them, let us look at them.

1. To those now married, however, I give this command (though it is not mine; it is the Lord's; a wife must not separate from her husband. If she does separate, she must either remain single or become reconciled to him again. Similarly, a husband must not divorce his wife. (1 Cor 7:10-11).

2. Then some Pharisees came up and as a test began to ask him whether it was permissible for a husband to divorce his wife. In reply he said, "What command did Moses give you?" They answered, "Moses permitted divorce and the writing of a decree of divorce." But Jesus told them: "He wrote that commandment for you because of your stubbornness. At the beginning of creation God made them male and female; for this reason a man shall leave father and mother and the two shall become as one. They are no longer two but one flesh. Therefore let no man separate what God has joined." Back in the house again, the disciples began to quetion him about this. He told them, "Whoever divorces his wife and marries another commits adultery against her; and the woman who divorces her husband and marries another commits adultery." (Mk 10:2-12).

3. What I say to you is: everyone who divorces his wife—lewd conduct is a separate case—forces her to commit adultery. The man who marries a divorced woman likewise commits adultery." (Mt 5:32).

4. Some Pharisees came up to him and said to him, "May a man divorce his wife for any reason whatsoever?" He replied, "Have you not read that at the beginning the Creator made them male and female and declared for this reason a man shall leave his father and mother and cling to his wife, and the two shall become as one? Thus they are no longer two but one flesh. Therefore, let no man separate what God has joined. They said to Him, "Then why did Moses command divorce and the promulgation of a divorce decree?" "Because of your stubbornness Moses let you divorce your wives," he replied, "but at the beginning it was not that way. I now say to you, whoever divorces his wife—lewd conduct is a separate case—and marries another, commits adultery, and the man who marries a divorced woman commits adultery." (Mt 19: 3-9).

5. Everyone who divorces his wife and marries another commits adultery. The man who marries a woman divorced from her husband likewise commits adultery." (Lk 18:16).

What can be said about these biblical passages? Most biblical scholars say:

1. Matthew, Mark, Luke and John's writings were written between 50-100 A.D.
2. Mark's gospel is the earliest of all the gospels.
3. Paul's writings are generally acknowledged to be written before the gospel writers wrote their accounts.
4. Matthew and Luke had access to the writings of Mark.
5. Paul and Mark's writings make no exceptions for divorce.
6. Matthew and Luke's writings do not allow divorce except for the case of lewd conduct. This exception clause (lewd conduct is a separate case) was not originally Jesus' statement. Probably, Matthew (Luke copied it from Matthew) inserted this exception clause because some members of the early church could not live by the strict command of Jesus.

Some early Christians may have been married to spouses who practiced the pagan code of excessive sexual infidelity. The exception granted in these latter passages parallels the modern Church's granting of annulments because a spouse did not comprehend the fidelity commitment required of a Catholic.

Therefore, the Catholic Church does not allow divorce because of the writings of Paul and Mark which are the earliest records of Jesus' ideas on divorce. A Catholic Marriage is indissoluble because it is the union in Christ of two persons capable of living together as man and wife. This union, however, is not just a union of bodies. It is a union of the totality of the persons.

B. Remarriage—While the Church does not allow divorce, it will grant what is called, an annulment. An annulment means that the marriage was invalid. It may be invalid for a number of reasons. For example, the Church court (Marriage Tribunal) may discover that one party entered marriage with the intention of withholding the right to have children from the other. In such a case, the marriage would be declared invalid and the person would be free to remarry. There are other reasons for annulments. They would be insanity, grave emotional disturbance, intention of not being faithful, lack of conjugal love, psychopathic or sociopathic personality and serious immaturity.

It is very difficult to discuss every possible circumstance which might be considered for an annulment case. The best piece of advice is to see your priest who will help you to the diocesan marriage tribunal which will review your case.

5. Open Marriage

Our final question is what about *Open Marriages?* One of the most popular books on redefining marriage is written by Nena and George O'Neill. It is called *Open Marriage.* The O'Neills say that an *Open Marriage* means a relationship between two people that is open and honest. The relationship is based on the equal freedom and identity of both partners. *Open Marriage* involves a verbal, intellectual and emotional commitment to the right of each to grow as an individual. Their central theme is personal growth. In addition to personal growth, they state these points:

1. Honest, free flowing communication. The way in which your partner walks, stands, smiles, tells us more than words.
2. Open Listening. It requires that you become transparent and let your partner in. You cannot respond properly unless you open yourself completely to what is being said.
3. Flexibility in Roles. From the moment we were born, we were trained for future roles. Little boys are trained to be aggressive and little girls are trained to be passive. These roles must change. If men and women are capable of doing one anothers tasks, they can benefit enormously. By gaining and practicing greater flexibility in roles, both husband and wife can be compassionate as well as resourceful, strong as well as sensitive.
4. Equality is necessary in *Open Marriages.* Equality of responsibility means that each partner has the equal right

to pursue his or her goals.

5. Identity. It means that you should know yourself. It destroys fears and it increases openness.

6. Trust. Without trust, an *Open Marriage* cannot grow. It is being open and honest with one another in your communication with each other.

7. Open companionship. If another person other than your partner adds to your self image, it is permissible to share that experience.

While the O'Neills have given some worthwhile ideas as stated above, yet the overall approach of *Open Marriage* must be rejected. Why? Let us consider these points:

1. *Open Marriage* minimizes the primacy of a permanent commitment. This new life created by marital love is meant to continue as long as the partner lives. Jesus said, "For this reason a man shall leave his father and mother and cling to his wife, and the two shall become as one flesh. Thus they are no longer two but one flesh" (Mt 19:5).

2. It minimizes self giving. A partner is a person to be loved and not a thing to be used for one's selfish purposes. A partner considers the value and dignity of the other person. A partner looks for the welfare of the other so that they may both grow and develop the love they share together.

3. It minimizes exclusive fidelity. For a permanent marriage there has to be complete loyalty. He who loves gives himself completely. He occupies the central part of his partner's life. If there is some infidelity, then, there cannot be a complete giving of self. It is cheating the spouse who deserves his or her complete loyalty.

4. It encourages "instant" happiness. In a Christian marriage, the husband and wife love each other and seek the continuous happiness of one another. This happiness grows and develops through mutual giving and sharing with one another. A happily married couple strives to be sensitive to their own needs as human beings and make constant efforts to meet and overcome them. Open Marriages seek the individual happiness of the individual

rather than the couple's happiness.

5. It emphasizes personal fulfillment as opposed to couple fulfillment. In Christian Marriages, each partner seeks the earthly happiness and the eternal salvation of the other partner. This love creates a relationship of giving and receiving which enables them to participate in the mystery of creation.

In the final analysis, there is no utopia. No marriage is without frustrations, disappointments and disillusionment. A good marriage takes a lot of giving and forgiving. It is open to growth with one another.

The Second Vatican Council put it this way:

> Let the spouses themselves made to the image of the living God and enjoying the authentic dignity of persons be joined to one another in equal affection, harmony of mind, and the work of mutual satisfaction. Thus, too, they will follow Christ who is the principle of life. Thus, too, by the joys and sacrifices of their vocation and through their faithful love, married people will become witnesses of the mystery of that love the Lord revealed to the world by His dying and His rising up to life again. (*Constitution on the Church in the Modern World*, art. 52).

Comment

There is no doubt that the institution of marriage is in trouble. If we are to believe statistics, twenty percent of first marriages will end in divorce. Young people are looking for an "instant happiness" marriage. Some say that traditional marriages are not the answer because they are restrictive. Some say that Open Marriages and Trial Marriages are the solutions for happiness in marriage. Obviously, many are searching for an answer.

It is true that our society is going through a dynamic phase of rapid change. A critical reevaluation of traditional values on every level has shaken the structure of American life to its very foundations. Individual identity has become more important than ever before. Gone are the old roles of "Mother," "Father," "Husband," and "Wife." Today relationships rather than roles are stressed. Despite the problems created, these new insights into the nature of man are a blessing rather than a curse. Marriage is a covenant relationship. Marriage is a personal relationship. Marriage is a love relationship. These relationships involve God, Jesus, the Church, our partner, relatives and friends. Within these relationships the couple develops potentialities. They grow in relationship to one another.

Summary

1. Eighty percent of marriages today are permanent and successful.
2. Every marriage is the union of two unique persons who are loving people, developing, enriching their abilities and who are aware of each other's needs for privacy and independence.
3. Every marriage is a covenant and not a contract.
4. Every marriage is a sacramental sign of Jesus.
5. Every marriage is a community of love.
6. Qualities for a stable, loving relationship are communication, honesty, commitment and permanence.
7. There is a rite for celebrating a marriage during Mass.
8. There is a rite for celebrating a marriage outside of Mass.
9. Interfaith marriages have increased in recent years.
10. Interfaith marriages may be celebrated with or without a nuptial Mass.
11. Divorce is not permitted in the Catholic Church.
12. St. Paul and St. Mark's writings reflect the earliest church writings about Jesus' opposition to divorce.
13. Remarriage in the Catholic Church is permitted if the previous marriage was invalid.
14. Open Marriage minimizes permanent commitment, self giving, exclusive fidelity.

Discussion Questions

1. Give six further reasons why marriages have failed.
2. Give examples of God's covenant with the Jewish people.
3. What are the differences between a contract and a covenant?
4. Discuss the old marriage ritual statement.
5. Discuss St. Paul's first letter to the Corinthians (Chapter 13) which says, Love is patient, and so forth.
6. Explain the terms "mixed Marriages" and "Interfaith Marriages."
7. Discuss the differences between Mark and Matthew's statement on divorce.
8. Cite several cases for Remarriage in the Catholic Church.
9. Discuss the weaknesses of *Open Marriage*.

Footnotes

1. In the Old Testamet times, God (Yahweh) made a covenant (an agreement) with Abraham (father of the Jewish people). He (God) would be their God and they (Jews) would be his people.
2. Landers, Ann. *Love and Sex*, Field Enterprises, Inc., 1976, 11-12.
3. Champlin, Joseph. *Together for Life*, Notre Dame, Indiana: Ave Maria Press, 1975, pp 67-78.
4. Putnan, Nina. "Divorce is No Solution" *Readers Digest*, August 1948, 60.

BIBLIOGRAPHY

Bosler, Raymond. *What they ask about Marriage*, Ave Maria Press, Notre Dame, Indiana, 1975.

Kindregan, Charles P. *A Theology of Marriage*, Benziger, Bruce & Glencoe, Inc., Beverly Hills, California, 1975.

Schreiber, Angela M. ed., *Marriage and Family in a World of Change*, Ave Maria Press, Notre Dame, Indiana, 1975.

Thomas, John L. *Beginning Your Marriage*. (interfaith Edition) Buckley Publications, Chicago, Ill., 1975.

Wrenn, Lawrence G. Ed., *Divorce and Remarriage in the Catholic Church*, Newman Press, New York, 1973.

We have studied the contemporary teaching of the Church on marriage and we have also looked at the problem of divorce and remarriage. One of the great pressures on contemporary Christian marriages is the modern attitude towards sexual conduct. There are many people in the world today who teach a sexual code of ethics which is quite different from the teaching of Jesus or the teaching of the Catholic Church. There are many pressures in today's society urging people to participate in pre-marital sex, homosexuality, bi-sexuality or open marriages. Such voices are not voices within the tradition of Christ, and yet they are very powerful voices. The following Chapter explores their arguments and also the Christian response to these arguments.

Chapter 9

CONTEMPORARY SEXUAL CONDUCT
Pre-Marital Sex, Group Sex, Homosexuality, Birth Control, and Sterilization

---

Introduction

God created the stars in the heaven and the earth below and all things on it. All things created are good and come from the loving hand of the Heavenly Father. The human body—male and female—and human sexuality, that is the joining of a man and woman in physical union, is meant to be a beautiful thing. It is not dirty or immoral. It is man and woman sharing in the creative love of God. The most correct attitude of a Catholic toward human sexuality is one of gratitude to the Heavenly Father for allowing us to share in His creative love. God has so made men and women that this act is one of great pleasure. Most people will say that the greatest pleasure of all is when a new born babe comes into the world as a result of this act of love. The Catholic teaching is that acts of human sexuality belong within a marriage between a man and a woman. The Church has taught in Vatican II that there is a dual purpose in marriage. One is the mutual enrichment of the two spouses and the other, which can never be separate from the first, is the bringing of children into the world. The Church has always taught that acts of human sexuality outside of marriage are morally wrong. Although Catholic moralists today are more lenient, it is important to realize that for many centuries most Catholic moralists held that no sin involving human sexuality was ever a light matter. It was always considered a grave sin. Some may feel that this teaching was very harsh, and that is why it has been somewhat changed in the more recent history of the Church. However, it does indicate the importance that Catholic moralists gave to the issue of human sexuality. The contemporary attitude in the world today is very different from the Church's traditional teaching. We live in an age that extols the value of sexual freedom. There are many reasons for this. Some of the reasons that have been given are: the invention and wide distribution of the birth control pill; the emergence of Women's Liberation; the new philosophy of personalism; the greater interest in self-fulfillment as opposed to self-sacrifice; the examples of media celebrities who often expound a viewpoint of sexual permissiveness; and today's prolonged adolescence in which young people reach physical maturity at a very early age, but are unable to financially raise a family until much later in life. Some conservative Catholics feel that the Church has accommodated itself too much to this era of sexual freedom. Others believe that the traditional teaching of the Church was too strict and made it impossible for anyone to obey the teaching in good conscience. Let us look at two views that are present today about human sexuality. Father Andrew Greeley talks about an exaggerated new freedom which people such as Eugene Fontinell and Norman O. Brown proclaim. He talks about their viewpoint, not to approve of them, but merely to state that many Christians have adopted their secular opinion as their own:

> But if the response of the old Christian sexuality was that you could do practically nothing, the response of the new Christian sexuality is that you can do anything—no holds barred. Premarital, extramarital (or in the slock euphemism of Eugene Fontinell, "co-marital") intercourse, homosexuality, necking and petting, mastur-bation, and everything else short of bestiality (and in some cases I suspect even that is not excluded)—all become legitimate forms of human behavior so long as they are "growth-producing." The polymorphous perversity lauded by Norman O. Brown now becomes the sign of Christian virtue. The birth control and divorce questions have long since been answered, of course, and the battle cry of the moment is "Enjoy! Find a mistress or a lover, take off your clothes, and begin to grow and develop as a human being." This is the new answer to the old question, and I think that I do not

caricature it, although I must add that its advocates would at all
times insist on "responsibility" in forming new and experimental
sexual liaisons. They are not willing to go quite so far as Professor
Brown, who has long since stopped being hung up on responsibility.[1]

In 1977, the Catholic Theological Society of America also
tried to wrestle with the question of sexual conduct in contemporary society. It issued a document[2] on human sexuality in which
theologians tried to explain what freedoms were permitted to
Catholics and what were not. This Document raised a great deal of
controversy in the Church. One such reaction to it was by William
Reel,[3] a columnist for the *Daily News*, who was very much against
the statement. He thought the Document failed to truly deal with
the issue of sexual responsibility. He believed that it was a sellout
to contemporary society and that it permitted many things which a
good Christian should not condone.

The 1977 award for pious poppycock is herewith tendered to the
Catholic Theological Society of America for its just released study of
human sexuality. The study espouses a sappy, sugary
Cosmopolitan woman morality and is certain to cause a sensation in
Catholic circles.

But what is truly scandalous about the study is its utter, total
capitulation to cant and cliche. It is the ultimate testimony to the
empty void of liberal Christianity. Read this numbing nonsense
produced by our leading Catholic theologians and you will
understand why so many churches are empty.

Here is a typical sentence: "Where sexual conduct becomes
personally frustrating and self-destructive, manipulative and
enslaving of others, deceitful and dishonest, inconsistent and
unstable, indiscriminate and promiscuous, irresponsible and non-
life-serving, burdensome and repugnant, ungenerous and un-
Christ-like, it is clear that God's ingenious gift for calling us to
creative and integrative growth has been seriously abused."

To that? Well, then, you are ready to go on to the next infallible
statement, in which these learned theologians (priests no doubt in
smoking jackets, nuns in pantsuits) explain that adultery 'seems to
contradict many of the characteristics of wholesome sexual inter-
relatedness and above all, to compromise the covenant fidelity

presented by Scripture as an ideal."

By the way, if you thought adultery was wrong because the Seventh Commandment says it is, well, that just proves what a stuffy old reactionary you are.

Homosexuality and premarital sex are okay with these trendy theologians. However—traditionalists, take heart!—they seem to draw the line at group sex. "Swinging," they say, is a "thinly veiled form of self-gratification, offensive to true Christian interpersonalism and devoid of the joy that characterizes good sexual relations." So there. Better not swing unless you want to offend true Christian interpersonalism, they caution you.

But enough of mindless drivel.

Mr. Reel says that the Catholic Theologians[4] in question have abandoned their obligation to defend traditional Catholic morality. It is important to realize that the moral questions involved are very delicate. This is because human sexuality deals with the very heart of someone's personality. How individuals deal with sexual love tells you a great deal about those individuals as persons. Their approach to sex tells you whether they are responsible or irresponsible, loyal or disloyal, tender or callous, loving or incapable of love. Sexual morality is not just a question of organs, but of a person's ability to love and to care.

In this chapter we will look at several specific questions involving sexual conduct in the contemporary world. In each case we will define the particular area of sexual conduct; we will note the traditional teaching on the matter and look at some contemporary attitudes toward that teaching.

1. *Pre-marital Sex:* Definition

Pre-marital sex refers to sexual intercourse between a couple before they are married. It usually means that the couple do intend to get married at some future date.

The teaching of the Church is that this is morally wrong and that sexual intercourse should only be done after marriage. There is an attitude in contemporary society that says: since young people

have to wait a much longer time than they did in the past before
they are financially able to get married, since modern methods of
birth control make it possible to prevent having children, and since
it is preferable to have sexual intercourse between two people that
are committed to one another rather than a promiscuous
relationship between two people who do not care for one another,
pre-marital sex in this situation is to be permitted. Let us look at
Fr. Greeley's[5] viewpoint about pre-marital sex. He says it is
important to understand the term "Yahwist." For Fr. Greeley this
means someone who has a personal and loving union with God,
not someone who is simply living by a legal code in order to please
a remote and impersonal God.

> I am frequently asked what I would say to young people who come
> to me asking whether it is "all right" to have pre-marital
> intercourse. Clearly, such a question represents an attempt to get off
> the New Agenda and back on the old. But I suppose it must be
> answered. My response is to say that it depends on who the young
> people are. If they are committed Yahwists who believe in the
> interpretation of Reality offered by the Yahwistic symbol system, I
> would say that we who are followers of Yahweh do not act in any
> way that reflects badly on the permanency, the implacable fidelity,
> and the public nature of Yahweh's commitment to us. Because of
> our religious convictions, we believe that our loving behavior
> should reflect His behavior, and that is fundamental and apart from
> all rigid, juridical moral imperatives; it is why we live our lives the
> way we do. With such committed Yahwists, I would then develop
> the symbolism of Yahweh's fidelity, as I do briefly in the remaining
> part of this chapter and at much greater length in my book, *Sexual
> Intimacy*.

> Unfortunately, most young people who profess to be Christians are
> not in fact committed Yahwists of the sort I have described. They do
> not "buy" to the very depths of their souls the world view contained
> in the Jewish and Christian symbol system. For them, then, a purely
> religious argument will not be enough, and in the face of the
> collapse of the old "sin morality" sexual imperatives, I would have
> to fall back on psychological arguments, which I believe have both
> validity and a moderate amount of persuasiveness. But I would not
> expect to be very successful. I would assume that in all likelihood the
> two young people in question had already made up their minds to
> bed down together—if they hadn't already. In part their question is a
> search for justification—the priest couldn't give them any "good

reasons" for not sleeping together. In part, it is an attempt to bait me, to impress and shock me with how modern and sophisticated they are. I don't know that this represents any important cultural change. In the past when young people were determined to sleep with each other, the moral arguments didn't have much effect, and now psychological arguments won't have much effect either. Only religious arguments will have weight under those circumstances, and then only with those who are already religiously convinced. The problem with the young professed Christian who is not in fact possessed by the Christian symbol system is that when he comes to seek reasons why he shouldn't sleep with his girl friend there is a religious barrier between him and me. He does not believe what I believe in, or at least he does not believe in it the way I believe in it. What we should be talking about is religion, not sex; about God, life and death, and the meaningfulness of human existence, not about pre-marital intercourse. Alas, only rarely does God enter his mind at such a time. I take consolation, however, from my conviction—which I do not think is either naive or fanciful—that he is on God's mind, and that under such circumstances, I am not obliged to "talk him out" of something called "mortal sin." If he comes away from a conversation with me feeling that I respect him as a person while adhering to my own religious integrity even though just now he doesn't "buy" it, then I think I have done all that I can as a priest. To attempt more would be false and dishonest.

2. *Extra-marital Sex:* Definition

Extra-marital sex refers to sexual intercourse outside of marriage by one or two spouses who are married and committed to a different person. Adultery traditionally means that the spouse had sexual intercourse with a person to whom he or she was not married. The modern term "swinging" refers to both partners approving of the extra-marital affairs of the other partner, and sometimes actually planning such liaisons together. The teaching of the Church has always been that such intercourse outside of marriage is morally wrong and it violates the virtue of justice because the partner has a commitment to the spouse with whom he or she has pronounced their marital vows.

3. *Group Sex*

This refers to a group of people that have sexual intercourse among all the members of the group. Such practices are common in some primitive tribal societies. The teaching of the Church has been that such conduct is morally wrong. There are some contemporaries who believe that the institution of marriage is outdated, that it would be easier to have a group of people committed to each other, who would raise each other's children, who would be financially responsible for each other, and who would have total sexual freedom among each other. This approach to communal living or group sexuality has sometimes led to very sick cults, such as the "Manson Family." Other people have not done the immoral and unjust things of the Manson family, but have made an honest attempt to create what they consider a new utopian society.

4. *Homosexuality*

The basic definition of homosexuality is sexual love between two persons of the same sex. Homosexuality can be divided into three categories. 1) Promiscuity which is temporary sexual liaisons between two people who have no emotional commitment to each other, or do it for payment. 2) Homosexual "marriage" refers to two people of the same sex that live in emotional and personal commitment to each other and also have sexual intercourse with one another. 3) Lesbianism is used to define women homosexuals. Traditionally, homosexuality has been considered a violation of the Church's teaching on the sanctity of marriage and human sexuality. Contemporary society feels that at a certain stage in a person's development, if they are homosexuals, they will not be able to change, that this is an emotional and psychological state that cannot be altered, and that such people should be treated with sympathy and understanding. Homosexuals themselves have become far more active in defending themselves and demanding their civil rights and also seeking to function in various job professions. There is even an organization of Catholic homosexuals trying to maintain an ongoing relationship with the Church. This group is called "Dignity." One common complaint of homosexuals with both the Church and the State is that they are frequently treated as criminals even when they make every effort to act as good citizens. There is a need for sympathy and understanding on the part of the larger society as a whole. However, the Church has insisted on its teaching that the homosexual is going against human nature and against the creative plan of God for human sexuality. At the same time it is important for informed Catholics today to understand that many homosexuals are caught in a situation, not necessarily of their own making, which has its roots in a very complex personal history. Such people should be treated with the love and concern that Jesus showed to those who were the outcasts in his society.

5. Bi-sexuality

Bi-sexuality refers to individuals who engage in both heterosexual and homosexual activity. Such people are also frequently promiscuous, that is, they have sexual relationships with many people rather than a permament one-to-one relationship. The traditional teaching of the Church is that bi-sexuality is morally wrong and is a denial of the natural sexuality of man and that it leads to a very callous approach to human relationships. Some segments of society have found bi-sexuality a very popular trend today. At times it has been fashionable for some celebrities to extol it as a form of popular pleasure. However, most studies indicate that there are no true bi-sexuals, that bi-sexuals are either heterosexual or homosexual. So, in some unions, they are actually doing the opposite of their sexual inclination, simply out of curiosity or for personal pleasure, but not because of a sexual orientation toward both sexes.

6. Sterilization

Sterilization is defined as a method which prevents either a man from fathering a child or a woman from conceiving a child. There are several different types of sterilization. There is surgical sterilization which is almost always permanent. For a woman, this would involve either the tying or the cutting of the Fallopian tubes so that the ovum could no longer descend toward the uterus and it would be impossible for her to conceive a child. For the man it is a vasectomy which is the cutting of the vas deferens tubes which bring the sperm into the penis. After this operation, although a man is capable of sexual intercourse, he can no longer ejaculate viable sperm so he can no longer be fertile and fertilize a woman's ovum. Both of these methods are permament though they can be reversed by a second more difficult operation.

The Church has constantly taught that sterilization, which is permanent, is a sin against the human body and the natural functions given to it by God.

7. *Birth Control*

Sometimes birth control is referred to as "temporary sterilization." This means that a person can prevent conception by using artificial means such as hormonal chemicals or certain devices. Artificial means of birth control include, for the woman, the birth control pill which makes it impossible for a woman to conceive, the diaphram, the IUD, or jellies which prevent the sperm from reaching the ovum; and for the man; a condom, which is placed over the penis and prevents the sperm from reaching the ovum. Natural birth control refers to following the fertility cycle of the couple. Normally a woman generates one ovum for a few days within a 28 day cycle and when the couple know, after proper charting, when the woman is fertile, they can abstain from intercourse at that time to prevent conception.

Artificial means of birth control are morally wrong. The natural means of birth control can be used when the couple has a good reason for preventing further pregnancies. Today some Catholic theologians[4] believe that a couple with a good reason for limiting the size of their family can use artificial means.

Comment

The Church has taught that sexual intercourse is a beautiful thing. It has taught that it has a place within marriage and that marriage has a dual purpose; the mutual personal growth of the spouses and the bringing forth of children. The teaching of the Church has been challenged by several contemporary views which stress that human sexuality is a harmless means of pleasure and that varieties of sexual intercourse are permissible and should be encouraged. There has been a weakening of the Church's teaching among some people. Many Catholics are confused about what is permissible and what is not. In its official stance, the Church has not changed any of its teaching, however there are many contemporary Catholics who challenge the Church's teachings. Some of the practices which have been encouraged in recent times include pre-marital sexual intercourse, extra-marital sexual intercourse, group sex or communal living, homosexuality, bi-sexuality and sterilization. In each of these cases the Church's teaching is that it is morally wrong to indulge in these practices. There was a time in society and in the Church when purity and sexual restraint were encouraged by the group. Modern society has seen many powerful groups extol the value of a variety of sexual pleasures. In this case, the social pressure on individuals to act in a way different than the Church teaching is very strong. Because of these strong pressures there are some Catholic moralists who feel that the Church must be sympathetic and understanding to those whose sexual practices are not in line with the Church's teaching. It is important for any student of Catholic morality to understand that for a long period of time it was believed by Catholic moralists that there was no such thing as light matter involved in sexuality, but that any sexual practice outside of marriage was objectively morally wrong and a serious sin.

Summary

1. There are two contemporary attitudes toward sexual freedom in the Catholic Church. A popular misconception of the

modern view is that Catholics are free to indulge in any sexual activity which they find pleasurable as long as they do not hurt the other persons involved. The second view is that traditional sexual responsibility is still valid and holds for all Catholics and that anything less is a denial of objective moral views. This view also holds that people are personally very damaged by living a life of promiscuous or unnatural sexual pleasures.

2. Pre-marital sex is sexual intercourse before marriage between a man and a woman who intend to get married. The traditional teaching is that this is wrong. The contemporary attitude of many people is that it is permissible.

3. Extra-marital sex refers to sexual intercourse between a person who is married with someone else to whom they are not married. Adultery traditionally meant that the sexual union was done without the knowledge of the other partner. "Swinging" today is a modern reference to adultery known and approved by the other partner. The traditional view is that adultery is morally wrong. Some contemporaries view the practice of extra-marital sex, with the knowledge of the other partner, as an "open marriage" and that this is permissible.

4. Group sex refers to a group of people who make a commitment to live together and support each other financially and emotionally. The group normally permits sexual intercourse among all the members of the group. This is very common in primitive tribal societies. Traditionally this has been considered a violation of the marriage vows. Today there are some groups that claim that it is a viable alternative to marriage.

5. Homosexuality refers to sexual union between two people of the same sex. Homosexual "marriages" refer to two people who have an emotional commitment to each other. Promiscuity refers to homosexual partners who are with each other on a temporary basis. Lesbianism refers to female homosexuality. The Church's teaching is that this is morally unacceptable. A contemporary view among some people is that it is impossible for these people to change their makeup and that the Church should be sympathetic to them and to help them live their lives as best they can.

6. Bi-sexuality refers to people who practice both heterosexual and homosexual relationships. The Church's view is that this

pleasure and needs are the most important things to be considered. Such an individual will do anything to maintain himself. In the play "A Man For All Seasons," Richard Rich was a symbol of this type of personality. Rich blew with the wind. He was loyal to whomever was in power. He was willing to sacrifice friends and conscience in order to rise in power. After Rich perjured himself in order that More could be condemned to death, More noticed a badge of office on his chest. He takes up the locket and he looks at it questioningly. One of the characters explains to him, "Sir Richard Rich has been made Chancellor of Wales." and Thomas More turns to Rich and says, "Not for all the world should a man lose his soul, but for *Wales?*"

Women's Liberation

Women's Liberation has grown increasingly popular within the last decade. Women have become conscious that many of their roles have been preconditioned for them by society. Now with the availability of birth control and better education, women are able to plan their families and decide what their career will be. They find that they are no longer dependent on a man in order to survive economically and there is less pressure on them to get married. They can choose to be single and independent. There are obviously many good and Christian values in the Women's Liberation Movement. Unfortunately, the early leaders of women's liberation have been among the exponents of abortion, lesbianism, parenthood without marriage and promiscuity. The Church teaches that women are independent and free persons. It was the first large institution to treat women as persons and not as chattel. The Church applauds the efforts of women to achieve equal rights before the civil law, and to become more involved in the ministry of service in ecclesiastical structures. It also approves of the justice of equal pay for equal work. However, the Church also, to be true to its own traditional teaching, must point out that there are dehumanizing and negative aspects of the women's liberation movement. Marriage is not simply for convenience, but has been instituted by God to enhance both man and woman. Bringing is immoral. There are some contemporaries that claim that it is permissible to have a variety of sexual experiences. Most psychologists feel that bi-sexuality is actually an artificiality, that a person is either a heterosexual or a homosexual and is simply practicing the other variety out of curiosity.

7. Sterilization refers to methods which are used to prevent a man from emitting viable sperm to fertilize an ovum or to prevent a woman from conceiving a child. There are permanent and temporary forms of sterilization. Surgical procedures are permanent; chemicals or instruments can be used to achieve temporary sterilization. The teaching of the Church is that all forms of sterilization are immoral. Contemporary Catholic moralists do teach that natural family planning can be used by a married couple who have good reasons for preventing further pregnancies. Some would permit permanent sterilization if there was a sufficient medical reason for it.

8. Birth control refers to the withdrawal method and all forms of artificial means of preventing conception. These artificial devices are intrauterine devices, anovulant pills, condom, diaphragm, douche, and tubal ligation. The Church condemns the withdrawal and artificial methods. The Church's teaching is that birth control in these cases is immoral. Some theologians differ with the Church's teaching. Their position reflects a transition from a Greek view of nature (the Church's position) to an evolutionary view of nature. They claim that man is changing nature not just reading nature.

Questions for Discussion

1. What is the Catholic teaching on sexual morality?
2. Why have teachings of the Church on purity been challenged in modern society?
3. Give reasons pro and con for pre-marital sexual intercourse. What is the Church's teaching on this subject?
4. Give reasons pro and con for extra-marital sexuality. What is the Church's position on this practice?
5. Give reasons pro and con for group sex. What is the Church's teaching on this practice?

6. Most adult homosexuals claim that it is totally impossible for them to seriously consider heterosexual relationships and therefore they cannot marry and they cannot follow the Church's teaching on human sexuality. They feel that if they are Catholic they should be allowed to attend the sacraments and practice in the worship of the Church. The Catholic teaching says that they are in mortal sin and cannot be admitted to active participation in the Church life. Discuss.

7. What is bi-sexuality? What do most psychologists think about it? What is the Church's teaching on this practice?

8. Discuss the various forms of sterilization and birth control and explain if any are permitted by the Church.

Footnotes

1. Excerpted from the New Agenda by Andrew Greeley. Copyright 1973 by Andrew Greeley. Reprinted by permission of Doubleday and Company, Inc.
2. The Catholic Theological Society of America did not issue the document. It originally commissioned the document to be written, but the individuals working on it became an entity unto themselves. They resisted suggestions and changes offered by the leadership of the Catholic Theological Society of America and the organization did not endorse the document as it was finally issued.
3. William Reel, "On Non-Life serving sex and such," *Daily News*, June 8, 1977. 46. Copyright 1977 (1978) New York News Inc. Reprinted by permission.
4. A Theologian's opinion is not the official teaching of the Church.
5. Andrew Greeley, *op cit.* note 5, 142-143.

BIBLIOGRAPHY

Boyle, John P. *Sterilization Controversy*, Ramsey, New Jersey: Paulist Press, 1977.

Duvall, Evelyn M. *Why Wait Till Marriage?* New York: Association Press, 1965.

Greeley, Andrew. *Sexual Intimacy*, Somers, Conn., Seabury, 1975.

Greeley, Andrew. *The New Agenda*, Garden City, New York: Image Books: Doubleday, 1975.

Kennedy, Eugene C. *The New Sexuality: Myths, Fables and Hang-Ups*, Garden City, New York: Doubleday, 1973.

Mugavero, Francis J. "Sexuality-God's Gift," *Catholic Update*, Cincinnati, Ohio: St. Anthony Messenger Press, July 1976.

Oraison, Marc. *Homosexual Question*, New York: Harper and Row, 1977.

Sarno, Ronald A. *Achieving Sexual Maturity*, Ramsey, New Jersey: Paulist Press, 1969.

We have explored the modern teaching on sexual morality and seen that there are many opinions and values that are different and contrary to the teachings of Jesus and His Church. However, a truly Catholic morality calls us not only to responsible sexual behavior but to authentic human behavior in all phases of life. We are called upon to be good stewards of our lives that have been given to us by our loving, creative Father.

This chapter will deal with the life and death issues of abortion and euthanasia. We will deal with the moral, medical and legal problems that surround these realities.

Chapter 10

THE ISSUES OF LIFE AND DEATH:
ABORTION AND EUTHANASIA

"Only a life lived for others is a life worthwhile"
                                          Albert Einstein

"Life is good when it is magical and musical, a perfect timing and
consent and when we do not anatomise it"
                                          Ralph Waldo Emerson

"I am the way, the truth and the life"
                                          Jesus Christ

The beauty and value of life is obvious. However, in our own
century men like Hitler and Stalin have abused and destroyed
millions of lives. In our own land, at the prsent time, many favor
the destruction of life by abortion and euthanasia. Why? Perhaps it
is because of the shifting attitudes of physicians, lawyers, feminists
and theologians. Maybe it is because of the growing sexual
permissiveness of our society, or because of the attitude in our
society that anything weak or non-productive has no value.

The first part of this chapter will focus on the abortion issue
and the second part will examine the euthanasia issue. What about
the abortion situation? It is not a Catholic issue alone, but a human
issue that affects everyone. It concerns Protestants, Jews, Moslems.
However, Catholics have been leading the fight against abortion.
Others have rallied behind the pro-life position of the Roman
Catholic Church.

For clarity, we have divided the abortion issue under several
headings: The Dilemma Crisis and Controversy of Abortion;

Abortion and Medicine; Abortion and the Law; Abortion and the Church, and Abortion and Morality.

PART I: THE ABORTION ISSUE

1. *The Dilemma Crisis and Controversy of Abortion*

Abortion has become a dilemma because there are diametrically opposing views by groups who have presented strong arguments. Whether and to what extent abortion should be permitted or encouraged or severely repressed has divided philosophers, legislators, doctors and theologians since the beginning of Western Civilization. Abortion and infanticide were practiced by the Greco-Roman World. Christianity condemned both practices. Throughout the ages, this condemnation was accepted by most people until the beginning of the 20th century.

Today, infanticide (an act of killing an infant) is condemned but abortion is not. What caused the change in attitude towards abortion? Briefly, the first important departure came from Russia in 1920. The post-revolutionary government authorized abortions at the request of the mother. By the mid 1960's American public opinion mounted in favor of legalizing abortions. Then, on January 22, 1973, the Supreme Court of the United States declared a woman had a legal right to dispose of the fetus for any reason during the first six months of pregnancy and at any other time if the physician certified that it was necessary to preserve her life and health.

Needless to say that the abortion issue has become more controversial and critical. Human lives are at stake. To promote thinking on this life and death issue we will examine four points: terminology; time, definitions and methods.

a. *Terminology*

When a woman conceives (the male sperm fertilizes the woman's ovum) scientists[1] refer to it as a zygote, after two weeks as an embryo, from the third month as a fetus. An *embryo* in humans is the stage of development between the 2nd and 8th weeks inclusive. A *fetus* is the more common term to designate a recognizable human form from the 3rd month to birth. A *person* is a human being who has developed from the first moment of conception to birth. The latter term will be discussed in the Abortion-Morality section. When used of an unborn child, it is a highly controversial term among the pro and anti-abortionist groups. Of the three terms mentioned, fetus is the most common and acceptable one used.

b. *Time*

When can a fetus exist independently? The fetus is normally viable 28 weeks after conception. At that point it can live independent of the mother's womb. With expert care it may be viable 20 to 24 weeks after conception. Therefore, if a fetus leaves the womb before the minimum of 20-28 weeks then it is a natural abortion. Natural abortion is the medical term for miscarriage. After that time, but before the full nine months, it is a premature birth. Expulsion of a dead fetus later in pregnancy is called stillbirth (spontaneous abortion).

c. *Definitions*

Then what is an abortion? An abortion may be defined as the termination of a pregnancy before independent viability of the fetus has been attained. The weakness of this definition is the absence of the word, "intentional" or "unintentional." Obviously, some pregnancies may not come to full term (9 months). For example a woman suffers a miscarriage (sometimes called a "natural abortion," (spontaneous abortion) during the early stages of her pregnancy and the fetus is expelled from the womb before it is viable. In this case, she did not intend the action and could not be held responsible for the consequences. Strictly speaking, it would not be an abortion. To be an abortion, the *intention* must be present. And so, a proper definition of abortion is that it is an *artificially* induced termination of a pregnancy prior to its natural termination in the course of events, and that this termination is effected with the express purpose of bringing about the death of the fetus which is aborted and that this intention is actually realized. Notice the elements of this definition: a) deliberate action; b) before the normal nine months; c) intended death of the fetus; d) actual death of the fetus. All four elements must be present for the fulfillment of this definition.

d. *Methods*

Medically, there are four general procedures used in abortion. First, there is the "D and C" (dilation and currettage) method which was most popular until recently. It is usually performed under general anesthesia and consists in opening the lining of the uterus with the curette or a scraping instrument. The fetus is removed from the uterine wall by scraping. Second, a new method is the vacuum aspiration. The cervix is dilated and a metal tube attached to a small vacuum pump is inserted and it sucks out the fetus. A third method is saline injection. It is usually performed after 16 weeks or more. A long needle is injected through the woman's abdomen to extract the amniotic fluid. This fluid is replaced with a toxic salt solution which burns the outer layers of the fetus. The fetus inhales and swallows the salt solution and goes into a coma and dies within an hour or two. Labor begins 24 to 28 hours later and the fetus is expelled.

Fourth, there are methods which are very dangerous and crude. There are three types: a) instrumentation—instruments such as coat hangers, knitting needles, telephone wires, etc. are inserted into the uterus of the woman; b) foreign objects—the opening of the cervix is packed with gauze or other materials which causes the cervix to dilate and the fetus is expelled; c) drugs—a variety of drugs such as ergot compounds are taken orally which kills and expels the fetus.

2. *Abortion and Medicine*

We have examined the brief history, terms, time and methods of abortion. Let us focus on the medical aspect of abortion. Medically speaking what happens with these aborted fetuses? They are either disposed of or used for research purposes—alive or dead.

What about doctor's opinions? They generaly agree that human life is present in the embryo (fetus) from the first moment of conception. Letters and articles in medical journals reveal that there is a new abortion-trauma in our country, not where one expects it, in the psyche of the pregnant woman, but in the psyche of the doctor who performs the abortions. In the *New England Journal of Medicine,* Dr. Bernard N. Nathanson, an advocate and pro-abortionist for many years, wrote an article saying that he was greatly disturbed that he had performed 60,000 abortions. Dr. Julius Fogel, a Freudian psychiatrist-obstetrician said:

> I think every woman whatever her age, her background, or sexuality, has a trauma at destroying a pregnancy. A level of humanness is touched. This is part of her own life. She destroys a pregnancy, she is destroying herself. . . One is dealing with the life force. It is totally beside the point whether or not you think a life is there. You cannot deny that something is being created and that this creation is physically happening.[2]

Yet there are doctors like Carol Nadelson who believe that an abortion is not as traumatic as giving up a child for adoption. Garrett Hardin, Professor of Human Ecology at the University of California at Santa Barbara says, "If you are pregnant, poor, unmarried, and frightened at the thought of having a child, you'll be better off having your pregnancy terminated."[3]

Most psychiatrists say that there is not sufficient medical data to state that women who have an abortion will not have psychological damage. Second, a woman's cultural, personal, social and religious background have an effect on her mental welfare. Third, each woman is distinct and unique. Therefore, it is dangerous to give overall solutions to a problem. Fourth, a state of mental stability is greatly preferred to a state of mental instability. And so phrases such as "highly unlikely" are not good enough.

Even if it can be *proven* that there will be no emotional problems for a given woman seeking an abortion, it is still an immoral action.

3. *Abortion and the Law*

Let us examine the legal aspect of the abortion issue. Supreme Court Justice Harry Blackmun said to the Senators during his confirmation hearings, "The Supreme Court is the terrible end of the line of litigation. There is no further place to go. The decision had better be right."

On January 22, 1973, the United States Supreme Court ruled by a 7 to 2 majority that states cannot pass laws prohibiting abortion. The court laid down three rules: 1. During the first three months of pregnancy the state must leave the decision whether to have an abortion and when and how to carry it out, to the woman and her doctor; 2. During the second three months the state may not forbid abortion but may regulate the procedure; 3. The state may prohibit abortion after six months except when necessary to preserve the life and health of the mother.

Several implications emerge from the Supreme Court decision: 1. During the first three months the right to privacy belongs to the woman and the doctor; 2. There is the right of the state to protect the woman's life during the second three months; 3. During the last three months, the state may preempt the life of the fetus for the woman's mental and physical health; 4. The fetus has no constitutional rights and protection until it is born and may be destroyed for several reasons; 5. The court has decided that the life and health of the mother prevails at all stages of pregnancy.

The Supreme Court decision is being challenged and fought primarily by Catholic Christians who deny the government's right to destroy the fetus' human life. Why? Because human life whether it is unborn or born is sacred to God who is the author of all life.

4. *Abortion and the Church*

The third aspect of the abortion issue concerns the Church.

What is the Church's position? For clarity, let us consider three areas: 1. the Judeo-Christian Bible; 2. the Christian tradition of the past; 3. the Church's position today.

While the Bible does not state the moment when human life begins in the woman's womb, it does mention the value of life. It also gives ideals and guides on how to preserve life. For example, what does the Old Testament say? Let us read:

> God created man in his image; in the divine image he created him; male and female he created them.
>
> Genesis 1:27.

> There shall be no temple harlot among the Israelite women, nor a temple prostitute among the Israelite men.
>
> Deuteronomy 23:18.

> Behold sons are a gift from the Lord; the fruit of the womb is a reward.
>
> Psalm 127:3.

These Old Testament writings reflect the love relationship between God (Yahweh) and his people (Hebrews). They exemplify the dignity of man and the sacredness of life.

Like the Old Testament, the New Testament also speaks of the value of life. Jesus showed many signs of compassion and love for people. For example:

> He (Jesus) then addressed the paralyzed man: "I say to you, get up. Take your mat with you and return to your house."
>
> Luke 5:24.

> Blest are they who show mercy; mercy shall be theirs.
>
> Matthew 5:7.

> Let the children come to me and do not hinder them. It is to just such as these that the kingdom of God belongs.
>
> Mark 10:14.

Second, the Roman Catholic Church's opposition is rooted in tradition. The *Book of Didache* (80 A.D.) states that the Christians will not procure an abortion nor destroy a new born child. The *Epistle of Barnabas* (138 A.D.) forbids abortion. St. Jerome's (d. 420 A.D.) and St. Augustine's (d. 430 A.D.) writings say that abortion was a grave sin. During the Middle Ages, men like Albert the Great and Thomas Aquinas wrote about the sacredness of human reproduction. Pope Pius IX (1864) excommunicated anyone involved in an abortion.

Third, what does the Church say today? The Code of Canon Law (1918) issued an excommunication for an abortion. Pope John XXIII's *Mater et Magistra* (1962) said that human life is sacred from its very beginning of conception. Pope Paul VI's *Humanae Vitae* (1968) condemns abortion. The Vatican Declaration on Abortion on November 18, 1974 reaffirms the Church's stand against abortion. It is clear that the present day Church continues its opposition to abortion.

5. *Abortion and Morality*

This final section on abortion considers the moral view. During the past years, the Roman Catholic Church in the United States has taken a strong stand in opposing the liberalization of abortion laws. While Roman Catholics have been the main force in the pro-life movement, other religious groups have also been active in opposing abortion. Protestant theologians like Albert Outler, professor of theology at Southern Methodist University; Paul Ramsey, professor of religion at Princeton University; George Huntston Williams, professor of Divinity at Harvard University, oppose abortion. Samuel Fox is neither a Catholic nor a Protestant. He is a Rabbi who is president of the Massachusetts Council of Rabbis, and a professor in the Religious Studies Department of Merrimack College in North Andover, Massachusetts. He leads the voice of those in the Jewish community who are also against abortion. Yet, there are many people who are in favor of abortion. Why? Some say that it is because of the sexual permissiveness of our times. Others think that the moral arguments against abortion are not clearly understood. It is a combination of the two ideas. What are the arguments against abortion? Let us recall what we mean by morality. It means the goodness or badness (right or wrong) of a particular action. Man is responsible for his actions whether they affect himself or others. He is responsible to himself, parents, friends strangers because of his social nature. He does not exist alone but in relation to others. Therefore his actions cannot be completely free and independent as if he lived alone on this earth. He must be a morally good person, otherwise he destroys the health and well being of society. That is why the abortion issue is so important. The consequences are crucial to everyone concerned.

What then are the arguments proposed by the anti-abortionists? First, there is the argument that the value of human life is grounded in the value God has placed on it. Every human life, whether born or unborn, is unique, distinct, and sacred to God, who is the author of all life. No human being has the right to put a value on another human being or potential human being. All human life is equal before God. Unfortunately, we live in a society that places a price tag on things and people. Who is to say that a fetus is less valuable than a newly born child? Certainly man does not have this right.

Second there is the helplessness argument. This idea says that the more helpless a person is, the more right one has to care and assistance from others. Normally, a person will feel obliged to help a less fortunate human being. For example, people will automatically help a blind person cross the street. Therefore, one should want to help a fetus who is completely dependent on the nourishment of the mother's body. Is it morally right to destroy a helpless unborn fetus for convenience and comfort?

Third, religiously minded people believe that a soul is infused into every fetus by God. When it happens has not been solved by theologians. Their opinions range from the first moment of conception to the end of the third month of pregnancy. Since it is impossible to prove the latter, it is reasonable to take the safer course, namely the first moment of conception. The fetus has, therefore, a spiritual-corporal nature. No human power has the right to destroy it for any reason. There is a sacredness about the human life of the fetus.

Fourth, the human form argument has gained more support

these days. Basically, it says that the genetic DNA code can only evolve into a human being and that the evolving fetus looks like a human being from the earliest state of its development. For example, the fetal development follows these steps:

1. 4 weeks—the head, rudimentary eyes, ears, brain, digestive tract, heart are present;
2. 6 weeks—the internal organs are present;
3. 8 weeks—brain waves, all essential organs are formed;
4. 10 weeks—the fetus is capable of spontaneous movement;
5. 12 weeks—the brain structure is complete.

Obviously, there is human life in potentiality or in actuality from the moment of conception when the completely unique genetic package (DNA code) is present.

The fifth argument is the most controversial among the pro and anti-abortion groups. The antiabortionists say that a fetus is a person who has rights. Dr. Eike-Henner Kluge, professor of philosophy at the University of Victoria presents a strong case for fetal personhood. His definition of a person is, "A person is an entity that is a rational being; that is to say, it is an entity that has the present capabilities of symbolic awareness in the manner characteristic of rational beings."[4] His definition is a genetic one rather than a physical or a biological orientated one. Personhood stems from the fetus' genetic structure. It follows that personhood brings rights. Therefore, the fetus has rights which must be protected since it is helpless at this point of its development. For example, the state will protect the rights of the mentally retarded and the insane. Why not the unborn fetus?

Comment

The abortion issue is far from over. Legislators, doctors, moralists will continue to discuss the pro and con of abortion arguments.

Our position should be with those who fight for life against death and for existence against extinction. The fight for life is not a

Catholic issue; it is not a Protestant issue; it is not a Jewish issue. It is a human issue. All human life, born and unborn, is sacred because God is the source of all human life. Human life, unlike animal and vegetable life, is unique and distinct. And so, it must be developed, cherished and protected.

The pro-lifers, as those who battle abortion call themselves, correctly say that any decision for abortion must take into account these points:

1. a fetus is an evolving human life;
2. even though a fetus does not have full status and rights, it is not just an organ of the woman's body;
3. the state must protect the rights of all its members, that is the healthy, the deformed, the insane and the fetus who is the most helpless of all.

In conclusion, let us remember that the weakest of those who possess human life are the unborn. They are subjected to the decisions of those who would destroy them for convenience and selfishness. The Church has vowed to defend the human dignity and human rights of man from the earliest moment of his conception.

Summary

1. Abortion and Infanticide were practiced by the Greco-Roman world.
2. Early Christians condemned abortion and infanticide.
3. While terms such as embryo, fetus and person are used to describe the unborn, fetus is the most common term.
4. A fetus is viable 28 weeks after conception, however, with special care, it may be viable 20-24 weeks after conception.
5. An abortion is an artificially induced termination of a pregnancy prior to its natural termination in the course of events and this termination is effected with the express purpose of bringing about the death of the entity.
6. There are four general methods of abortion: dilation and currettage; vacuum aspiration; saline injection and use of

intruments, foreign bodies, or drugs.

7. Most psychiatrists think that women who have an abortion will have some psychological damage.

8. On January 22, 1973, the United States Supreme Court stated that states may not pass laws prohibiting abortion.

9. The Bible extols the value of life.

10. The Old and New Testaments give ideals and guides on preserving life.

11. Throughout the centuries, Catholic tradition has condemned abortion.

12. Catholic, Protestant and Jewish voices speak against abortion.

13. The antiabortionists' position is grounded in these points: 1. value of human life; 2. the fetus' helplessness; 3. the soul of the fetus; 4. the human form of the fetus; 5. the fetus' rights.

PART II—THE DILEMMA OF EUTHANASIA

The second part of this chapter focuses on the Euthanasia Issue. Internists, surgeons, nurses, psychiatrists, lawyers, patients and clergymen are intimately involved in this problem. The physician's dilemma in this modern age of medical technology has caused moments of guilt and anxiety. The patient worries about the heavy financial burden on his family. The lawyer is concerned about his client's legal rights. The clergyman cries out against the evils of euthanasia.

For clarity, let us consider the legal, medical and moral aspects of euthanasia. First of all, what is it?

Definition of Euthanasia

Euthanasia is not a new word, but its meaning has changed over the years. The word is from the Greek *Eu*, meaning good and *Thantatos*, death. So euthanasia means "a good death." During the Hitler regime (1933-1945) in Germany, it became associated with genocide or legalized mass murder. He exterminated the mentally ill, the crippled and the retarded. Because these people served no useful purpose to society, they were eliminated. Some called it "mercy killing." Eventually, this meaning was applied to cases of the incurably ill, the comatose, the sedated and the "human vegetables." Today, this is the more common term used when speaking about euthanasia.

Obviously there is some confusion about what euthanasia means. For our purpose, euthanasia means the deliberate though painless killing of a person for the sake of that person rather than that of anyone else.

Euthanasia can be either direct or indirect. It is direct when a person actually kills another by direct means. For example, a doctor administers a drug that will painlessly kill a patient. It is indirect when extraordinary medical procedures that could prolong the patient's life are stopped in order to allow a patient to die. For example, a respirator must be used to keep a comatose patient alive, even though there is no hope that the patient will ever recover.

First, let us examine the legal questions of euthanasia. From the criminal point of view, direct euthanasia can result in a charge of murder. But the real problem is the indirect euthanasia case, that is, when a doctor or someone else pulls the life-support machine to allow the patient to die.

Since the Supreme Court has legalized abortions, there has been mounting pressure by physicians, legislators and clergymen to have a "death with dignity" law in every state of the union. At the present time, no state has passed a law legalizing euthanasia. However, there are many states which have a "death with dignity" bill in their state legislatures. Men like Dr. Sackett, the Florida doctor-legislator, have proposed this type of bill in the Florida state legislature.

Ever since the Euthanasia Society of America was founded in 1938, there has been increased concern about the "right to die." The Euthanasia Society of America became known as the Euthanasia Educational Council in 1967 to undertake a program of public and professional education. Presently, there are a half million members. Because of their voices, the states of Oregon and

Pennsylvania are discussing a Death Definition type bill. In the states of Hawaii and Montana, a Direct Euthanasia type bill is being considered. States such as Iowa, Wisconsin, Virginia, Massachusetts, Illinois, Rhode Island, Maryland, Florida, Idaho and Delaware are examining a Living Will type bill. The Living Will document says, "If the time comes when I can no longer take part in decisions for my own future, let this statement stand as an expression of my wishes, while I am still of sound mind. If the situation should arise in which there is no reasonable expectation of my recovery from physical or mental disability, I request that I be allowed to die and not be kept alive by artificial means or heroic measures. I do not fear death itself as much as the indignities of deterioration, dependence and hopeless pain. I therefore ask that medication be mercifully administered to me to alleviate suffering even though this may hasten the moment of death." It must be signed before two witnesses and renewed every five years. Advocates of the document say that it relieves the physician and relatives of any guilt feelings or the legal charge of negligent homicide. Opponents claim that the Living Will restricts rather than broadens a patient's right. The latter opinion is also the Roman Catholic Church's position. Thus far, there have been two million requests for this document. However, it is not legally binding. There are legislators who predict a legal status for the Living Will by 1983.

However, there is a Catholic version of the Living Will which reads: "I believe in the Resurrection of the body and if I ever reach a physical condition in which I am unable to communicate with my family or relatives, I release both physicians and family from using any extraordinary means to preserve my life." Obviously, this version does not allow for the administering of any drug which hastens the time of death. This Catholic Living Will allows the patient to refuse any extraordinary means of preserving life.

Euthanasia is not only a controversial and a popular topic among legislators but also among physicians. What do doctors think? Some are clearly in favor of it, others are just as strongly opposed. The rest will not talk about it but quietly do what they think they should do. Here are a few typical physicians' comments:

1. Dr. Colin Harrison, Royal College of Physicians says, "We are our brother's keeper, and it is only love, ultimately, that can sustain the keeping. In obvious, if unconscious, recognition of that fact, we divide ourselves among various avocations that, in the main provide the necessities of life, prevent its tragedies and preserve its amenities. . . . Existence remains the central theme of man's endeavor, and upon it depends all else. By corollary, death is the enemy to whom will go victory in the end. Death is not just another way of being a more comfortable absence of something. It is the absence of everything, utter disaster. It is the enemy forever waiting without the gates.

The economy of human existence, then, is supported by various avocations, each of which is aimed at some particular threat to our life and the enjoyment thereof. Each has its own proper contribution, each its own proper limitations. The fireman saves from fire, the physician from disease and more remotely, the farmer from hunger, the construction worker from exposure, the sanitary contractor from contagion and so on. None is the lifesaver. If the average length of life from birth is a criterion, this system effectively postpones the enemy's victory, and the greatest threat to its continued success is the possibility that some kindly, well-intentioned, good-hearted humanitarian will open the gates and invite friend death amongst us."[5]

2. Dr. Bernard Towers, professor of pediatrics and anatomy at the University of California—Los Angeles School of Medicine says, "I think society has to recognize that we have a responsibility to that fellow member of our community, and if the parents are unable to discharge the responsibility, then society must do it for them.

I think they're acting unprofessionally from a medical point of view because all they're doing is extending the dying process; I would hope their application to the courts in such a case would not be successful."[6]

3. Dr. William May, an ethicist and co-chairman of a program on death and dying at the Hasting Center for Society, Ethics and the Life Sciences says, "We act and reflect as if the patient does not have a moral life but is the object of the things that we do in our morality. The virtues and courage of patients may be as important to death with dignity as any environment we can offer."[7]

4. Dr. Samuel Klagsburn, psychiatrist at Columbia University College of Physicians and Surgeons says, "I think patients should be

expected, as all the rest of us are, to handle suffering, but without having to go out of the way to participate in prolonged suffering.

Death for which a family is prepared is better for everyone than an unexpected death, but that should be no excuse for prolonging dying. Families I have treated where dying has been agonizing have been hurt in long-term-ways—wives can't remarry, husbands escape into alcoholism, children act out and literally ruin their lives. Therefore, I find myself respecting a patient's wish to take his or her family into consideration and, quite literally, for the sake of the family, for the greater good of someone else, entertain the possibility of ending life."[8]

Clearly then, physicians are divided on the euthanasia issue. What is alarming is the slow but steady support for some form of a legal-medical euthanasia bill. Because of advanced medical technology, physicians can prolong their patients' lives almost indefinitely. What bothers some physicians is the quality of life. The "Death with Dignity" syndrome means a fast, clean and painless death. Other physicians believe life has meaning to the last breath. Physicians are faced with the following questions: Should they prolong the patients who are incurable and in severe pain? Should they not preserve life with all the art and skill of their profession? Are they maintaining good track records by keeping patients technically "alive" as long as possible for their own personal pride? Must they not be primarily concerned with health and disease rather than death?

Modern medicine, then, must find the balance between the two extremes of allowing patients to die because they are incurable and preserving them with long, expensive and painful medical procedures.

We have examined the legal and medical viewpoint on euthanasia. What is the Catholic moralist's position? To the Christian, human life is a God-given gift. The Christian believes there is a dignity to suffering and death. The Christian's suffering is tied in with Christ's suffering, death and resurrection. The Christian's death is the beginning of a new life. Naturally, the Christian is concerned about the dignity of man. However, the Christian's view of suffering and death is quite different from the humanist's view. The humanist looks at the corporal side of man while the Christian looks at the corporal-spiritual composition of man.

It is clear, then, that Catholic moralists reject "direct euthanasia" as a solution to the problem. There are five basic reasons:

First, there is the command of God that we take no human life. The fifth commandment expressly says, "Thou shalt not kill. It does not allow any exceptions.

Second, there is the moral code. While I am free, I am not morally free to cut off my life for any reason or use it any way I wish. My life is my own but it also belongs to others.

Third, there is the merit reason. Each person must have the opportunity to gain and develop the virtues of patience, perseverance, humility, love, compassion and understanding. If a person is deprived of these moments, how can he mature? Challenges make man rise to his fullest potentiality.

Fourth, there is the ordinary and extraordinary medical-moral argument, this is sometimes known as indirect euthanasia. When the term "indirect euthanasia" is used for deciding to stop employing extraordinary means to preserve life, it is permitted by Church teaching. We are under no obligation to use extraordinary means of preserving life. The Church has always maintained this position. The problem is to determine what extraordinary means are. For example, machines, surgical procedures, treatments and drugs which would be expensive and offer little hope of success would not have to be used to preserve life. A person is bound to the ordinary means of life according to his circumstances, place, time and culture.

Fifth, there is the "hospice approach" moral argument. The hospice approach emphasizes the value of patient care when cure is not possible. This includes:

1. comforting and caring for the sick and dying;
2. looking at the whole person seeking to alleviate the spiritual, psychological, social and physical pain;
3. extensive research on pain-killing drugs;
4. improving the patient's environment whether it be at home or in the hospital;

5. encouraging the commitment of nurses, physicians, relatives of the sick and dying.

A final note to the moral viewpoint on euthanasia is the approach of the moral theologian, Richard McCormick, S.J. He suggests that the meaning of human life is found primarily in human relationships. He says:

> Life is a value to be preserved only insofar as it contains some potentiality for human relationships. When in human judgment, this potentiality is totally absent or would be, because of the condition of the individual, totally subordinate to the mere effort for survival, that life can be said to have achieved its potential.[9]

The Jesuit Theologian is saying that as long as a person is capable of human relationships or actually having human relationships he/she is a person and has all the rights of human relationships. When they no longer have the capacity for human relationships, then extraordinary means no longer have to be used to preserve their life.[10]

On the other hand, Paul Ramsey, Professor of Religion at Princeton University, a Protestant ethician believes Christians cannot deny extraordinary means to preserve life, since God, not man is the author and preserver of life. He says:

> When have Christians—or medical ethics in the Judeo-Christian tradition—heretofore reasoned that when a human being has achieved his potential, this can be taken as a sign that God is calling his servant home? that his duty to preserve life ceases? (I deny) . . . that our duty to preserve life ceases when to the seeing eye (one's own or another's) it appears that that life's earthly potential has been achieved.[11]

Comment

The whole problem of euthanasia has raised many perplexing questions. Who is to decide that a patient's life should not be prolonged unnecessarily? Will "mercy killing" open the door to the large scale killing of the retarded, handicapped and the terminally ill person? What about man's commitment to preserving life rather than destroying it?

The answers to these questions and others are not simple. They will have to take into account a number of factors, namely, the real possibility of misuse; the element of possible recovery; the uniqueness of each person, and the sacredness of life. Finally, in light of Jesus' teachings, there is no life meaningless or useless. Just as suffering and death were part of Jesus' life so are they for the Christian's life. We must be very careful in not slipping into simple answers.

Summary

1. Euthanasia is a confusing term. From its Greek roots, it means "a good death." More recently, it means "mercy killing."
2. Practically speaking, euthanasia means the deliberate though painless killing of a person for the sake of that person rather than that of anyone else.
3. Direct euthanasia means that a person actually kills another by direct means. Indirect euthanasia means that extraordinary means are stopped in order to allow the patient to die. Direct euthanasia is forbidden by the Church. Indirect euthanasia is not.
4. The Euthanasia Educational Council (1967) formerly the Euthanasia Society of America (1938) gives programs of public and professional education.
5. There are 14 State Legislatures discussing a Death Definition bill, a Direct Euthanasia bill or a Living Will bill. Those documents which encourage direct euthanasia are morally unacceptable to Catholics.
6. The Living Will document must be signed by two witnesses and renewed every five years. It is not legally binding.
7. The Roman Catholic Church opposes the Living Will document because it restricts rather than broadens a patient's rights.

8. Some legislators and physicians are opposed to euthanasia.
9. Christians must use ordinary not extraordinary means to preserve life.
10. There is a slow but steady support for some form of a legal-medical euthanasia bill.
11. The two extreme positions of the euthanasia issue are not the answers to the problem.
12. Christians believe there is a dignity to their suffering and death which is linked to Jesus' suffering, death and resurrection.
13. Catholic Moralists reject direct euthanasia for five reasons: 1) the fifth commandment of God; 2) the moral code does not allow one to do just as he wishes with his own life; 3) merit may be gained through the virtues of patience, humility, etc.; 4) ordinary not extraordinary means of preserving life are demanded; 5) the hospice approach for the sick and dying may be an alternative to euthanasia.
14. A Catholic Living Will is permissible.

Questions for Discussion

1. How would you describe human life, human person and actual life?
2. Should a mother be the one to make the final decision on whether to have an abortion?
3. Would you consider abortion murder? Explain.
4. Does a fetus have rights?
5. When in your opinion does human life begin?
6. Give examples of direct and indirect euthanasia.
7. Do you think a doctor should preserve the terminally ill patient?
8. What consequences can result from a legal Living Will document?
9. Do you think Protestants have a different view of euthanasia?
10. Is "mercy killing" moral or immoral? Give reasons for your answer.

Footnotes

1. Clarence W. Taber, Taber, *Taber's Cyclopedia Medical Dictionary*, Philadelphia: F.A. Davis Co., 1970, p. E-16: F-14.
2. Paul Marx, *The Death Peddlers—War on the Unborn*, Collegeville: St. John's University Press, 1971, 28.
3. Garret Hardin, "Abortion vs. the Right to Life: The Evil of Mandatory Motherhood," *Psychology Today*, 8, 1974, 42.
4. Eike-Henner W. Kluge, *The Practice of Death*, New Haven and London: Yale University Press, 1975, 91.
5. Colin P. Harrison, "Medicine Terminal Illness and the Law: A Physician's View," *The Medical-Moral Newsletter*, Vol. 14, No. 9, Nov. 1977, 33.
6. Bernard Towers, "When Death Threatens the Young: A Look at Some Perplexing Issues," *Euthanasia News*, Vol. 3, No. 4, Fall 1977, 3.
7. William F. May, "Issues of Natural Death, Mercy Killing: Two Views," *Euthanasia News*, Vol. 3, No. 4, Fall 1977, 1.
8. Samuel C. Klagsburn, "Issues of Natural Death, Mercy Killing: Two Views," *Euthanasia News*, Vol. 3, No. 4, Fall 1977, 2.
9. This is a theological opinion and not the teaching of the Church.
10. Richard A. McCormick, S.J. "To Save or Let Die: The Dilemma of Modern Medicine," *AMERICA*, July 13, 1974, pp. 6-10.
11. Paul Ramsey, *Ethics at the Edge of Life: Medical and Legal Intersections*, New Haven: Yale University Press, 1978, 175.

BIBLIOGRAPHY

Allen, William F. *Sexuality Summary*, Canfield, Ohio: Alba House Communications, 1977.

Ernst, Siegfried. trans. Sr. M. Mathe, *Man the Greatest of Miracles*, Collegeville, Minn.: The Liturgical Press, 1976.

Jersild, Paul: Johnson, Dale, eds. *Moral Issues and Christian Response*. New York: Holt, Rinehart and Winston, Inc., 1971.

Kluge, Eike-Henner W. *The Practice of Death*, New Haven and London: Yale University Press, 1975.

Marx, Paul. *Death Without Dignity: Killing for Mercy*, Collegeville, Minn.: The Liturgical Press, 1975.

Rachels, James, ed. *Moral Problems*, New York: Harper and Row Publishers, 1971.

Ramsey, Paul. *Ethics at the Edge of Life: Medical and Legal Intersections*, New Haven: Yale University Press, 1978.

Stevens, Edward, S.J. *Making Moral Decisions*, New York Paulist
Press, Dues Books, 1969.

Thiroux, Jacques. *Ethics Theory and Practice*, California:
Glencoe Press, 1977.

Van der Poel, Cornelius. *The Search for Human Values*, New
York: Paulist Press, 1971.

We have just seen the modern world's teaching on abortion and euthanasia and also how very frequently these viewpoints are diametrically opposed to the teachings of Jesus and the Catholic Church. One of the reasons why these opposing viewpoints are so powerful in today's world is the contemporary mass media. The mass media has become a means for people to influence others to do wrong and to belittle those people who are trying to do good. This is an unfortunate situation, but it indicates how powerful an institution the mass media has become in contemporary life. The following chapter is an exploration of the mass media, how, in many ways, it has replaced the traditional role of Scripture in society, and the need that Christians have to very carefully evaluate the powerful influence that it has on their lives.

Chapter 11

THE MASS MEDIA AS THE MODERN BIBLE: THE CONTEMPORARY CONFIDENCE GAME

1. *The Role of the Bible in the Ancient, Medieval and Renaissance World*

For a large part of human history, the Bible has played the role of being the source of Truth and a guide for how people were to live their moral life. The Church quoted from the Scriptures, and the people read or heard the Word of God. From it they learned the examples of Judaeo-Christian virtues. In many ways the Bible formed the unconscious assumptions of people's lives. They looked to it for values and examples of moral behavior. Today, in many ways, the Bible has been replaced by mass media. Modern man looks to mass media for examples of moral behavior and he looks for it also to give him the "truths" by which he lives his life. These "truths" unfortunately are not also the eternal Truths revealed in the Scriptures.

2. *The Confidence Game*

The popular movie "The Sting" depicted several examples of a confidence game. Confidence games basically depend on having the victim earn the confidence of a cheater, who will eventually take a great deal of money away from the victim. There are usually three characters involved in a confidence game. The first is the con artist, who is the one responsible for gaining the confidence of the victim. The second is the false victim, who is actually a partner of the con artist; and the third is the victim, who is sometimes called "the mark." A confidence game can be played for very small stakes or for very large stakes. It can be done with three people or it can be done by several institutions. Several years ago, a major insurance company was indicted for pretending to have large sums of money which it did not have. In a confidence game played among three people, the usual procedure is for the con artist to flash a large amount of money. This awakens the interest and greed of the victim. The money has supposedly been found or is from a number of receipts from an illegal gambling operation. The victim is led to believe that the funds can be shared if none of them notify the legal authorities about the money. It is obvious that only people who are very greedy and are willing to disobey the law, can fall into a confidence game trap. The victim is allowed to handle the large sum of money which he has seen. This gives him the feeling that he is being trusted. Usually, he is handling a very small amount of money on top which has either false money or paper clippings underneath which looks like money in large stacks. A third person joins the group. This third person is let in on the secret and is then allowed to handle the "money" as well. Together the three decide how best they can share the money. The "confidence" man requests that the others demonstrate some faith in him by putting up some money of their own. The false victim puts up a large sum of "money" too.

Then the victim is usually led to draw out a large amount of real money from a savings account to put up as his part of the trust money. Several things are done in the course of the game which has the false victim make mistakes and cause problems. The con artist instructs the real victim that the other man is too stupid to follow directions and that they should cheat him by switching bags. Eventually the game reaches a point where the victim is told to hold the "money" while the con artist tries to find the false victim who has disappeared. He finds himself alone with a large amount of "money." When he opens the money, he actually finds that the sum he is holding is only newspaper clippings. The real con artists, who were working together all along, have disappeared with his real money. Most victims of a con are unwilling to inform the police because they do not wish to look foolish and all along they were doing something which was supposedly illegal. They are left "holding the bag" of fake money.

3. *The Modern Media*

One of the best explanations that can be given of contemporary media is that it is a form of a confidence game played between the producers and the consumers. The advertiser takes on the role of the confidence artist. The false victim is someone in a commercial presentation not using the product or service being advertised, and "the mark" (victim) is the consumer who is watching the show. The flash of "money" which the confidence game uses is translated into scenes of happy people who are using the product, and precisely because they are using the product, are happy. The greed that is awakened in the consumer is by exciting a need for something which the person really does not need. The "confidence" is to have the consumer and the seller earn trust and confidence in one another. This can be achieved by having the announcer or one of the sellers instruct the consumer on a personal level of the value of the product and how inexpensive it really is. "The Sting" is a term used in the confidence game when the victim is left holding the bag with no money. "The Sting" in the mass media confidence game is the consumer purchasing a product with his own money that he really does not need.

4. *The Modern Media Numbness*

The Greeks told the story of "Narcissus." Narcissus was a beautiful youth who looked at his reflection in a pool. As he leaned over to look at his handsome face more closely he fell into the pool and drowned. Narcissus is a symbol of selfishness drawn to such an extent that one destroys oneself. Marshall McLuhan, who is a contemporary educator and who has analyzed the effect of modern media on mankind, says that we are all living at the present time the Narcissus myth. Each of the media that we have invented is an extension of one of our powers or functions. McLuhan teaches that once these powers are extended, the central nervous system compensates by numbing the senses. The overall effect, then, of the barrage of mass media in the contemporary world is to create a population which is too benumbed and hypnotized by the constant extension of so many of their senses to think clearly:

> With the arrival of electric technology, man extended, or set outside himself, a live model of the central nervous system itself. To the degree that this is so, it is a development that suggests a desperate and suicidal autoamputation, as if the central nervous system could no longer depend on the physical organs to be protective buffers against the slings and arrows of outrageous mechanism. It could well be that the successive mechanizations of the various physical organs since the invention of printing have made too violent and superstimulated a social experience for the central nervous system to endure.
>
> In relation to that only too plausible cause of such development, we can return to the Narcissus theme. For if Narcissus is numbed by his self-amputated image, there is a very good reason for the numbness. There is a close parallel of response between the patterns of physical and psychic trauma or shock. A person suddenly deprived of loved ones and a person who drops a few feet unexpectedly will both register shock. Both the loss of family and a physical fall are extreme instances of amputations of the self. Shock induces a generalized numbness or an increased threshold to all types of perception. The victim seems immune to pain or sense.[1]

McLuhan is saying that modern media extend mankind's powers of perception to such an extent that they put a strain on his ability to assimilate all of the input. To compensate, man dulls or benumbs his sense of awareness. He becomes hypnotized. He is like Narcissus, so in love with his own image that he drowns in his own sense of awareness.

5. *A Comparison Between the Modern World of Mass Media and the Medieval World of the Holy Scripture*

Medieval World View	Modern World View
a. Man saw himself with an eternal soul, having spiritual powers.	a. Man sees himself as a consumer who can buy products.

b. The soul was engaged in an eternal battle between the forces of good and evil. Both God and Satan were struggling to posses the eternal soul.

b. Companies compete to create certain needs in the consumer to take their share of his market dollar.

c. Man has obligation to work in cooperation with God's grace to earn his eternal salvation.

c. Man must work to earn money so that he will have the purchasing power to buy goods and services.

d. The reward which is offered to man is Grace in this life and eternal union with God in heaven. Once in heaven all his needs and desires are fulfilled.

d. The reward of modern life is to possess products or services which supposedly will bring happiness. Since they cannot do this (Augustine says, "Our hearts are restless until they rest in thee"—God) man is left frustrated and he must begin all over again. Therefore, his desires are for more and more expensive products or services. Contemporary media, rather than satisfy this need, really stimulate it for more and more purchasing.

e. In order to earn heaven, man was urged to live a moral life and to follow the ethical code of the Christian tradition.

e. The new morality is an unconscious one in which man is encouraged to be selfish and greedy and to be concerned more about his own needs than those of others.

its activities from the direction of the Mass Media. Modern Mass Media urge us to be *consumers, indifferent to moral questions.* This militates against the Christian vocation to be a free moral individual who is responsible for one's actions.

6. *The Church's Teaching on Modern Media*

During Vatican Council II, the Fathers debated the effect of mass media on the contemporary world. They issued a document on their findings called "The Decree on the Instruments of Social Communication." The   Fathers noted the requirement that everyone involved in mass media have a moral conscience when using these instruments:

> A special need exists for everybody concerned to develop an upright conscience on the use of these instruments, particularly with respect to certain issues which are rather sharply debated in our times.
>   (Decree on Social Communications #5)

One of the difficult problems of the modern world is that many institutional governments use the mass media only to inform their citizens of the news which they want them to hear. This distorted information is called "propaganda." Also, every individual person, no matter what he has done, has a right to his reputation. He cannot be falsely accused of something which cannot be proven. Therefore, there is a "right to know" and "a right to privacy." Both these rights are fundamental human rights. Since they are sometimes in conflict, there is a need for discernment and courage when deciding which "right" is to take precedence. However, the Fathers clearly teach that it is wrong for any institutional government to use the mass media to give false information to people.

> The first question pertains to what is called "information," i.e., the search for news and the publication of it. Indeed because of the advances of contemporary society and the closer bonds linking its members together, the information process has clearly grown very useful and generally necessary. For an open and timely revelation of events and affairs provides individuals with a grasp of them which is

sustained and considerably detailed. As a result, men can actively contribute to the common good and all can more easily foster the development of the whole civic community.

Hence there exists within human society a right to information about affairs which affect men individually or collectively, and according to the circumstances of each. The proper exercise of this right demands that the matter communicated always be true, and as complete as charity and justice allow. The manner of communication should furthermore be honorable and appropriate; this means that in the gathering and publication of news the norms of morality and the legitimate rights and dignity of a man must be held sacred. For knowledge is sometimes unprofitable, "but charity edifies" (1 Cor 8:1).

                          (Decree on Social Communication #5)

The Fathers note that there is a special obligation for those involved in producing the programs of mass media, to be men and women of virtue. They are especially concerned because of the temptation to follow commerical reasons for deciding on programming.

They are specifically concerned that people with little or no moral conscience will be those producing programs with a wide range of audiences:

Special duties bind those readers, viewers, or listeners who personally and freely choose to receive what these media have to communicate. For good choosing dictates that ample favor be shown to whatever fosters virtue, knowledge, or art. People should reject whatever could become a cause or an occasion of spiritual harm to themselves, whatever could endanger others through bad example, and whatever would impede good selections and promote bad ones. The last effect generally results when financial support is given to men who exploit these media for commercial reasons.

If those who use these media are to honor the moral law, they must not neglect to inform themselves in good time of the judgments they should respect according to the requirements of a good conscience. By taking pains to guide and settle their conscience with appropriate help, they will more readily thwart less honorable influences and amply support those which are worthy.

                          (Decree on Social Communication #9)

The Fathers of the Council believed strongly that there should be a professional association of people involved in producing the programs in mass media. These professional associations should have a code of ethics in the same way that groups of doctors and lawyers do. It is especially important that the producers remember that they have an obligation to the public good rather than to commercial interests. It is also important for such producers to realize that a large number of their audience are young children who do not have the ability to discern carefully messages given to them. Furthermore, it is important to present religious messages in a respectful manner:

> The chief moral duties respecting the proper use of instruments of social communication fall on newsmen, writers, actors, designers, producers, exhibitors, distributors, operators, and sellers, critics, and whoever else may have a part of any kind in making and transmitting products of communication. For it is quite clear what heavy responsibilities are given to all such persons in the present state of affairs. By molding and activating the human race they can lead it upward or to ruin.
>
> On these persons, then, will lie the task of regulating the commercial, political, and artistic aspects of these media in ways which will never conflict with the common good. They will merit praise if they aim to secure this goal more certainly by joining professional groups which expect from their members reverence for moral laws in the affairs and regulations of their art. If necessary, these associations should require adherence to a code of ethical conduct.
>
> In any case, these responsible persons should never forget that much of their audience consists of young people who have need for literature and shows that can give them decent amusement and inspiration. They should also see to it that worthy and competent men are put in charge of religious features and that such matters are handled with proper reverence.
>
> (Decree on Social Comunication #11)

The Fathers of the Council also had to deal with the issue of government monitoring and freedom of the press. The purpose of government monitoring is seen as insuring that the public good is upheld. The purpose of "freedom of the press" is to see that the communications people have the right to report news which may be embarrassing to the government. On the one hand, it is important that government prevent the communications media from abusing their public trust. On the other hand, it is vital that governments do not suppress the right of communications media to report truthfully on news and events. Sometimes the term "censorship" is misunderstood. It is part of the American tradition to encourage freedom of expression. However, it is an abuse of that freedom—never intended by the Founders of the Constitution—to permit any source of information to use its access to the public to glorify violence, sexual aberration, or misconduct:

> In this whole field, civil authority is bound by special duties in terms of the common good, to which these instruments are subordinate. This authority is duty bound to defend and protect a true and just availability of information; the progress of modern society utterly depends on this, especially as regards freedom of the press. This authority should foster religion, culture, and fine arts; it should protect consumers in the free exercise of their lawful rights. It should also assist the undertaking of projects which could not otherwise be initiated, despite their extreme usefulness, especially for young people.
>
> Finally public authority, which properly concerns itself with the health of its citizens, has the duty of seeing to it in a just and vigilant manner that serious danger to public morals and social progress do not result from a perverted use of these instruments. This goal should be achieved by enactment of laws and their energetic enforcement. The freedom of individuals and groups is not at all infringed upon by such watchful care, especially if those have taken on themselves the responsibility of using these media have failed to observe sensible cautions.
>
> (Decree on Social Communication #12)

Vatican II made a distinct effort to foster the development of mass media and, at the same time, to challenge it to present us with ideals and programs worthy of the art. It is an unfortunate commentary that in our contemporary world, the ideals presented by the Fathers of Vatican II were, for the most part, ignored. Too often, only commercial interests and the audience size has a determining factor in what programs will or will not be on the air.

7. *Two Views of the Effect of Television on Modern Society*

a) "Fred Silverman: The Vast Wasteland of Mindless Entertainment"

At nine o'clock on any winter Sunday night, there are television sets turned on in more than two thirds of the homes in the United States. Ninety percent of the people watching those sets are watching one of the three national networks. Next winter, it is quite possible that all those people, most of America, will be watching shows originally selected by one man.

His name of course, is Fred Silverman. On June 8, 1978 when his contract as president of the entertainment division of the American Broadcasting Company expires, he will take over as president of the entire National Broadcasting Company. Hundreds of years ago, it would have been almost as if one man controlled most of the printing presses most of the time.

. . . My sense tells me that, in its infancy, television has created at least three confusingly intertwined social and cultural conditions of real concern. First: Boorstin's "democratized experience" and the likelihood that Americans to some extent depend on television to determine acceptable behavior, how other Americans behave in diverse situations. Second: the effects of the passivity of television watching on child development and education, and on the energy and creativity of the total society. And finally: the chance that television conditions thinking and frustrates large numbers of viewers who find out the hard way that real-life problems cannot be resolved, laughingly, in thirty or sixty minutes.

. . . The point is that dealing with real life always requires time and nuance. If confusions develop in real lives conditioned by six hours a day of watching unreal living, then television is potentially more dangerous than its most hostile critics imagine.

Television, of course, *is* dangerous. But that does not mean it is necessarily bad. The sea is dangerous, so is weather. I prefer weather as an analogy; I think television is much more than a communications medium. It is our new environment and, like the weather, it often determines whether we stay home or not. But there are many analogies: theologian Harvey Cox thinks it fills the classic functions of a religion; Peter B. Wood of Duke University likens it to dreams, "a vivid projection of our collective subconscious." The fact is that we do not yet know what we're talking about—it is still too new, too pervasive.

What we do know is that it is here to stay and that it is controlled by a very small number of men, of whom Fred Silverman happens to be the most successful at the moment. The same Fred Silverman who was invited to a dinner party a couple of years ago along with Tom Wicker and Russell Baker of the *New York Times* and whose host had to explain who Wicker and Baker were. *That* Fred Silverman, who will now be in charge of NBC news.[3]

It is possible that by the time students read this passage Mr. Silverman will no longer be in charge of NBC programming. It is a world of volatile appointments and if ratings go down, even one or two percentage points, whole staffs are changed. Mr. Reeves, who is a political reporter for *Esquire* magazine, is concerned about having a man in charge of news who does not even know who the major political reporters are for one of the largest newspapers in the country. His point is that such a man does not fit the qualifications that are needed for objective reporting. It can also be said that Mr. Silverman has neglected to provide that inspiration and uplift which the Fathers of Vatican II urged upon the mass media community. It may be unfair to single out one person as a symbol of such blatant misuse of the mass media, however, Mr. Silverman has handpicked most of the programs in prime time television. He is certainly one of the most powerful men in the contemporary world. And if those programs fail to uplift and inspire, a good part of the responsibility for this failure can be laid at his doorstep.

b) Pseudo-science—The modern world can no longer think about what is true or what is false.

Another problem with our commercialized entertainment is that we have been sold a bill of goods by advertisers. Even though we think we have the sophistication to distinguish true from false claims, for the most part we can be easily fooled. Claims reach our subconscious and there they work with insidious force. Dr. James S. Trefil, a physicist at the University of Virginia, is quite concerned that we have lost the ability to think. He says that we have become so mesmerized by commercial claims and pseudo-scientific entertainment that we can no longer distinguish between what is proven fact and what is fancy. It is obvious that our society is in great danger if those of us who are responsible for making moral and free decisions cannot even decide for ourselves what is true or false.

> As a physicist, I realize that today's flights of fancy may well be tomorrow's scientific orthodoxy. But it worries me that a public ill equipped to distinguish between razzle-dazzle and sound speculation is swallowing whole many pseudo-scientific notions that strike me as silly at best and as a species of intellectual junk food at worst.

> My concern here is not, incidentally, altogether cool and disinterested; I still brood about the time several years ago when my son, then ten, was watching a TV "documentary" about ancient civilizations that had been visited by extra-terrestrials. When I ventured something mildly skeptical about the show, my son turned on me and cried, "But didn't you *see*? They *proved* it!"

> Repeated experiences like this with my children, my students and my contemporaries have left me convinced that the world could use a kind of do-it-yourself guide to getting one's bearings in the Alice-in-Wonderland realm of unorthodox scientific claims.[4]

Dr. Trefil's point is not that it is true or false that ancient astronauts once visited the earth. His point is that the TV show which was purported to give clear evidence of it was a mish-mash of half-truths and deductions which came from false premises. As a scientist, he is concerned that certain opinions are being given the stamp of scientific proof which they really do not deserve. Whether or not it is true that ancient astronauts once visited the earth, his point was that such a claim had not been substantiated by a television program. His son, fascinated by the images on the screen and the firm authoritarian voice of the announcer immediately accepted what he was seeing as a scientific proof. What he was seeing was good entertainment. He was not seeing a scientific thesis that began with a hypothesis, was proven by sundry examples, and then showed a conclusion which had been validated. All of these are necessary for scientific truths to be established. His son's willingness to believe something that really had not been proven to him is a very serious error, both in education and in entertainment. Who of us would like to take a medicine whose inventors *thought* it might be useful for our health? One of the unfortunate effects of the quasi-scientific claims of most products advertised on television is that we have accepted them as the new "gospel," just as medieval man did not challenge the "truths" that were told him in Scripture even when, in some cases, they were false. (As Galileo proved when he pointed out that the ancients did not comprehend that the sun did not literally run across the top of the sky.) Even in these mistaken notions there was an underlying truth, the truth that God was the Creator of all things visible and invisible, and that man was the center of His love and concern. The claims that are made in the modern media for certain products have no basis in fact whatsoever. One of the most distressing things to consumer advocates is to find out that products that have been conclusively proven to be useless are still purchased by Americans, because they are still advertised in the media.

8. *Modern Media: Present Misuse and Future Potential*

1. *Medium*	2.Present Usage	3. Future Potential
a) *Television*	Device for increasing marketing. Propaganda for government lies.	Present great art and literature for ordinary people. Create inspiration to work for economic and social improvements. Provide education on health, childcare and nutrition for a wide range of people who cannot receive this information at the present time.
b) *Radio*	Music and news reporting aimed at special and limited markets such as ethnic groups.	Can be used for language training, foreign language education, and can be highly influential in instructing in moral values.

c) Cinema	Frequently used to depict the attractiveness of violence and sexual aberrations.	Can be used to portray the virtue of courage and the value of high ideals.
d) Telephone	Frequently used for gossip or for communicating business news.	Can be ideal for instructing the deaf, bringing comfort to the lonely and displaced.
e) Telegraph	Linked with large metropolitan newspapers and frequently communicates information about wars, violence, terrorism and poverty.	Can be a device for fostering international cooperation and for creating civic pride among local groups.
f) Phonograph	Means of distributing popular and romantic songs. Frequently used to foster self-interest and narcissism.	Can be used to bring great music and plays to those who cannot afford to attend concerts or the theater.

It may be argued that all of the things under future potential are things that the media are doing right now, but that the public is not accepting them or using them in this way. However, it is also true that an audience of any kind can be gradually educated to high art and also that high art can be very entertaining and very fulfilling. The argument always is that due to the present commercial interests in media, such programming does not "sell" and the public will not "buy it" from the producer. As Richard Reeves pointed out in his article on Fred Silverman, the choices that have been given the American public are so limited that many of the things that can be the future potentiality of the networks and of other forms of media are not given a chance to work. The Catholic Church teaches that church members have an obligation to struggle to improve the quality of programming in all forms of entertainment. This does not mean a mindless censorship "crusade" to take everything that one does not personally like off the air, but it does mean a continual commitment to improve the quality of media productions.

Comment

Contemporary mass media have created a very passive generation in our modern world. The Christian vocation is to be a free and independent person capable of making moral decisions. In our modern society we accept what is told to us, not what we have discovered for ourselves. By not thinking for ourselves, we do not have the moral strength of character to make value judgments. People who cannot make value judgments, cannot decide on the proper moral choices which are before them. They are willing to let others make the decisions. We live in a society which has substituted the mass media for the Bible. Just as a victim can be fooled by a confidence man, we are continually being fooled by the media into becoming a mindless consumer. The Church teaches that we must take an active and decisive role in our lives. In order to do this, we must be conscious of the effect that media are having on our subconscious. We must also be willing in some ways to be a "counter-culture" to the over-riding values which our society accepts without question.

Summary

The Bible was the unconscious source of values for ancient, medieval and Renaissance man. Today, this role has been assumed by the mass media. Contemporary mass media work a confidence game on today's consumer. Marshall McLuhan teaches that media are extensions of the powers and functions of the human body. Like the ancient myth of "Narcissus," once man creates an extension of himself he must dull his awareness and sense of that extension. The overall effect of a great number of media is to numb or mesmerize modern man to the point where he is unconscious of what is happening to him. The medieval world view had man as an eternal soul struggling between good and evil to achieve his eternal salvation. The modern world view has man as a consumer, who is constantly urged to purchase more and more products that he does not need. Vatican II has taught that the news which is disseminated through the modern media should be true and not false propaganda. It urges that producers of mass media programming be men and women of virtue; that they have a standard professional code of ethical conduct, and that the government has the dual responsibility to monitor media and also to foster freedom of the press.

Mr. Fred Silverman is an example of a television executive who selects programs solely on the basis of their appeal to mass audiences and has done little to improve the quality of television programming.

Dr. James S. Trefil believes that most contemporary Americans confuse pseudoscience with genuine science. He believes that modern man, mesmerized by commerical programming, is unable to distinguish between what can be proven as true and what is simply asserted as true. Most modern media today are being misused and could be adapted and changed and used to greatly enhace contemporary culture. We have unconsciously become part of a system which makes us unaware of the influences of advertising and commercials on our attitudes. Our ability to think and decide for ourselves and to choose what we really want is compromised. Rather than being free and independent persons, we have become blind consumers who work to earn money to buy more and more products which satisfy us less and less. The Church teaches that Catholics have a moral obligation to work to improve the quality of the products of mass media in which they find themselves immersed. It is also important to realize that our contemporary society is living in an environment which is not conducive to Christian values. It is important that, in some ways, a Catholic is able to act as "a counter culture" to the over-commercialized society in which he finds himself. This does not mean that a practicing Catholic must divorce himself from the world of which he is a part, in the way that ancient hermits did when they ran off from the society of their day. It does mean, however, that to truly live a life of virtue and moral rectitude it is necessary to, in some way, "separate" oneself from the false values of the world.

Work Project on Violence in Television

In 1974 a TV movie was made about a young woman in a reform school. In the course of the movie, which was about peer rejection, she was sexually assaulted by a gang of girls. It was the most powerful scene in the movie and left an indelible impression on the audience. What did such a scene do to the youth who watched it? Unlike movies and theater shows, TV enters the home of families, and what it chooses to show or not to show leaves a lasting impression on people. More and more educators are becoming concerned about the effect of TV on young minds. The following are three reactions to the show, which became a legal issue in 1978, when the Supreme Court ruled that a mother could sue a local television station and a national network on the claim that her daughter suffered an attack modeled on the movie scene. Is it legitimate to claim that the act of violence would never have happened in real life if the attackers did not have a model for such sick behavior? Kay Gardella is a television critic for the *Daily News*, Dr. Edward H. Ross is a pediatric clinical psychologist who treats abnormal children, and David Gerber is the producer of the television series *Police Story*. Read over the excerpts and then answer the following questions:
1. Does television foster violence in minds disposed to aberrant behavior?
2. Does television encourage sexual abnormality?
3. If "sex and violence" guarantees high ratings, what does that say about us as a people?
4. If ratings are the only norm by which productions are judged what does that say about our producers and artists?
5. Is there a Christian reaction to this problem? Does the Church offer any guidelines on the issues of sex and violence in the media?

The Wages of Violence by Kay Gardella[5]

Television is now beginning to reap what it has been sowing for years—violence.

The last thing the industry expected was to find itself on the defensive in a courtroom. After all, television had its First Amendment rights just like everybody else. How could anyone possibly blame a medium for the increase in violent crimes in our nation?

A lawyer in Miami, a flamboyant fellow named Ellis Rubin, attempted to do just that in the murder trial of 15 year old Ronny Zamora last October, and failed. He made TV a co-defendant when he claimed the boy's addiction to crime shows on TV drove him to murder an elderly woman. The boy was convicted. TV was exonerated. But television now is in another serious legal tangle. Earlier this week, the U.S. Supreme Court cleared the way for a California girl to press an 11 million damage suit against NBC and KRON-TV in San Francisco on the basis that a rape scene in the NBC film "Born Innocent" inspired a similar attack on her.

The scene from the 1974 TV movie, starring Linda Blair as a teenager in a reform school who is raped by other girls with the handle of a plumber's plunger, has been branded into the psyche of every viewer who saw it. Critics still debate the merit of showing that scene on the tube. Those connected with the production defend it. The network permitted it.

Now the mother of a 9 year old child contends that the sexual assault upon her daughter with a bottle by four older girls on a California beach was inspired by the movie. So she is fighting for her daughter's rights in court. And once more TV will be called to account for its lack of social responsibility.

Violent Shows are Destroying Our Kids
by Edward N. Ross[6]

In letting the San Francisco television sex case go to trial, the Supreme Court last week may have provided those of us fighting against television violence with the major break we've been waiting for.

Implicit in the justices' refusal to hear the network's appeal is a decision to recognize that TV violence may indeed play a major role in the rise of juvenile crime in this country.

There is no doubt of the relationship in my mind. Study after study through the years—including a report by the National Commission on the Causes and Prevention of Vionece and the Surgeon General's Report—have linked violent crime to television viewing.

. . . The ones that get into the press are usually the most shocking: the doctor who recently reported treating a kid who set a house on fire after watching a program about arson; two children who jumped from a roof playing "Batman," the boy who got hold of a loaded handgun after watching a police program, etc.

What you don't read in the press are about the thousands of children who are psychologically tormented and riddled with various kinds of anxieties as a result of violence or sex. I have lost count of the cases I have personally seen over the years—it must be in the hundreds.

. . . The problem we face is that children—even "normal" children—are easily receptive to outside stimulation like television. They frequently aren't capable of separating good from bad, reality from fantasy, and all children show a need to act out fantasy. (The boys who jumped off the roof playing Batman.) Of course, the healthier the child, the less the likelihood for violence, but all children emulate what they see to some extent.

Powerful Lobbies are Destroying Our Rights
by David Gerber[7]

. . . But there is something I fear even more than what would happen to television, which, after all, could survive nicely on its quiz and gimmick shows. I am quite concerned about what would happen to America. For if the plaintiff should win here in California it would sound the death knell for free speech in every medium of expression.

. . . What the social scientists call violence has already been watered down. Now they are working on the elimination of the "heavy sex" that they say pervades the television medium.

The fact is that children today see more in the streets than they ever see on their television screens. New York City runs six high schools for pregnant teenagers. It appears the kids might be better off spending more time in front of the television than in their other pursuits.

Not long ago, we depicted a rape on a "Police Story" program. It showed no nudity and no simulation. What the viewer saw was the look of anguish on the victim's face. Thirty million people watched it. Six letters of protest came in.

When the network asked me to make some changes for the reruns, I protested. The program wound up being praised by Women Against Rape for demonstrating the plight of rape victims.

There has never been any real, hard evidence that violence and sex on TV cause crimes. Still those in the industry who believe as I do don't advocate violence and sex—just reality. The past has shown us that violence for violence's sake doesn't work. People get bored with it, and the shows go off.

Yes there is a lot of junk on television—and parents should be concerned about the programs their children watch. But the way of showing that concern is by being strict about TV and choosing what programs can be viewed by youngsters.

Every television comes equipped with an on-off button. By not using it more often, parents are abdicating their responsibility.

Healthy children come from good parenting not by advocating censorship.

Discussion Questions

1. Explain the role of the Bible in the medieval world and contrast it with the role of mass media in the modern world.
2. Explain how a confidence game works.
3. In what ways are modern mass media a new version of the old confidence game?
4. What does Marshall McLuhan have to say about the Narcissus myth and its relationship to mass media?
5. Contrast the world view of the medieval Christian with that of the modern Christian.
6. Define media, the effects of mass media and consumerism.

7. Give the salient points of the teachings of the Fathers of Vatican II on mass media.

8. Compare and contrast Richard Reeves and Dr. James Trefil's views on the effect of television on modern society.

9. Cite some present examples of how modern media are used and contrast them with future potentialities.

Footnotes

1. Marshall McLuhan, *Understanding Media: The Extensions of Man*, New York: The New American Library, 1964, 53.
2. Jim Wallis, *Agenda for Biblical People*, New York: Harper & Row, 1976, 84.
3. Richard Reeves, "The Dangers of Television in the Silverman Era: Something is forcing the quality of television down—and Fred Silverman is the instrument," *Esquire Magazine*, April 25, 1978, 45, 54, 57. First published in *Esquire Magazine*.
4. James S. Trefil, "A Consumer's Guide to Pseudo-science" *Saturday Review*, April 29, 1978, 16.
5. Kay Gardella, "Wages and Violence," *Daily News*, April 28, 1978, 71. Copyright 1977 (1978) New York News Inc. Reprinted by permission.
6. Edward N. Ross, "Violent Shows Are Destroying Our Kids," *Daily News*, April 30, 1978, 57. Reprinted with permission of the New York *Daily News*.
7. David Gerber, "Powerful Lobbies Are Destroying Our Rights," *Daily News*, April 30, 1978, 57.

BIBLIOGRAPHY

Abbott, Walter, ed. "Decree on Social Communications" *Documents of Vatican II*, New York: America, 1966.

McLuhan, Marshall. *Understanding Media: The Extensions of Man*, New York: The New American Library, 1964.

Muggeridge, Malcolm. *Christ and the Media*, Grand Rapids, Michigan: Eerdmans, 1978.

Ong, Walter. *The Presence of the Word*, New Haven: Yale University Press, 1967.

Wallis, Jim. *Agenda for Biblical People*, New York: Harper & Row, 1976.

The previous chapter explored the influence that mass media had on contemporary Christians; it also indicated that very frequently, these influences can be used for evil rather than for good. The commercial aspects of mass media have also inclined people to be self-centered and greedy. It has also formed a cultural pattern that has made people very passive and very willing to accept the decisions that are made for them by other people. This leads again to the question of freedom and authority. It is extremely important for each individual Christian to realize that he participates in the freedom won for him by Jesus Christ and that he is responsible for the moral decisions which he makes. Yet at the same time there is a need to be obedient to the correct laws of both the State and the Church, and therefore, very frequently there are conflicts between freedom and authority. This final chapter is an exploration of these conflicting roles and how the individual Christian tries to resolve them in the contemporary world.

Chapter 12

FREEDOM AND AUTHORITY

Introduction: The Problem of Freedom

In our present day society, there are two major problems. They are freedom and authority. It does not matter whether you are twenty or sixty years old. Perhaps it stems from our American heritage. Our country was founded on the principle of freedom for every person regardless of his or her race, color or creed. During the two hundred years of our history there have been numerous incidents which endangered this freedom. There was the American Civil War. There were the First and the Second World Wars. And there were other similar difficult situations.

By no means are we saying that freedom is a prerogative of the American people. Every human being strives and yearns for freedom when it has been limited or taken away. Freedom is a basic element in the nature of man. He wants it; he fights for it; he dies for it. Freedom will remain a problem for mankind as long as there are people who misuse the power entrusted to them. Power or authority can be good or bad, depending how it is applied. Unfortunately, we have seen too many cases where power has corrupted people. For example, how can we forget the American Watergate scandal?

At this point, let us consider the first of the two problems, namely, Freedom.

FREEDOM

In recent years, there has been a boom in books and movements dedicated to increasing man's freedom. They assume that independence is good and dependence is bad. They assume that there should not be any restrictions placed on a person. So often we hear expressions like: "do your own thing"; "born free"; "I must find myself."

There is nothing wrong with wanting to be free. The problem is how to keep a balance between individual freedom and the laws of society. At the present time, the pendulum seems to have swung far to the left, namely the supremacy of the individual's freedom. We might note that it is as dangerous to swing to the left as it is to the right (Supremacy of the Law). A balance is needed. It is difficult, but it is possible with man's ingenuity and adaptability.

Let us examine three points:

  I   the idea of freedom;

  II the types of freedom and;

  III the problems with freedom.

I. The Idea of Freedom

Two philosophers exemplify the extreme positions on freedom.

On one side there is Jean Paul Sartre who emphasized the supremacy of the individual's freedom. For him the individual must maintain his freedom at all cost. In practice, a person would not have to obey the laws of the government, church, state, city, etc., if they did not benefit him. From this philosophy, civil disobedience and revolution are the logical results.

On the other side, there is Thomas Hobbes' philosophy. It is that the law is supreme. Without law, there is chaos. Therefore, man must obey the civil and religious laws. Society cannot function without obedience to the law. Tyranny is the logical result of this system.

Neither of these philosophies has the absolute solution, for obvious reasons. Man is not an island. He is part of the human race. He cannot be completely free. Likewise institutions (civil or religious) cannot impose absolute laws. These institutions exist to serve, guide and develop the potentialities of a human being.

We believe that there is a third philosophy of freedom which preserves the best elements of Sartre and Hobbes' philosophies. It is Jesus' philosophy of love. It creates the balance between the supremacy of the individual's freedom and the supremacy of the law. It was the basis for the political systems of Christian Europe. Jesus' philosophy of love is the guiding principle for man's freedom. And so the essence of Christian freedom is the power to do good. This power comes from the fact that man is made in the image and likeness of God. It is God who has created man free. While man has the power to do good, he can choose evil. It is the free will of man which determines the choice. He is ultimately responsible for his decisions. If he uses his freedom well, it will grow and develop. Freedom is like a seed. It has to be nurtured if it is to grow into a healthy plant. The Second Vatican Council said:

> It is in accordance with their dignity as persons, that is, beings endowed with reason and free will and therefore privileged to bear personal responsibility, that all men should be at once impelled by nature and also bound by a moral obligation to seek the truth, especially religious truth. They are also bound to adhere to the truth, once it is known, and to order their whole lives in accord with the demands of truth.
>
> (Declaration of Religious Freedom #2)

II. Types of Freedom

From what we have said, it is evident that there are several types of freedom.

First, there is *Physical freedom*. It is the freedom of choice. If man is not really free then our discussion on freedom has been useless. For example, a student may or may not go to class. If he chooses to go, he may hear something that may change the course of his life.

Second, there is *Psychological freedom*. It is the freedom of the will. Man's motives influence his will. But it is his free will that decides.

Third, there is *Moral freedom*. It is the ability to judge what is right or wrong. Because of man's relationship with God and his fellow human beings, he has to choose to fulfill his moral obligations.

Fourth, there is *Religious freedom*. It is the right to be free from coercion in matters of faith.

Since man does not exist in a vacuum, his freedom is influenced by the institutions of society. Institutions like government and church can interfere with his freedom. Of the two institutions, the Church has often been accused of hampering man's freedom. In reality, this is rarely true. In fact, the Church has often safeguarded his freedom. One has only to read some of the documents of Vatican II Council to prove this point:

The Vatican II Fathers stated:

This Vatican Synod declares that the human person has a right to religious freedom. This freedom means that all men are to be immune from coercion on the part of individuals or of social groups and of any human power, in which wise that in matters religious no one is to be forced to act in a manner contrary to his own beliefs. Nor is anyone to be restrained from acting in accordance with his own beliefs, whether privately or publicly, whether alone or in association with others, within due limits.

(Declaration on Religious Freedom #2)

It is the special duty of government to provide this protection. However, government is not to act in arbitrary fashion or in an unfair spirit of partisanship. Its action is to be controlled by juridical moral order.

(Declaration on Religious Freedom #7)

Revelation does not indeed affirm in so many words the right of man to immunity from external coercion in matters religious. It does, however, disclose the dignity of the human person in its full dimension. It gives evidence of the respect which Christ showed toward the freedom with which man is to fulfill his duty of belief in the Word of God.

(Declaration on Religious Freedom #9)

III. Problems with Freedom

Since freedom is important in our lives, any threat to it can lessen or destroy our human dignity. We will review six major threats.

1) *Force*

First there is force or violence. It urges us inwardly or outwardly towards a certain direction. For example, prejudice seriously harms the Christian's dignity of man. For years the black man has been denied equal opportunities in many areas of life, housing and education in particular. In some cases, he was forcefully subdued into submission. In the early nineteen sixties, America's consciousness of this problem was awakened. There were peaceful demonstrations by Christians and non-Christians, black and white. Today the black man's freedom has been allowed to grow and expand. His God-given human dignity is being restored.

2) *Fear*

Second, there is fear. It can weaken or destroy a person's pursuit of freedom. It intimidates the free will of a person. Because of this fear, he may no longer be in complete control of his actions. Take the case of a terrorist who threatens his victim. Under these conditions, the victim's actions are not completely free.

3) *Passion*

Third, there is passion. Passion or emotions such as joy, love, fear, hate, hope, etc., are natural and good. Yet, they can diminish our freedom. In some cases, they may completely overpower our will and temporarily destroy our freedom. For example, an erotic sexual desire not controlled by human reason may lead to rape or sexual perversion. In other cases, the emotions can help to develop our freedom. The employer, for example, may give a compliment to his employee for a fine job. He has acknowledged the worth of this person, and rewarded his free choice to achieve high standards in his job.

4) *Ignorance*

Fourth, there is ignorance. It can be deliberate or inadvertent. It can make one feel imprisoned. It limits one's freedom. For example, a physician who fails to keep up with his medical knowledge stunts his own potentiality, and may do harm to his patients.

5) *Drugs*

Fifth, there are drugs. Dangerous drugs can be categorized into five major divisions. They are stimulants, depressants, hallucinogens, and narcotics. While some drugs are medically necessary, others are not. In either case, drugs do diminish or destroy freedom. The persistent use of drugs can produce addiction. The addict eventually loses control of his will power. He is no longer a free person who can realize or determine his own destiny.

6) *Mass Suggestion*

Sixth, there is mass suggestion. Today we are afflicted with this subtle threat to freedom. It can affect students in an auditorium, television viewers at home, workers in a factory and shoppers in supermarkets. By continuous repetition of an idea, a person's will can be weakened. After a while, he accepts it without challenge. Then he believes it. For example, Adolf Hitler convinced millions of German and non-German people that the Jews were responsible for the economic problems of Germany. We know the tragic results. Six million Jews were killed.

To determine the degree of responsibility in actions involving force, fear, passions, ignorance, drugs and mass suggestion, we say that these threats lessen accountability but does not destroy it.

Summary: Human Freedom in the Church

A final note to this notion of freedom is that it characterizes the people of God. The Vatican II Fathers expressed it in this manner:

> It is one of the major tenets of Catholic doctrine that man's response to God in faith must be free. Therefore no one is to be forced to embrace the Catholic faith against his own will. This doctrine is contained in the Word of God and it was constantly proclaimed by the Father's of the Church. The act of faith is of its very nature a free act.
>
> (Declaration on Religious Freedom #10)

> The Church therefore is being faithful to the truth of the gospel and is following the way of Christ and the apostles when she recognizes, and gives support to, the principle of religious freedom as benefiting the dignity of man and as being in accord with divine revelation.
>
> (Declaration on Religious Freedom #12)

AUTHORITY

Introduction: The Problem of Authority

Now let us consider the second major problem of our times, namely, authority. For some people, authority is a bad word. They think of restriction, harassment or confinement.

Needless to say, everyone wants to be free. We hear expressions like "let me do my own thing"; "don't tell me what to do"; "I have to experiment."

Individuals want to be free. Institutions, families, societies likewise fight to be independent. Politicians, sociologists and religious leaders debate the pro and con aspects of the authority issue. Because of the violent and fervent authority struggle, some people believe that mankind is on the verge of collapse. Without authority, society cannot function. Will our society collapse? Probably not. History records many incidents of man's continual struggle between freedom and authority. Like our predecessors, we have to adapt these notions to the concrete problems of our times.

Man grows and develops through the ages. He learns more about himself and his world. New sciences such as psychology and advanced technology give man new insights into the nature of things. The authority-freedom conflict is an age old conflict. It remains a challenge for us to reinterpret the notion of authority in light of our present day situations.

Like the issue on freedom, we will consider three aspects of authority:

I   the idea of authority;
II   the types of authority;
III the problems with authority.

I. The Idea of Authority

What is authority? Let us consider two definitions.

Cornelius Van der Poel says, "the primary task of authority is not to impose values or regulations; rather its primary task is to be the central organism in the common search for human values . . . authority in its proper sense is possible only in relation to free human beings . . . authority is the means to define the undefined possibilities of the human being."[1]

Authority has been defined, "primarily as the service of guiding persons in their efforts to reach personal fulfillment for authenticity. It takes on a negative or prohibitive form only in those situations in which individuals refuse to respect the rights of others."[2]

The two definitions use similar words such as "search" and "guide." Neither definition uses the idea of dominance. Therefore, all authority figures such as politicians, teachers, parents, religious leaders, government representatives, are responsible for guiding or protecting human beings, not dominating them. It is their function to help people so that they can become all they can possibly be and do all they can possibly do. The Vatican II Fathers stated:

> He (Jesus) acknowledged the power of government and its rights when He commanded that tribute be given to Caesar. But He gave clear warning that the higher rights of God are to be kept inviolate.
> (Declaration on Religious Freedom #11)

> Therefore, government is to assume the safeguard of the religious freedom of all its citizens, in an effective manner, by just laws and by other appropriate means. Government is also to help create conditions favorable to the fostering of religious life, in order that the people may be truly enabled to exercise their religious rights and to fulfill their religious duties. . . .
> (Declaration on Religious Freedom #6)

Authority is necessary if society is to function well. Now we will review four types of authority.

II. Types of authority

1. *Natural Law*

First, there is the natural law authority. Nature is what man discovers in the world before he changes it. It demands respect and responsibility. While man is a keeper, developer and discoverer of nature, he does not have the right to violate or destroy it. For example, animals never eat more than they need. There are overweight animals only because man has deliberately overfed them. Yet, man does get fat because he consumes more energy than he needs. He violates the law of nature.

There are countless other examples of how man has violated the natural law. Ecologists constantly remind us how we are polluting our rivers and air. Man has abused nature many times and eventually he pays the price.

2. *Civil Law*

Second, there is civil law authority. Civil laws come from society which means fellowship. Society is, therefore, a group of people who live together with common needs, desires and values. There are many societies such as a school, a family, a club, a nation, a state, a city, etc. Each of these societies has rules and regulations. All their members must be treated fairly and decently. Every society, therefore, has basic laws which are called fundamental and functional laws. A fundamental law is, for example, the right of every man to life. A functional law is a traffic light which helps to protect the lives of citizens.

Unfortunately, some people make bad civil laws out of ignorance or deliberateness. The consequences of these laws are tragic because they harm the dignity of the human being. Fortunately, there are people who strive to correct these laws.

3. *Divine Law*

Third, there is the Divine law authority. This law comes from God's revelation. For Christians it has been revealed in three stages: 1) Abraham the father of the Hebrew people; 2) Moses the father of the Mosaic law (the Ten Commandments); 3) Jesus who gave us the law of love for God and neighbor. Christians are obliged to obey the Divine law because of their special relationship with God and His Son, Jesus. The Ten Commandments are applications of Jesus' law of love. To obey the Divine law is really to practice love in a specific way. Love is not coercion. It is the basis of good authority.

4. *Church Law*

Fourth, there is the Church law. In our age, the teaching authority of the Chuch is under severe attack. In recent times national surveys give statistics on the rebellion of some Catholics on issues such as birth control, Papal infallibility, pre-marital sex, and Sunday Mass obligation. Why? The answers vary, depending on whom you ask.

We believe one of the reasons for the rebellion against the Church is the misunderstanding of the teaching authority of the Church.

It was previously stated, but worth repeating, that the teaching authority of the Church is a spiritual authority. She has received her authority from Jesus. It was Jesus who founded the Church and therefore the Church has an obligation to see that His teachings are carried out. The Second Vatican Council stated:

> The Church therefore is being faithful to the truth of the Gospel, and is following the way of Christ and the apostles when she recognizes and gives support to, the principle of religious freedom. . .
>
> (Declaration on Religious Freedom #12)

The Church is a society composed of the Pope, bishops, clergy and laity. All are pilgrims on their way to the Kingdom of Heaven. All are obliged to help one another to fulfill their temporal and spiritual destiny. All share in the teaching authority of the Church but in different ways. Parents are the primary teachers of their children. The Pope possesses the highest teaching authority in the Church. He is the successor of St. Peter, whom Jesus chose to be the head of the Church. Bishops and priests have the authority to teach and preach the message of the Gospels. Theologians have the authority to teach and speak responsibly. The laity have the authority to share their knowledge and ability with the entire Christian community. All Church members must exercise their authority mutually and respectfully.

How does the Church exercise this authority?[3] There are four ways: (1) infallible teachings; (2) non-infallible teachings; (3) private opinions; (4) disciplinary rules.

(1) *Infallible Teachings*

First the question of infallible teachings is under reexamination today. There is no doubt that the Church possesses infallibility in matters central to the faith. What about the past statements of Papal infallibility? Some of these statements are presently being reinterpreted in light of the new knowledge of our times.

(2) Non-infallible Teachings

Second, there are certain Church teachings which are classified as non-infallible teachings. Yet these are authoritative teachings of the Church. An example of this type of teaching is an encyclical of the Pope. Because of the Church's vast wisdom and knowledge, Catholics would be unwise to disregard these teachings. For example, the Church has preached for many years against the birth control pill. It has created a tremendous uproar in Catholic circles. However, it is interesting to note that many medical physicians today are against the pill. Why? Medical studies have shown the harmful effects of the birth control pill.

(3) Private Teachings

Third, there are private teachings such as opinions of bishops, priests, lay people and theologians. How are these teachings to be accepted? Catholics must weigh these opinions in light of the people who give them. These teachings are not binding on the Catholic community. Yet, a person should be open to listening to new ideas.

(4) Disciplinary Rules

Fourth, there are disciplinary rules in the Church, e.g. fast laws. Disciplinary rules are necessary in any society for the common good of its members. So, too, for the Church society. Remember, no one is forced to join the Church. However, to choose to be a member is to agree to work for the good of its members.

The Vatican II Council stated:

> From the beginning, the subject and the goal of all social institutions is and must be the human person, which for its part and by very nature stands completely in need of social life. This social life is not something added on to man. Hence, through his dealings with others, through reciprocal duties, and through fraternal dialogue, he develops all his gifts and is able to rise to his destiny.
> (Pastoral Constitution on the Church in the Modern World #25)

We have considered four types of authority. But what about the problems with authority?

III. Problems With Authority

In order to insure the self-awareness of every human being, authority is necessary. But we know there are problems with authority. Too often, people have harmed, damaged or even destroyed the dignity of man by the misuse of authority. The same can be said about some institutions. Let us consider these two points.

1. *People*

It goes without saying that some people have abused their authority. There are parents who have been too permissive with their children. The results have been devastating to witness: disruption, defiance, and general confusion. Unfortunately, these parents have stymied their children's maturity.

2. *Institutions*

What about institutions? Once again, it happens that some institutions (schools, corporations, churches, etc.) at times forget their primary purpose. It is to guide, not dominate, their members.

In conclusion, we say that authority is a gift and a burden.

Comment

Whether it be the African state of Zaire, or a group of senior citizens, or a private college, we hear the cry for independence. We all want to control our own destiny.

Today's world is crying out to be free. It is searching for new symbols, new ideals, and new visions. It is facing new problems such as nuclear energy, cloning, and space adventure. How will it meet these problems? If it heeds the message of Jesus' ethics of love, then it will meet with a reinterpretation of freedom and authority. Responsible freedom and authority will replace irresponsible freedom and authority.

Freedom means to be aware of man's potentialities and those of others. It will create an inner ability to control, direct and harmonize our emotions, needs, fears and weaknesses. Authority fosters freedom by setting guidelines. It encourages maturity by demanding personal involvement. It accepts the rights and responsibilities of another human being. It responds to real needs of people. It listens to the ideas of people.

Summary

1. Freedom and Authority are major problems of our society.
2. Jean Paul Sartre's philosophy is the supremacy of the individual's freedom.
3. Thomas Hobbes' philosophy is the supremacy of the law.
4. Jesus' philosophy is the law of love leading to true freedom and authentic authority.
5. There are four types of freedom: physical, psychological, moral and religious.
6. There are six major threats to freedom: force, fear, passion, ignorance, drugs, and mass suggestion.
7. Authority means to search and guide a human being.
8. There are four types of authority: natural law, civil law, Divine law, and Church law.
9. The Church is composed of the Pope, bishops, clergy, and lay people.

10. The Church exercises her authority in four ways: infallible teachings, non-infallible teachings, private teachigs and disciplinary rules.
11. There are two problems with authority: abuse by people and abuse by institutions.

Discussion Questions

1. Explain the advantages and disadvantages of Sartre and Hobbes' philosophies.
2. Compare and contrast Vatican II Council's ideas on Religious Freedom with Jesus' ethics of love.
3. Discuss the mass suggestion threat to freedom.
4. Show the weaknesses in Cornelius Van der Poel's definition of authority.
5. Give some examples of the infallible teachings of the Church.
6. Give examples of institutions violating their authority.

Footnotes

1. Cornelius Van der Poel, *The Search for Human Values*, New York: Paulist Press, 1971, 72.
2. Bernard Haring, *The Law of Christ*, Maryland: The Newman Press, 1961, Vol. I, 99.
3. Robert Hater and Judy Ball, *Catholic Update*, "What's Happening to the Teaching Authority of the Church?", Feb. 1978, I-4.

BIBLIOGRAPHY

Deedy, John. *What A Modern Catholic Believes About Conscience, Freedom and Authority*, Chicago, Illinois: The Thomas More Press, 1972.

Dobson, James. *Dare to Discipline*, Wheaton, Illinois: Tyndale House Publishers, 1972.

Haring, Bernard. *The Law of Christ*, Maryland: The Newman Press, Vol. I, 1961.

Janssen, Louis. *Freedom of Conscience and Religious Freedom*, New York: Alba House, 1965.

Regan, George. *New Trends in Moral Theology*, New York: Newman Press, 1971.

Strommen, Merton ed. *Research on Religious Development*, New York: Hawthorn Books, Inc., 1971.

Van der Poel, Cornelius. *The Search for Human Values*, New York: Paulist Press, 1971.

The previous six chapters have examined contemporary moral issues.

This chapter is a summary of some of those issues and a reflection on some others.

Conservative Christians usually believe that practicing members of the Church can be pesonally involved and can benefit from the economic structure of the present capitalistic system in the West. Some Christians—either Liberal or Conservative—instead hold that Christians should form a "counter culture" to the present economic system which they believe is intrinsically immoral. One such writer is the evangelical Protestant Jim Wallis, who believes that the super-consumer society created by the media has caused widespread poverty in the Third World:

> We are finally coming to understand a discomforting but central fact of reality—the people of the nonindustrialized world are poor because we are rich; the poverty and brutalization of the wretched masses is maintained and perpetuated by our systems and institutions and by the way we live our lives. In other words, the oppressive conditions of life in the poor countries, like the causes of poverty and misery in our own land, are neither merely accidental nor because of the failures of the poor. Our throw-away culture of affluence and wasteful consumption fragments and privatizes our lives. Our consumer orientation lulls us into primary concern for ourselves and into a passive acceptance of the suffering of others—horrors committed in our name in Indochina and elsewhere. At home, our consumerism supports corporate interests that exploit the poor, profit from war, and destroy the environment. Peace, justice, and ecological survival are sacrificed for the rewards and pleasures of affluence. Our present standard and style of life can be maintained or expanded only at the cost of the suppression of the poor of the world.[2]

Discuss the pros and cons of this view.

Definitions

Media: Media or the means of communication are extensions of some human power such as speech, or hearing or vision.

Electronic Mass Media make possible communicating the same message to very large groups of people. *The effects of mass media* are so pervasive that most of us are unconscious of their power. Therefore, we make many decisions, not as free moral individuals, but as part of a mass society which takes its values and

Chapter 13

SUMMARY:
Reflections on Contemporary Moral Issues in School, the Economy, Politics, and Mass Communication

In the early 1960's when John Kennedy was President of the United States and Pope John XXIII was the Supreme Pontiff of the Roman Catholic Church, idealism and stableness were the popular themes of American life. But those days were soon to end.

Today, the American scene is different. The attitude of American youths on sex, patriotism, work, politics, church and family life differ greatly from their predecessors. We might add that the attitudes of adults have also changed. Some have labeled our times, an age of egotism and individualism.

In order to understand the marketplace better, we will consider four aspects:

1) the college scene;
2) the economy
3) politics; and
4) mass communications.

1. *The College Scene*

The American college students (17 to 24 age group) comprise 40 million people which make up about a fifth of the population. Today's students come from the homes of white collar workers; black, Hispanic, and Mexican ghettos; bank presidents; truck drivers; poor and middle class parents, and so forth. College is no longer restricted to the wealthy and very intelligent student. Today's students study computers, space technology and psychological sciences, which did not exist in their parents' generation. Through various media, but especially television, the college student has been exposed to all aspects of life such as sex, money, divorce, various marital life styles, violence, dishonesty, and scandal. Generally speaking, most college students are aware of the social, political, and religious problems of the day. They search for the truth. They desire rational solutions. They are religiously minded.

Many studies have been done to analyze the contemporary attitudes and values on American college campuses. For clarity and brevity, we have summarized them as follows:

1. College students have greater sexual freedom today.
2. They do not believe that living a clean moral life is very important.
3. Church institutions are not so important as religion.
4. Money is the most important factor in life.
5. Drugs and rock music pervade the college campus.
6. Every day should be lived as if it were the last.
7. Alcoholism is an acute problem for the college student.
8. Suicide rates are the highest among the college age group.
9. College students marry at a later age; for women at 21 years; for men at 24 years.
10. The crime rate is greater among the college students than any other age group.
11. The car is the college status symbol.
12. Patriotism is the lowest of their priorities.
13. Most college students believe that the American political system needs major reform.
14. College students, in general, say that their parents should be "modern" and not old fashioned.
15. Colleges need better qualified professors.
16. World affairs are very important.

These sixteen attitudes and/or values give a key to the mind of today's college student. Because of their frustrations, some educators believe that the college scene will witness great confrontation. We hope not, because man's greatest gift, intelligence, can be the guiding norm in resolving problems.

2. *The Economy*

The second point under consideration is the economy.

Eli Ginsberg, the noted economist and educator wrote, "Today's workers, higher paid and better educated than ever before, won't put up with being 'ordered arouund' on the job."[1]

Barbara Ward, economist and Third World advocate says that Christians must, "give the sign that all this wealth, all this technology, can be made to work for life, not death."[2]

Daniel Yankelovich, research professor of psychology at New York University, states, "A new breed of Americans, born out of the social movements of the 60's and grown into a majority in the 70's holds a set of values and beliefs so markedly different from the traditional outlook that they promise to transform the character of America in the 80's."[3]

Every day of our lives, we are confronted with a barrage of statistics, explanations and announcements about economics. Whether you be a student or an adult, everyone is affected by the economic tides. We are aware of the double-digit inflation of 1973-74 and the near double digit inflation of our present times.

Politicians, business leaders, labor experts, produce conflicting cures for our economic problems. Problems such as supply and demand, debts and savings, and the loss of the purchasing power of the dollar are our primary concerns. However, we will not discuss these problems. Nor will we discuss the growing impact of government; the stock market's trading in securities and commodities; the unions' power and the foreign world trade. These problems are subjects for an economics class.

We are interested in the moral aspect of this economic question, namely Christian charity. What should be the Christian's attitude to the national and world economy? It should be one of love for the neighbor as Jesus commanded. He must be interested and concerned about the neighbor's welfare. And it does not matter whether that neighbor be from his own neighborhood, city, state, country, or a foreign country.

The Second Vatican Council stated:

> People hounded by hunger call upon those better off. Whether they
> have not yet won it, women claim for themselves an equity with men
> before the law and in fact. Laborers and farmers seek not only to
> provide for the necessities of life but to develop the gifts of their
> personality by their labors, and indeed to take part in regulating
> economic, social, political, and cultual life. Now, for the first time
> in human history, all people are convinced that the benefits of
> culture ought to be and actually can be extended to everyone.
> (Pastoral Constitution on the Church in the Modern World #1)

More recently, Barbara Ward, foremost Catholic economist,
advisor to Pope Paul and the President of the World Bank, advisor
to the former Presidents Kennedy and Johnson, proposed a World
Marshall Plan for the economic ills of the world. Based on the
European Recovery Plan of the Secretary of State George C.
Marshall in 1947, Mrs. Ward believes that another Marshall Plan is
needed now. Christians must support the idea but it means
sacrifices. She said, "Let's have several more Marshall Plans.
What's wrong? We're twice as rich as we were then. What are we
waiting for? I'd like to hear Christians above all saying, 'Look, I'm
quite prepared to have a smaller car and have part of my income in
tax bonds which will be repaid in 20 years.' "[4]

Do you think she is right or wrong? We hope the former. You
ask, "What does this idea have to do with me?" Precisely this:
awareness awakens our consciousness and consciousness awakens
our responsibility to the needs of our neighbor.

3. Politics

The third area to be considered is politics. For some people,
politics means corruption, graft, bribes, and so forth. Very few
people believe politicians can be honest people. Obviously, some
are and some are not. What makes some honest is the love of God
and neighbor.

Ever since the days of the Watergate scandal, legislative bodies all over the country are working to bring politics and ethics together.

What is the political scene today? These three men are examples of a Christian awareness for Christian values in politics:

Ralph C. Chandler, professor of political science and a Presbyterian clergyman writes,

> The houses of Congress, however, have not only passed comprehensive codes for their own members, but are currently taking steps to have the provisions of these codes enacted into statutory law to cover all federal employees. President Carter has asked Congress to require annual public financial disclosure statements from top Executive Branch officials and to prohibit them from lobbying their former agencies for at least one year after leaving government. He also asked that a special prosecutor's office he created to prosecute misconduct by high ranking Executive Branch officials and an Office of Ethics be established within the Civil Service Commission...
>
> For ethics presupposes a context of personal principle and of moral commitment which rules and rules-makers cannot touch.[5]

Joseph Califano, a Catholic, who is Secretary of Health, Education and Welfare, wants the government more sensitive to the needs of the family. He said in an interview for a Catholic magazine,

> Restore trust and confidence in American families as the basic unit of society. The government should not be telling families that they lack the competence to handle things when in fact they have been meeting the physical, mental and spiritual needs of their children for centuries . . . Programs that hurt families should be revised like welfare policies which encourage a father to desert his home and social security provisions which penalize a retired couple for getting married . . . (he advises) individuals and parish groups who are interested in things like pro-life legislation, food stamps, and welfare reform to make their views heard.[6]

Governor Jerry Brown of California, a former Jesuit seminarian, asked a group of religious leaders these two questions: "Where are the saints of the Middle Ages who kissed the sores of the Lepers?" "Do you still teach the corporal works of mercy?" He went on to say, "the Church can help spark a revolution, if it inspires some committed men and women to bear their neighbors' burdens instead of dumping everything on the government."[7]

He believes that a new spirit depends on a new faith, a new fervor and a new spark. He says, "If the spark is there, then we'll see the fire. Faith in the broadest sense of the word is the determinant of action. Action is preceded by thought or faith or will. If that's not there, forget it. It's not going to happen."[8]

Brown's message is simple: "volunteerism is not a luxury, it is a necessity for a civilized society that wants to truly meet its human needs—that as Christians we believe the Good News that that energy or Spirit is there."[9]

These Christians, one Protestant and two Catholics, have given us an insight into the need of Christians in politics. Politics can be Christianized if we want to do it. What is needed is determination and spirit.

4. Mass Communications

Our fourth point is mass communications. In the past fifteen years, mass communication has vastly expanded. In the 1920's the radio came into the American scene. Thirty years later television gave a new dimension to mass communication. Programs of entertainment are interspersed with commercials. Paperback books proliferate in the book market. Magazines such as *Playboy* and *Playgirl*, etc. flaunt their hedonist philosophies.

Albert Speer,[10] onetime Nazi official, said:

> Mass media are taking away the right to think. The wardens in Spandau, I was sometimes shocked at the way they took everything for granted that they saw on television. The cruelty in some detective stories or Western stories (on television) is certainly not contributing to respecting human beings, and human life. For those who are open to it, it is doing more damage . . . writers such as Rachel Carson and Ralph Nader have alerted many people to the danger of molding ourselves and our environment to the needs of technology instead of to human beings . . . and technological developments have many good sides if they are mastered and used in a cautious way . . . I learned in Spandau the tremendous possibilities

of human beings to adapt to other conditions . . . that distinguishes us from the animals.[11]

Susan Ogden, an instructor of business administration at Georgetown University wrote, "it is estimated that the typical American family is exposed to 1,500 bits of advertising, in some form or other, each day. In many cases, as much as 60 percent of the sales dollar is spent on advertising, and many other companies regularly spend 20 to 40 percent."[12]

Her advice to consumers is, "it doesn't take a lot of training, just a careful eye, a bit of practice and the firm commitment not to believe all you read and hear on the TV, on the radio, and in the newspaper and magazines."[13]

Another writer, Dolores Curran[14] gave the following statistics about television. She said: 1) children graduating from high school spend 15,000 hours in front of television; 2) children spend more time watching television than any other activity except sleeping; 3) television leads all other traditional influences on us; 4) the average home has the television set on for 44 hours a week; 5) the White House, the Supreme Court and Television were listed as the top three powerful institutions in American society.

Dr. Herbert Schiller, professor of communications at the University of California wrote,

> Is your mind being manipulated, controlled or bent out of shape, at least a little bit, by the mass media? Is the six o'clock news molding your mind by the way the program organizes "reality"? Is your consciousness being managed by TV Guide, National Geographic, Kojak, or even the Super Bowl? Do opinion polls present you with the "facts" or with a snow job? Are Walt Disney or Charlie's Angels value free entertainment? In short, how often are our minds being managed today by the media?[15]

He makes the following observation:

> The media put on what they think will make money. The networks are interested in their balance sheets. And they do anything to make sure their balance sheets show as impressive a profit as possible . . . whether it's a matter of presenting a pretty woman like Farrah Fawcett-Majors or a virile type of private eye like Kojak or some tye of speedy and highly aggressive activity like a pro football game.[16]

Can it be that mass communication controls our minds? There is no doubt that it does. It may be argued as to what extent. Obviously mass media is good when it is used well. When it is misused, it is bad. Therefore, we must use it for the growth and development of people's potentialities. Mass media communicates a new language blending image and word; it can be an instrument for good relations among nations; it can help to bring a broad general culture to the people; it can give better educational, political, sociological and religious knowledge to people; it can help develop the personality of a person.[17]

In conclusion, let us quote what the Second Vatican Council Fathers said,

> The chief moral duties respecting the proper use of instruments of social communication fall on newsmen, writers, actors, designers, producers, exhibitors, distributors, operators, and sellers, critics, and whoever else may have a part of any kind in making and transmitting products of communication. For it is quite clear what heavy responsibilities are given to all such persons in the present state of affairs. By moldng and activating the human race they can lead it upward or to ruin.
>
> (Decree on the Instruments of Social Communication #11)

Discussion Questions

1. Discuss the sixteen attitudes and values of American Youths.
2. What do you think of Daniel Yankelovich's statement?
3. Outline the advantages of Barbara Ward's Marshall Plan?
4. Compare Dr. Califano and Governor Brown's government plans.
5. As a student, how can you fit into the Governor's plan of Volunteerism?
6. List the advantage of television.
7. Is mass media making us robots? Discuss.

Summary

1. Four aspects of the summary are the college scene, the economy, politics, and mass communications.
2. College students' attitudes and values differ from their parents and predecessors.
3. College students search for the truth and desire rational solutions.
4. Man's greatest gift is his intelligence.
5. The moral aspect of economics rests on Jesus' command to love thy neighbor.
6. Barbara Ward recommends a new Marshall Plan for the economic ills of the world.
7. Legislative bodies all over the country are working to bring politics and ethics together again.
8. Dr. Joseph Califano wants the government to be more sensitive to the needs of the family.
9. Governor Brown believes Christians can Christianize politics.
10. Television is the leading media of mass communication.
11. Consumers must not believe everything they hear, read or see.

Comment

Today's marketplace needs Christians who are heroes. We seem to be fresh out of heroes. In the past, what made heroes? One thing, for certain, was courage and conviction in what they believe in. Because of our "soft-living" and other reasons, we have compromised Jesus' commandment to love God and our neighbor. As Governor Brown aptly expressed it, Christians must have determination and spirit. Without it we are lost. To put it bluntly, we need to put Christian moral values based on Jesus' commandment back in our schools, economy, politics, and mass communications.

There are some bright signs on the horizon. For example, in mid-December of 1977, representatives of the Chicago Catholic

social and political organizations signed a statement calling for a
Catholic social action vision.
     Perhaps this epilogue[18] summarizes it:

> Toynbee has written of the builders of our modern technical
> civilization that one day this may be carved on their tombstones:
> Here lie the technicians who built or destroyed modern civilization.
> The modern technical civilization may well turn out inhuman,
> leading to despair. It may also turn out more human and more
> agreeable to man: Here lie the men who used or failed to use the
> wonderful means of the modern age to spread the Kingdom of God.

Footnotes

1. Eli Ginsberg, *U.S. News and World Report*, "Economy," Jan. 23, 1978, p. 47.
2. John Bank, *St. Anthony Messenger*, "Barbara Ward: Economist and World
    Watcher," November 1977, II.
3. Daniel Yankelovich, *Psychology Today*, "The New Psychological Contracts at
    Work," May 1978, 46.
4. *Op. cit.*, Bank, 12.
5. Ralph C. Chandler, *Commonweal*, "Ethics and Public Policy," May 12, 1978,
    306-308.
6. Barbara Beckwith, *St. Anthony Messenger*, "Making Government Pro-Family:
    An Interview with Joseph Califano," September 1977, 28-36.
7. Jack Wintz, *St. Anthony Messenger*, "We Need More Saints—Governor Brown
    Launches His New Volunteer Plan," August 1977, 20.
8. *Ibid.*, 25.
9. *Ibid.*, 24-25.
10. Albert Speer was the only high ranking Nazi leader who willingly accepted his
    guilt in the Nazi Regime. During his twenty years of imprisonment, he spoke of
    his remorse for his part in the Nazi Regime.
11. Michael Malloy, *The National Observer*, "Albert Speer on Today's Dic-
    tatorship," November 15, 1975, 4.
12. Susan Ogden, *St. Anthony Messenger*, "Games Advertisers Play—And How to
    Beat Them," June 1975, 29.
13. *Ibid.*, 32.
14. Dolores Curran, *St. Anthony Messenger*, "Television, Who Owns the Knob—
    Parents or Children?", January 1977, 16.
15. Jack Wintz, *St. Anthony Messenger*, "Who's Managing Your Mind?",
    September 1977, 13.
16. *Ibid.*, 17.
17. Edmond Becker, *The Medellin Papers*, "Mass Communications and
    Catechetics," Manila, Philippines: East Asian Pastoral Institute, 95-98.
18. *Ibid.*, 103.

BIBLIOGRAPHY

Fletcher, Joseph. *Situation Ethics*, Philadelphia: The Westminsiter Press, 1975.

Hofinger, Johannes and Sheridan, Terence, eds. *The Medellin Papers*, Manila, Philippines: East Asian Pastoral Institute, 1969.

Kennedy, Eugene. *Fashion Me A People—Man, Woman, and The Church*, New York: Sheed and Ward, 1967.

Newland, Mary Reed. *Youth: What Happened?*, Notre Dame, Indiana: Ave Maria Press, 1970.

O'Malley, William. *The Roots of Unbelief*, New York: Paulist Press, 1976.

Stevens, Edward. *The Morals Game*, New York: Paulist Press, 1974.

Epilogue

THE NEED FOR PRAYER

We have studied a great deal about morality in this book. We have looked at the teachings of Jesus, the history of the Church, the purpose of the Church. We have studied the teachings of Church moralists on conscience, marketplace ethics, sexual behavior. We have tried to comprehend how each of us is influenced by different sources of morality: family, friends, social groups, media, education.

We have read several different authors, all of whom have various opinions about what is good and bad for the contemporary Catholic.

We have tried to explore the different tensions that are part of a contemporary Catholic's life: the tensions between the personal and communal, the mystical and organizational, the charismatic and the institutional. We have seen some writers who are considered "liberal" or "conservative" or "moderate."

We have looked at a Church to which we belong and which is often uncertain about the way to approach the modern world. And we have looked at a Church which strives mightily to continue to teach the Ethics of Jesus in a world which often turns a deaf ear to His pleas.

The book is over. The authors hope they have accomplished their original purpose to give the reader a general introduction to the teachings of Christ, the moral tradition of the Catholic Church, and the various contemporary views on how to apply these ethical concerns to today's life.

As the reader closes the book, perhaps he is looking at the text as simply another school book: memorize the important parts, concentrate on what the teacher thinks is important, and pray that you guess right on the final examination.

We hope that the book is more than that. We sincerely pray that we have helped you on your road to becoming a mature and thoughtful Christian who will use this text and others as tools for making adult moral decisions about how to live out the teachings of your faith in the modern world.

All the authors can communicate to you is knowledge. The *desire* to do good, the *will* to imitate Jesus, the courage to follow the teachings of the Church come only from divine grace. It is the work of the Holy Spirit, God's free and loving gift to His children. The authors are instruments, teachers who hope they have acted as good guides on the road of life.

No one can walk that road but you. Every moral choice which you make as you travel that journey is yours alone. It is not your parents or your teachers or your clergy. Moral decisions are made by each individual who has the courage to face the point in his life when he must decide.

The ability to choose the good over evil is a gift of God. It is a special grace which we receive when we open our hearts to His influence.

The tradition of the Church—through all the ages—by saints and sinners, wise men and fools, insitutional Catholics and charismatic Catholics, by the powerful and the weak, by those acclaimed by other men, and those despised—has always been the same: we all choose the good as the fruit of prayer.

Prayer can be private, or public. It can be liturgical or personal. It can be recited or it can be meditated. It can follow a format or be spontaneous. It can be done in silence or it can be done aloud. There is a form of prayer for every temperament. Prayer is the first acknowledgement by a creature that he *is* a creature, and depends on the Creator. The Creator is the source of divine grace. Prayer brings the gift of grace, and grace enlightens all moral decisions.

Christians never make moral decisions in a vacuum. Their own consciousness is crowded with the Triune Community of God, the urgings of the good spirit and the temptings of evil spirit, the saints and historical figures of the Church. Prayer links us with the long line of pray-ers who have gone before us and who serve as models of ethical decisions. The ethics of Jesus and the teaching of the Church is not just *knowledge*; it is wisdom, the ability to live our lives before the Throne of God, to make decisions in light of our personal loving relationship with the risen Jesus.

If the authors have given some of the tools needed for that chore, they have done their task. They have written more than a textbook. They have written a guide to the journey of life.

A moral life is the way *to* God and the way *of* God.

As the Scriptures proclaim:

Fret not yourself because of the wicked,
    be not envious of wrongdoers
For they will soon fade like the grass,
    and wither like the green herb.

Trust in the LORD, and do good;
    so you will dwell in the land and enjoy security.
Take delight in the LORD,
    and he will give you the desires of your heart.
                                        (Ps 38:1-4 RSV version)

                                        Rev. Leonard F. Badia, Ph.D.
                                        Ronald A. Sarno, M. Div.